The Ramayan Of Valmiki
Book VI
Translated Into English Verse

by

Ralph T. H. Griffith

The Ramayan Of Valmiki
Book VI
Translated Into English Verse
by Ralph T. H. Griffith

ISBN: 978-93-59951-53-9

Published by

DOUBLE 9 BOOKS

2/13-B, Ansari Road
Daryaganj, New Delhi – 110002
info@double9books.com
www.double9books.com
Tel. 011-40042856

ABOUT THE AUTHOR

Ralph Thomas Hotchkin Griffith (1826-1906) was a member of the Indian education service and one of the first Europeans to transcribe the Vedas into English. He lived in the United Kingdom (Oxford) and India (Benares and Nilgiris). Griffith was born on May 25, 1826, in Corsley, Wiltshire. He was a B.A. of Queen's College and was chosen Boden Professor of Sanskrit on November 24, 1849. He was the son of Reverend R. C. Griffith (Chaplain to the Marquess of Bath 1830). Lieutenant Colonel Joseph Boden contributed money to the university in 1832 to aid in the conversion of the people of India to Christianity, and the Boden Sanskrit professorship was created in 1832. Griffith pursued this goal by translating the Vedic scriptures into English. He also translated other Sanskrit works, including a verse version of the Ramayana and Kalidasa's Kumara Sambhava. He was the principal of Benares College in India and later settled in Kotagiri, Nilgiri. Griffith was more interested in translating Vedic works into English, and he completed the majority of them while living, teaching, and researching in Kotagiri, Nilgiris.

CONTENTS

BOOK VI

Canto I
Ráma's Speech

The son of Raghu heard, consoled,
The wondrous tale Hanumán told;
And, as his joyous hope grew high,
In friendly words he made reply:
"Behold a mighty task achieved,
Which never heart but his conceived.
Who else across the sea can spring,
Save Váyu 896 and the Feathered King? 897
Who, pass the portals strong and high
Which Nágas, 898 Gods, and fiends defy,
Where Rávaṇ's hosts their station keep,—
And come uninjured o'er the deep?
By such a deed the Wind-God's son
Good service to the king has done,
And saved from ruin and disgrace
Lakshmaṇ and me and Raghu's race.
Well has he planned and bravely fought,
And with due care my lady sought.
But of the sea I sadly think,
And the sweet hopes that cheered me sink.
How can we cross the leagues of foam
That keep us from the giant's home?
What can the Vánar legions more
Than muster on the ocean shore?"

Canto II
Sugríva's Speech

He ceased: and King Sugríva tried
To calm his grief, and thus replied:
"'Be to thy nobler nature true,
Nor let despair thy soul subdue.
This cloud of causeless woe dispel,
For all as yet has prospered well,
And we have traced thy queen, and know
The dwelling of our Rákshas foe.
Arise, consult: thy task must be
To cast a bridge athwart the sea,
The city of our foe to reach
That crowns the mountain by the beach;
And when our feet that isle shall tread,
Rejoice and deem thy foeman dead.
The sea unbridged, his walls defy
Both fiends and children of the sky,
Though at the fierce battalions' head
Lord Indra's self the onset led.
Yea, victory is thine before
The long bridge touch the farther shore,
So fleet and fierce and strong are these
Who limb them as their fancies please.
Away with grief and sad surmise
That mar the noblest enterprise,
And with their weak suspicion blight
The sage's plan, the hero's might.
Come, this degenerate weakness spurn,

And bid thy dauntless heart return,
For each fair hope by grief is crossed
When those we love are dead or lost.
Arise, O best of those who know,
Arm for the giant's overthrow.
None in the triple world I see
Who in the fight may equal thee;
None who before thy face may stand
And brave the bow that arms thy hand,
Trust to these mighty Vánars: they
With full success thy trust will pay,
When thou shalt reach the robber's hold,
And loving arms round Sítá fold."

Canto III
Lanká

He ceased: and Raghu's son gave heed,
Attentive to his prudent rede:
Then turned again, with hope inspired,
To Hanumán, and thus inquired:
"Light were the task for thee, I ween,
To bridge the sea that gleams between
The mainland and the island shore.
Or dry the deep and guide as o'er.
Fain would I learn from thee whose feet
Have trod the stones of every street,
Of fenced Lanká's towers and forts,
And walls and moats and guarded ports,
And castles where the giants dwell,
And battlemented citadel.
O Váyu's son, describe it all,
With palace, fort, and gate, and wall."
He ceased: and, skilled in arts that guide
The eloquent, the chief replied:
"Vast is the city, gay and strong,
Where elephants unnumbered throng,
And countless hosts of Rákshas breed
Stand ready by the car and steed.
Four massive gates, securely barred,
All entrance to the city guard,
With murderous engines fixt to throw
Bolt, arrow, rock to check the foe,
And many a mace with iron head

That strikes at once a hundred dead.
Her golden ramparts wide and high
With massy strength the foe defy,
Where inner walls their rich inlay
Of coral, turkis, pearl display.
Her circling moats are broad and deep,
Where ravening monsters dart and leap.
By four great piers each moat is spanned
Where lines of deadly engines stand.
In sleepless watch at every gate
Unnumbered hosts of giants wait,
And, masters of each weapon, rear
The threatening pike and sword and spear.
My fury hurled those ramparts down,
Filled up the moats that gird the town,
The piers and portals overturned,
And stately Lanká spoiled and burned.
Howe'er we Vánars force our way
O'er the wide seat of Varuṇ's 899 sway,
Be sure that city of the foe
Is doomed to sudden overthrow,
Nay, why so vast an army lead?
Brave Angad, Dwivid good at need,
Fierce Mainda, Panas famed in fight,
And Níla's skill and Nala's might,
And Jámbaván the strong and wise,
Will dare the easy enterprise.
Assailed by these shall Lanká fall
With gate and rampart, tower and wall.
Command the gathering, chief: and they
In happy hour will haste away."

Canto IV
The March

He ceased; and spurred by warlike pride
The impetuous son of Raghu cried:
"Soon shall mine arm with wrathful joy
That city of the foe destroy.
Now, chieftain, now collect the host,
And onward to the southern coast!
The sun in his meridian tower
Gives glory to the Vánar power.
The demon lord who stole my queen
By timely flight his life may screen.
She, when she knows her lord is near,
Will cling to hope and banish fear,
Saved like a dying wretch who sips
The drink of Gods with fevered lips.
Arise, thy troops to battle lead:
All happy omens counsel speed.
The Lord of Stars in favouring skies
Bodes glory to our enterprise.
This arm shall slay the fiend; and she,
My consort, shall again be free.
Mine upward-throbbing eye foreshows
The longed-for triumph o'er my foes.
Far in the van be Níla's post,
To scan the pathway for the host,
And let thy bravest and thy best,
A hundred thousand, wait his hest.
Go forth, O warrior Níla, lead

The legions on through wood and mead
Where pleasant waters cool the ground,
And honey, flowers, and fruit abound.
Go, and with timely care prevent
The Rákshas foeman's dark intent.
With watchful troops each valley guard
Ere brooks and fruits and roots be marred
And search each glen and leafy shade
For hostile troops in ambuscade.
But let the weaklings stay behind:
For heroes is our task designed.
Let thousands of the Vánar breed
The vanguard of the armies lead:
Fierce and terrific must it be
As billows of the stormy sea.
There be the hill-huge Gaja's place,
And Gavaya's, strongest of his race,
And, like the bull that leads the herd,
Gaváksha's, by no fears deterred
Let Rishabh, matchless in the might
Of warlike arms, protect our right,
And Gandhamádan next in rank
Defend and guide the other flank.
I, like the God who rules the sky
Borne on Airávat 900 mounted high
On stout Hanúmán's back will ride,
The central host to cheer and guide.
Fierce as the God who rules below,
On Angad's back let Lakshman show
Like him who wealth to mortals shares, 901
The lord whom Sárvabhauma 902 bears.
The bold Sushen's impetuous might,
And Vegadarsí's piercing sight,
And Jámbaván whom bears revere,

Illustrious three, shall guard the rear."
He ceased, the royal Vánar heard,
And swift, obedient to his word,
Sprang forth in numbers none might tell
From mountain, cave, and bosky dell,
From rocky ledge and breezy height,
Fierce Vánars burning for the fight.
And Ráma's course was southward bent
Amid the mighty armament.
On, joyous, pressed in close array
The hosts who owned Sugríva's sway,
With nimble feet, with rapid bound
Exploring, ere they passed, the ground,
While from ten myriad throats rang out
The challenge and the battle shout.
On roots and honeycomb they fed,
And clusters from the boughs o'erhead,
Or from the ground the tall trees tore
Rich with the flowery load they bore.
Some carried comrades, wild with mirth,
Then cast their riders to the earth,
Who swiftly to their feet arose
And overthrew their laughing foes.
While still rang out the general cry,
"King Rávaṇ and his fiends shall die,"
Still on, exulting in the pride
Of conscious strength, the Vánars hied,
And gazed where noble Sahya, best
Of mountains, raised each towering crest.
They looked on lake and streamlet, where
The lotus bloom was bright and fair,
Nor marched—for Ráma's hest they feared
Where town or haunt of men appeared.
Still onward, fearful as the waves

Of Ocean when he roars and raves,
Led by their eager chieftains, went
The Vánars' countless armament.
Each captain, like a noble steed
Urged by the lash to double speed.
Pressed onward, filled with zeal and pride,
By Ráma's and his brother's side,
Who high above the Vánar throng
On mighty backs were borne along,
Like the great Lords of Day and Night
Seized by eclipsing planets might.
Then Lakshman radiant as the morn,
On Angad's shoulders high upborne.
With sweet consoling words that woke
New ardour, to his brother spoke:
"Soon shalt thou turn, thy queen regained
And impious Rávan's life-blood drained,
In happiness and high renown
To dear Ayodhyá's happy town.
I see around exceeding fair
All omens of the earth and air.
Auspicious breezes sweet and low
To greet the Vánar army blow,
And softly to my listening ear
Come the glad cries of bird and deer.
Bright is the sky around us, bright
Without a cloud the Lord of Light,
And Śukra 903 with propitious love
Looks on thee from his throne above.
The pole-star and the Sainted Seven 904
Shine brightly in the northern heaven,
And great Triśanku, 905 glorious king,
Ikshváku's son from whom we spring,
Beams in unclouded glory near

His holy priest 906 whom all revere.
Undimmed the two Visákhás 907 shine,
The strength and glory of our line,
And Nairrit's 908 influence that aids
Our Rákshas foemen faints and fades.
The running brooks are fresh and fair,
The boughs their ripening clusters bear,
And scented breezes gently sway
The leaflet of the tender spray.
See, with a glory half divine
The Vánars' ordered legions shine,
Bright as the Gods' exultant train
Who saw the demon Tárak slain.
O let thine eyes these signs behold,
And bid thy heart be glad and bold."
The Vánar squadrons densely spread
O'er all the country onward sped,
While rising from the rapid beat
Of bears' and monkeys' hastening feet.
Dust hid the earth with thickest veil,
And made the struggling sunbeams pale.
Now where Mahendra's peaks arise
Came Ráma of the lotus eyes
And the long arm's resistless might,
And clomb the mountain's wood-crowned height.
Thence Dasaratha's son beheld
Where billowy Ocean rose and swelled,
Past Malaya's peaks and Sahya's chain
The Vánar legions reached the main,
And stood in many a marshalled band
On loud-resounding Ocean's strand.
To the fair wood that fringed the tide
Came Dasaratha's son, and cried:
"At length, my lord Sugríva, we

Have reached King Varuṇ's realm the sea,
And one great thought, still-vexing, how
To cross the flood, awaits us now.
The broad deep ocean, that denies
A passage, stretched before us lies.
Then let us halt and plan the while
How best to storm the giant's isle."
He ceased: Sugríva on the coast
By trees o'ershadowed stayed the host,
That seemed in glittering lines to be
The bright waves of a second sea.
Then from the shore the captains gazed
On billows which the breezes raised
To fury, as they dashed in foam
O'er Varuṇ's realm, the Asurs' home: 909
The sea that laughed with foam, and danced
With waves whereon the sunbeams glanced:
Where, when the light began to fade,
Huge crocodiles and monsters played;
And, when the moon went up the sky,
The troubled billows rose on high
From the wild watery world whereon
A thousand moons reflected shone:
Where awful serpents swam and showed
Their fiery crests which flashed and glowed,
Illumining the depths of hell,
The prison where the demons dwell.
The eye, bewildered, sought in vain
The bounding line of sky and main:
Alike in shade, alike in glow
Were sky above and sea below.
There wave-like clouds by clouds were chased,
Here cloud-like billows roared and raced:

Then shone the stars, and many a gem
That lit the waters answered them.
They saw the great-souled Ocean stirred
To frenzy by the winds, and heard,
Loud as ten thousand drums, the roar
Of wild waves dashing on the shore.
They saw him mounting to defy
With deafening voice the troubled sky.
And the deep bed beneath him swell
In fury as the billows fell.

Canto V
Ráma's Lament

There on the coast in long array
The Vánars' marshalled legions lay,
Where Níla's care had ordered well
The watch of guard and sentinel,
And Mainda moved from post to post
With Dwivid to protect the host.
Then Ráma stood by Lakshmaṇ's side,
And mastered by his sorrow cried:
"My brother dear, the heart's distress,
As days wear on, grows less and less.
But my deep-seated grief, alas,
Grows fiercer as the seasons pass.
Though for my queen my spirit longs,
And broods indignant o'er my wrongs,
Still wilder is my grief to know
That her young life is passed in woe.
Breathe, gentle gale, O breathe where she
Lies prisoned, and then breathe on me,
And, though my love I may not meet,
Thy kiss shall be divinely sweet.
Ah, by the giant's shape appalled,
On her dear lord for help she called,
Still in mine ears the sad cry rings
And tears my heart with poison stings.
Through the long daylight and the gloom
Of night wild thoughts of her consume
My spirit, and my love supplies

The torturing flame which never dies.
Leave me, my brother; I will sleep
Couched on the bosom of the deep,
For the cold wave may bring me peace
And bid the fire of passion cease.
One only thought my stay must be,
That earth, one earth, holds her and me,
To hear, to know my darling lives
Some life-supporting comfort gives,
As streams from distant fountains run
O'er meadows parching in the sun.
Ah when, my foeman at my feet,
Shall I my queen, my glory, meet,
The blossom of her dear face raise
And on her eyes enraptured gaze,
Press her soft lips to mine again,
And drink a balm to banish pain!
Alas, alas! where lies she now,
My darling of the lovely brow?
On the cold earth, no help at hand,
Forlorn amid the Rákshas band,
King Janak's child still calls on me,
Her lord and love, to set her free.
But soon in glory will she rise
A crescent moon in autumn skies,
And those dark rovers of the night,
Like scattered clouds shall turn in flight."

Canto VI
Rávan's Speech

But when the giant king surveyed
His glorious town in ruin laid,
And each dire sign of victory won
By Hanumán the Wind-God's son,
He vailed his angry eyes oppressed
By shame, and thus his lords addressed:
"The Vánar spy has passed the gate
Of Lanká long inviolate,
Eluded watch and ward, and seen
With his bold eyes the captive queen.
My royal roof with flames is red,
The bravest of my lords are dead,
And the fierce Vánar in his hate
Has left our city desolate.
Now ponder well the work that lies
Before us, ponder and advise.
With deep-observing judgment scan
The peril, and mature a plan.
From counsel, sages say, the root,
Springs victory, most glorious fruit.
First ranks the king, when woe impends
Who seeks the counsel of his friends,
Of kinsmen ever faithful found,
Or those whose hopes with his are bound,
Then with their aid his strength applies,
And triumphs in his enterprise.
Next ranks the prince who plans alone,

No counsel seeks to aid his own,
Weighs loss and gain and wrong and right,
And seeks success with earnest might.
Unwisest he who spurns delays,
Who counts no cost, no peril weighs,
Speeds to his aim, defying fate,
And risks his all, precipitate.
Thus too in counsel sages find
A best, a worst, a middle kind.
When gathered counsellors explore
The way by light of holy lore,
And all from first to last agree,
Is the best counsel of the three.
Next, if debate first waxes high,
And each his chosen plan would try
Till all agree at last, we deem
This counsel second in esteem.
Worst of the three is this, when each
Assails with taunt his fellow's speech;
When all debate, and no consent
Concludes the angry argument.
Consult then, lords; my task shall be
To crown with act your wise decree.
With thousands of his wild allies
The vengeful Ráma hither hies;
With unresisted might and speed
Across the flood his troops will lead,
Or for the Vánar host will drain
The channels of the conquered main."

Canto VII
Rávan Encouraged

He ceased: they scorned, with blinded eyes,
The foeman and his bold allies,
Raised reverent hands with one accord,
And thus made answer to their lord:
"Why yield thee, King, to causeless fear?
A mighty host with sword and spear
And mace and axe and pike and lance
Waits but thy signal to advance.
Art thou not he who slew of old
The Serpent-Gods, and stormed their hold;
Scaled Mount Kailása and o'erthrew
Kuvera 910 and his Yaksha crew,
Compelling Śiva's haughty friend
Beneath a mightier arm to bend?
Didst thou not bring from realms afar
The marvel of the magic car,
When they who served Kuvera fell
Crushed in their mountain citadel?
Attracted by thy matchless fame
To thee, a suppliant, Maya came,
The lord of every Dánav band,
And won thee with his daughter's hand.
Thy arm in hell itself was felt,
Where Vásuki 911 and Śankha dwelt,
And they and Takshak, overthrown,
Were forced thy conquering might to own.
The Gods in vain their blessing gave

To heroes bravest of the brave,
Who strove a year and, sorely pressed,
Their victor's peerless might confessed.
In vain their magic arts they tried,
In vain thy matchless arm defied
King Varuṇ's sons with fourfold force,
Cars, elephants, and foot, and horse,
But for a while thy power withstood,
And, conquered, mourned their hardihood.
Thou hast encountered, face to face,
King Yáma 912 with his murdering mace.
Fierce as the wild tempestuous sea,
What terror had his wrath for thee,
Though death in every threatening form,
And woe and torment, urged the storm?
Thine arm a glorious victory won
O'er the dread king who pities none;
And the three worlds, from terror freed,
In joyful wonder praised thy deed.
The tribe of Warriors, strong and dread
As Indra's self, o'er earth had spread;
As giant trees that towering stand
In mountain glens, they filled the land.
Can Raghu's son encounter foes
Fierce, numerous, and strong as those?
Yet, trained in war and practised well,
O'ermatched by thee, they fought and fell,
Stay in thy royal home, nor care
The battle and the toil to share;
But let the easy fight be won
By Indrajít 913 thy matchless son.
All, all shall die, if thou permit,
Slain by the hand of Indrajít."

Canto VIII
Prahasta's Speech

Dark as a cloud of autumn, dread
Prahasta joined his palms and said:
"Gandharvas, Gods, the hosts who dwell
In heaven, in air, in earth, in hell,
Have yielded to thy might, and how
Shall two weak men oppose thee now?
Hanúmán came, a foe disguised,
And mocked us heedless and surprised,
Or never had he lived to flee
And boast that he has fought with me.
Command, O King, and this right hand
Shall sweep the Vánars from the land,
And hill and dale, to Ocean's shore,
Shall know the death-doomed race no more.
But let my care the means devise
To guard thy city from surprise."
Then Durmukh cried, of Rákshas race:
"Too long we brook the dire disgrace.
He gave our city to the flames,
He trod the chambers of thy dames.
Ne'er shall so weak and vile a thing
Unpunished brave the giants' king.
Now shall this single arm attack
And drive the daring Vánars back,
Till to the winds of heaven they flee,
Or seek the depths of earth and sea."
Then, brandishing the mace he bore,
Whose horrid spikes were stained with gore,

While fury made his eyeballs red,
Impetuous Vajradanshtra said:
"Why waste a thought on one so vile
As Hanúmán the Vánar, while
Sugríva, Lakshman, yet remain,
And Ráma mightier still, unslain?
This mace to-day shall crush the three,
And all the host will turn and flee.
Listen, and I will speak: incline,
O King, to hear these words of mine,
For the deep plan that I propose
Will swiftly rid thee of thy foes.
Let thousands of thy host assume
The forms of men in youthful bloom,
In war's magnificent array
Draw near to Raghu's son, and say:
"Thy younger brother Bharat sends
This army, and thy cause befriends."
Then let our legions hasten near
With bow and mace and sword and spear,
And on the Vánar army rain
Our steel and stone till all be slain.
If Raghu's sons will fain believe,
Entangled in the net we weave,
The penalty they both must pay,
And lose their forfeit lives to-day."
Then with his warrior soul on fire,
Nikumbha spoke in burning ire:
"I, only I, will take the field,
And Raghu's son his life shall yield.
Within these walls, O Chiefs, abide,
Nor part ye from our monarch's side."

Canto IX
Vibhishan's Counsel

A score of warriors 914 forward sprang,
And loud the clashing iron rang
Of mace and axe and spear and sword,
As thus they spake unto their lord:
"Their king Sugríva will we slay,
And Raghu's sons, ere close of day,
And strike the wretch Hanúmán down,
The spoiler of our golden town."
But sage Vibhishaṇ strove to calm
The chieftains' fury; palm to palm
He joined in lowly reverence, pressed 915
Before them, and the throng addressed:
"Dismiss the hope of conquering one
So stern and strong as Raghu's son.
In due control each sense he keeps
With constant care that never sleeps.
Whose daring heart has e'er conceived
The exploit Hanumán achieved,
Across the fearful sea to spring,
The tributary rivers' king?
O Rákshas lords, in time be wise,
Nor Ráma's matchless power despise.
And say, what evil had the son
Of Raghu to our monarch done,
Who stole the dame he loved so well
And keeps her in his citadel;
If Khara in his foolish pride
Encountered Ráma, fought, and died,

May not the meanest love his life
And guard it in the deadly strife?
The Maithil dame, O Rákshas King,
Sore peril to thy realm will bring.
Restore her while there yet is time,
Nor let us perish for thy crime.
O, let the Maithil lady go
Ere the avenger bend his bow
To ruin with his arrowy showers
Our Lanká with her gates and towers.
Let Janak's child again be free
Ere the wild Vánars cross the sea,
In their resistless might assail
Our city and her ramparts scale.
Ah, I conjure thee by the ties
Of brotherhood, be just and wise.
In all my thoughts thy good I seek,
And thus my prudent counsel speak.
Let captive Sítá be restored
Ere, fierce as autumn's sun, her lord
Send his keen arrows from the string
To drink the life-blood of our king.
This fury from thy soul dismiss,
The bane of duty, peace, and bliss.
Seek duty's path and walk therein,
And joy and endless glory win.
Restore the captive, ere we feel
The piercing point of Ráma's steel.
O spare thy city, spare the lives
Of us, our friends, our sons and wives."
Thus spake Vibhishaṇ wise and brave:
The Rákshas king no answer gave,
But bade his lords the council close,
And sought his chamber for repose.

Canto X
Vibhishan's Counsel

Soon as the light of morning broke,
Vibhishan from his slumber woke,
And, duty guiding every thought,
The palace of his brother sought.
Vast as a towering hill that shows
His peaks afar, that palace rose.
Here stood within the monarch's gate
Sage nobles skilful in debate.
There strayed in glittering raiment through
The courts his royal retinue,
Where in wild measure rose and fell
The music of the drum and shell,
And talk grew loud, and many a dame
Of fairest feature went and came
Through doors a marvel to behold,
With pearl inlaid on burning gold:
Therein Gandharvas or the fleet
Lords of the storm might joy to meet.
He passed within the wondrous pile,
Chief glory of the giants' isle:
Thus, ere his fiery course be done,
An autumn cloud admits the sun.
He heard auspicious voices raise
With loud accord the note of praise,
And sages, deep in Scripture, sing
Each glorious triumph of the king.
He saw the priests in order stand,

Curd, oil, in every sacred hand;
And by them flowers were laid and grain,
Due offerings to the holy train.
Vibhishaṇ to the monarch bowed,
Raised on a throne above the crowd:
Then, skilled in arts of soft address,
He raised his voice the king to bless,
And sate him on a seat where he
Full in his brother's sight should be.
The chieftain there, while none could hear,
Spoke his true speech for Rávaṇ's ear,
And to his words of wisdom lent
The force of weightiest argument:
"O brother, hear! since Ráma's queen
A captive in thy house has been,
Disastrous omens day by day
Have struck our souls with wild dismay.
No longer still and strong and clear
The flames of sacrifice appear,
But, restless with the frequent spark,
Neath clouds of smoke grow faint and dark.
Our ministering priests turn pale
To see their wonted offerings fail,
And ants and serpents creep and crawl
Within the consecrated hall. 916
Dried are the udders of our cows,
Our elephants have juiceless brows, 917
Nor can the sweetest pasture stay
The charger's long unquiet neigh.
Big tears from mules and camels flow
Whose staring coats their trouble show,
Nor can the leech's art restore
Their health and vigour as before.
Rapacious birds are fierce and bold:

Not single hunters as of old,
In banded troops they chase the prey,
Or gathering on our temples stay.
Through twilight hours with shriek and howl
Around the city jackals prowl,
And wolves and foul hyænas wait
Athirst for blood at every gate.
One sole atonement still may cure
These evils, and our weal assure.
Restore the Maithil dame, and win
An easy pardon for thy sin."
The Rákshas monarch heard, and moved
To sudden wrath his speech reproved:
"No danger, brother, can I see:
The Maithil dame I will not free.
Though all the Gods for Ráma fight,
He yields to my superior might."
Thus the tremendous king who broke
The ranks of heavenly warriors spoke,
And, sternly purposed to resist,
His brother from the hall dismissed.

Canto XI
The Summons

Still Rávan's haughty heart rebelled,
The counsel of the wise repelled,
And, as his breast with passion burned,
His thoughts again to Sítá turned.
Thus, to each sign of danger blind,
To love and war he still inclined.
Then mounted he his car that glowed
With gems and golden net, and rode
Where, gathered at the monarch's call,
The nobles filled the council hall.
A host of warriors bright and gay
With coloured robes and rich array,
With shield and mace and spear and sword,
Followed the chariot of their lord.
Mid the loud voice of shells and beat
Of drums he raced along the street,
And, ere he came, was heard afar
The rolling thunder of his car.
He reached the doors: the nobles bent
Their heads before him reverent:
And, welcomed with their loud acclaim,
Within the glorious hall he came.
He sat upon a royal seat
With golden steps beneath his feet,
And bade the heralds summon all
His captains to the council hall.
The heralds heard the words he spake,

And sped from house to house to wake
The giants where they slept or spent
The careless hours in merriment.
These heard the summons and obeyed:
From chamber, grove, and colonnade,
On elephants or cars they rode,
Or through the streets impatient strode.
As birds on rustling pinions fly
Through regions of the darkened sky,
Thus cars and mettled coursers through
The crowded streets of Lanká flew.
The council hall was reached, and then,
As lions seek their mountain den,
Through massy doors that opened wide,
With martial stalk the captains hied.
Welcomed with honour as was meet
They stooped to press their monarch's feet,
And each a place in order found
On stool, on cushion, or the ground.
Nor did the sage Vibhishaṇ long
Delay to join the noble throng.
High on a car that shone like flame
With gold and flashing gems he came,
Drew near and spoke his name aloud,
And reverent to his brother bowed.

Canto XII
Rávan's Speech

The king in counsel unsurpassed
His eye around the synod cast,
And fierce Prahasta, first and best
Of all his captains, thus addressed:
"Brave master of each warlike art,
Arouse thee and perform thy part.
Array thy fourfold forces 918 well
To guard our isle and citadel."
The captain of the hosts obeyed,
The troops with prudent skill arrayed;
Then to the hall again he hied,
And stood before the king and cried:
"Each inlet to the town is closed
Without, within, are troops disposed.
With fearless heart thine aim pursue
And do the deed thou hast in view."
Thus spoke Prahasta in the zeal
That moved him for the kingdom's weal.
And thus the monarch, who pursued
His own delight, his speech renewed:
"In ease and bliss, in toil and pain,
In doubts of duty, pleasure, gain,
Your proper path I need not tell,
For of yourselves ye know it well.
The Storm-Gods, Moon, and planets bring
New glory to their heavenly king, 919
And, ranged about your monarch, ye

Give joy and endless fame to me.
My secret counsel have I kept,
While senseless Kumbhakarṇa slept.
Six months the warrior's slumbers last
And bind his torpid senses fast;
But now his deep repose he breaks,
The best of all our champions wakes.
I captured, Ráma's heart to wring,
This daughter of Videha's king.
And brought her from that distant land 920
Where wandered many a Rákshas band.
Disdainful still my love she spurns,
Still from each prayer and offering turns,
Yet in all lands beneath the sun
No dame may rival Sítá, none,
Her dainty waist is round and slight,
Her cheek like autumn's moon is bright,
And she like fruit in graven gold
Mocks her 921 whom Maya framed of old.
Faultless in form, how firmly tread
Her feet whose soles are rosy red!
Ah, as I gaze her beauty takes
My spirit, and my passion wakes.
Looking for Ráma far away
She sought with tears a year's delay
Nor gazing on her love-lit eye
Could I that earnest prayer deny.
But baffled hopes and vain desire
At length my patient spirit tire.
How shall the sons of Raghu sweep
To vengeance o'er the pathless deep?
How shall they lead the Vánar train
Across the monster-teeming main?
One Vánar yet could find a way

To Lanká's town, and burn and slay.
Take counsel then, remembering still
That we from men need fear no ill;
And give your sentence in debate,
For matchless is the power of fate.
Assailed by you the Gods who dwell
In heaven beneath our fury fell.
And shall we fear these creatures bred
In forests, by Sugríva led?
E'en now on ocean's farther strand,
The sons of Daśaratha stand,
And follow, burning to attack
Their giant foes, on Sítá's track.
Consult then, lords for ye are wise:
A seasonable plan devise.
The captive lady to retain,
And triumph when the foes are slain.
No power can bring across the foam
Those Vánars to our island home;
Or if they madly will defy
Our conquering might, they needs must die."
Then Kumbhakarṇa's anger woke,
And wroth at Rávaṇ's words he spoke:
"O Monarch, when thy ravished eyes
First looked upon thy lovely prize,
Then was the time to bid us scan
Each peril and mature a plan.
Blest is the king who acts with heed,
And ne'er repents one hasty deed;
And hapless he whose troubled soul
Mourns over days beyond control.
Thou hast, in beauty's toils ensnared,
A desperate deed of boldness dared;
By fortune saved ere Ráma's steel

One wound, thy mortal bane, could deal.
But, Rávan, as the deed is done,
The toil of war I will not shun.
This arm, O rover of the night,
Thy foemen to the earth shall smite,
Though Indra with the Lord of Flame,
The Sun and Storms, against me came.
E'en Indra, monarch of the skies,
Would dread my club and mountain size,
Shrink from these teeth and quake to hear
The thunders of my voice of fear.
No second dart shall Ráma cast:
The first he aims shall be the last.
He falls, and these dry lips shall drain
The blood of him my hand has slain;
And Sítá, when her champion dies,
Shall be thine undisputed prize."

Canto XIII
Rávan's Speech

But Mahápárśva saw the sting
Of keen reproach had galled the king;
And humbly, eager to appease
His anger, spoke in words like these:
"And breathes there one so cold and weak
The forest and the gloom to seek
Where savage beasts abound, and spare
To taste the luscious honey there?
Art thou not lord? and who is he
Shall venture to give laws to thee?
Love thy Videhan still, and tread
Upon thy prostrate foeman's head.
O'er Sítá's will let thine prevail,
And strength achieve if flattery fail.
What though the lady yet be coy
And turn her from the proffered joy?
Soon shall her conquered heart relent
And yield to love and blandishment.
With us let Kumbhakarṇa fight,
And Indrajít of matchless might:
We need not other champions, they
Shall lead us forth to rout and slay.
Not ours to bribe or soothe or part
The foeman's force with gentle art,
Doomed, conquered by our might, to feel
The vengeance of the warrior's steel."
The Rákshas monarch heard, and moved

By flattering hopes the speech approved:
"Hear me," he cried, "great chieftain, tell
What in the olden time befell, —
A secret tale which, long suppressed,
Lies prisoned only in my breast.
One day—a day I never forget—
Fair Punjikasthalá 922 I met,
When, radiant as a flame of fire,
She sought the palace of the Sire.
In passion's eager grasp I tore
From her sweet limbs the robes she wore,
And heedless of her prayers and cries
Strained to my breast the vanquised prize.
Like Naliní 923 with soil distained,
The mansion of the Sire she gained,
And weeping made the outrage known
To Brahmá on his heavenly throne.
He in his wrath pronounced a curse, —
That lord who made the universe:
"If, Rávaṇ, thou a second time
Be guilty of so foul a crime,
Thy head in shivers shall be rent:
Be warned, and dread the punishment."
Awed by the threat of vengeance still
I force not Sítá's stubborn will.
Terrific as the sea in might:
My steps are like the Storm-Gods' flight;
But Ráma knows not this, or he
Had never sought to war with me.
Where is the man would idly brave
The lion in his mountain cave,
And wake him when with slumbering eyes
Grim, terrible as Death, he lies?
No, blinded Ráma knows me not:

Ne'er has he seen mine arrows shot;
Ne'er marked them speeding to their aim
Like snakes with cloven tongues of flame.
On him those arrows will I turn,
Whose fiery points shall rend and burn.
Quenched by my power when I assail
The glory of his might shall fail,
As stars before the sun grow dim
And yield their feeble light to him."

Canto XIV
Vibhishan's Speech

He ceased: Vibhishaṇ ill at ease
Addressed the king in words like these:
"O Rávaṇ, O my lord, beware
Of Sítá dangerous as fair,
Nor on thy heedless bosom hang
This serpent with a deadly fang.
O King, the Maithil dame restore
To Raghu's matchless son before
Those warriors of the woodlands, vast
As mountain peaks, approaching fast,
Armed with fierce teeth and claws, enclose
Thy city with unsparing foes.
O, be the Maithil dame restored
Ere loosened from the clanging cord
The vengeful shafts of Ráma fly,
And low in death thy princes lie.
In all thy legions hast thou one
A match in war for Raghu's son?
Can Kumbhakarṇa's self withstand,
Or Indrajít, that mighty hand?
In vain with Ráma wilt thou strive:
Thou wilt not save thy soul alive
Though guarded by the Lord of Day
And Storm-Gods' terrible array,
In vain to Indra wilt thou fly,
Or seek protection in the sky,
In Yáma's gloomy mansion dwell,

Or hide thee in the depths of hell."
He ceased; and when his lips were closed
Prahasta thus his rede opposed:
"O timid heart, to counsel thus!
What terrors have the Gods for us?
Can snake, Gandharva, fiend appal
The giants' sons who scorn them all?
And shall we now our birth disgrace,
And dread a king of human race?"
Thus fierce Prahasta counselled ill:
But sage Vibhishan's constant will
The safety of the realm ensued;
Who thus in turn his speech renewed:
"Yes, when a soul defiled with sin
Shall mount to heaven and enter in,
Then, chieftain, will experience teach
The truth of thy disdainful speech.
Can I, or thou, or these or all
Our bravest compass Ráma's fall,
The chief in whom all virtues shine,
The pride of old Ikshváku'a line,
With whom the Gods may scarce compare
In skill to act, in heart to dare?
Yea, idly mayst thou vaunt thee, till
Sharp arrows winged with matchless skill
From Ráma's bowstring, fleet and fierce
As lightning's flame, thy body pierce.
Nikumbha shall not save thee then,
Nor Rávan, from the lord of men.
O Monarch, hear my last appeal,
My counsel for thy kingdom's weal.
This sentence I again declare:
O giant King, beware, beware!
Save from the ruin that impends

Thy town, thy people, and thy friends;
O hear the warning urged once more:
To Raghu's son the dame restore."

Canto XV
Indrajít's Speech

He ceased: and Indrajít the pride
Of Rákshas warriors thus replied:
"Is this a speech our king should hear,
This counsel of ignoble fear?
A scion of our glorious race
Should ne'er conceive a thought so base,
But one mid all our kin we find,
Vibhishaṇ, whose degenerate mind
No spark of gallant pride retains,
Whose coward soul his lineage stains.
Against one giant what can two
Unhappy sons of Raghu do?
Away with idle fears, away!
Matched with our meanest, what are they?
Beneath my conquering prowess fell
The Lord of earth and heaven and hell. 924
Through every startled region dread
Of my resistless fury spread;
And Gods in each remotest sphere
Confessed the universal fear.
Rending the air with roar and groan,
Airávat 925 to the earth was thrown.
From his huge head the tusks I drew,
And smote the Gods with fear anew.
Shall I who tame celestials' pride,
By whom the fiends are terrified,
Now prove a weakling little worth,

And fail to slay those sons of earth?"
He ceased: Vibhishaṇ trained and tried
In war and counsel thus replied
"Thy speech is marked with scorn of truth,
With rashness and the pride of youth.
Yea, to thy ruin like a child
Thou pratest, and thy words are wild.
Most dear, O Indrajít, to thee
Should Rávaṇ's weal and safety be,
For thou art called his son, but thou
Art proved his direst foeman now,
When warned by me thou hast not tried
To turn the coming woe aside.
Both thee and him 'twere meet to slay,
Who brought thee to this hall to-day,
And dared so rash a youth admit
To council where the wisest sit.
Presumptuous, wild, devoid of sense,
Filled full of pride and insolence,
Thy reckless tongue thou wilt not rule
That speaks the counsel of a fool.
Who in the fight may brook or shun
The arrows shot by Raghu's son
With flame and fiery vengeance sped,
Dire as his staff who rules the dead?
O Rávaṇ, let thy people live,
And to the son of Raghu give
Fair robes and gems and precious ore,
And Sítá to his arms restore."

Canto XVI
Rávan's Speech

Then, while his breast with fury swelled,
Thus Rávaṇ spoke, as fate impelled:
"Better with foes thy dwelling make,
Or house thee with the venomed snake,
Than live with false familiar friends
Who further still thy foeman's ends.
I know their treacherous mood, I know
Their secret triumph at thy woe.
They in their inward hearts despise
The brave, the noble, and the wise,
Grieve at their bliss with rancorous hate,
And for their sorrows watch and wait:
Scan every fault with curious eye,
And each slight error magnify.
Ask elephants who roam the wild
How were their captive friends beguiled.
"For fire," they cry, "we little care,
For javelin and shaft and snare:
Our foes are traitors, taught to bind
The trusting creatures of their kind."
Still, still, shall blessings flow from cows, 926
And Bráhmans love their rigorous vows;
Still woman change her restless will,
And friends perfidious work us ill.
What though with conquering feet I tread
On every prostrate foeman's head;
What though the worlds in abject fear

Their mighty lord in me revere?
This thought my peace of mind destroys
And robs me of expected joys.
The lotus of the lake receives
The glittering rain that gems its leaves,
But each bright drop remains apart:
So is it still with heart and heart.
Deceitful as an autumn cloud
Which, though its thunderous voice be loud,
On the dry earth no torrent sends,
Such is the race of faithless friends.
No riches of the bloomy spray
Will tempt the wandering bee to stay
That loves from flower to flower to range;
And friends like thee are swift to change.
Thou blot upon thy glorious line,
If any giant's tongue but thine
Had dared to give this base advice,
He should not live to shame me twice."
Then just Vibhishan in the heat
Of anger started from his seat,
And with four captains of the band
Sprang forward with his mace in hand;
Then, fury flashing from his eye,
Looked on the king and made reply:
"Thy rights, O Rávan, I allow:
My brother and mine elder thou.
Such, though from duty's path they stray,
We love like fathers and obey,
But still too bitter to be borne
Is thy harsh speech of cruel scorn.
The rash like thee, who spurn control,
Nor check one longing of the soul,
Urged by malignant fate repel

The faithful friend who counsels well.
A thousand courtiers wilt thou meet,
With flattering lips of smooth deceit:
But rare are they whose tongue or ear
Will speak the bitter truth, or hear.
Unclose thy blinded eyes and see
That snares of death encompass thee.
I dread, my brother, to behold
The shafts of Ráma, bright with gold,
Flash fury through the air, and red
With fires of vengeance strike thee dead.
Lord, brother, King, again reflect,
Nor this mine earnest prayer reject,
O, save thyself, thy royal town,
Thy people and thine old renown."

Canto XVII
Vibhishan's Flight

Soon as his bitter words were said,
To Raghu's sons Vibhishan fled. 927
Their eyes the Vánar leaders raised
And on the air-borne Rákhshas gazed,
Bright as a thunderbolt, in size
Like Meru's peak that cleaves the skies.
In gorgeous panoply arrayed
Like Indra's self he stood displayed,
And four attendants brave and bold
Shone by their chief in mail and gold.
Sugríva then with dark surmise
Bent on their forms his wondering eyes,
And thus in hasty words confessed
The anxious doubt that moved his breast:
"Look, look ye Vánars, and beware:
That giant chief sublime in air
With other four in bright array
Comes armed to conquer and to slay."
Soon as his warning speech they heard,
The Vánar chieftains undeterred
Seized fragments of the rock and trees,
And made reply in words like these:
"We wait thy word: the order give,
And these thy foes shall cease to live.
Command us, mighty King, and all
Lifeless upon the earth shall fall."
Meanwhile Vibhishan with the four

Stood high above the ocean shore.
Sugríva and the chiefs he spied,
And raised his mighty voice and cried:
"From Rávaṇ, lord of giants, I
His brother, named Vibhishaṇ, fly.
From Janasthán he stole the child
Of Janak by his art beguiled,
And in his palace locked and barred
Surrounds her with a Rákshas guard.
I bade him, plied with varied lore,
His hapless prisoner restore.
But he, by Fate to ruin sent,
No credence to my counsel lent,
Mad as the fevered wretch who sees
And scorns the balm to bring him ease.
He scorned the sage advice I gave,
He spurned me like a base-born slave.
I left my children and my wife,
And fly to Raghu's son for life.
I pray thee, Vánar chieftain, speed
To him who saves in hour of need,
And tell him famed in distant lands
That suppliant here Vibhishaṇ stands."
The Rákshas ceased: Sugríva hied
To Raghu's noble son and cried:
"A stranger from the giant host,
Borne o'er the sea, has reached the coast;
A secret foe, he comes to slay,
As owls attack their heedless prey.
'Tis thine, O King, in time of need
To watch, to counsel, and to lead,
Our Vánar legions to dispose,
And guard us from our crafty foes.
Vibhishaṇ from the giants' isle,

King Rávaṇ's brother, comes with guile
And, feigning from his king to flee,
Seeks refuge, Raghu's son, with thee.
Arise, O Ráma, and prevent
By bold attack his dark intent.
Who comes in friendly guise prepared
To slay thee by his arts ensnared."
Thus urged Sugríva famed for lore
Of moving words, and spoke no more.
Then Ráma thus in turn addressed
The bold Hanúmán and the rest:
"Chiefs of the Vánar legions each
Of you heard Sugríva's speech.
What think ye now in time of fear,
When peril and distress are near,
In every doubt the wise depend
For counsel on a faithful friend."
They heard his gracious words, and then
Spake reverent to the lord of men:
"O Raghu's son, thou knowest well
All things of heaven and earth and hell.
'Tis but thy friendship bids us speak
The counsel Ráma need not seek.
So duteous, brave, and true art thou,
Heroic, faithful to thy vow.
Deep in the scriptures, trained and tried,
Still in thy friends wilt thou confide.
Let each of us in turn impart
The secret counsel of his heart,
And strive to win his chief's assent,
By force of wisest argument."
They ceased and Angad thus began:
"With jealous eye the stranger scan:
Not yet with trusting heart receive

Vibhishaṇ, nor his tale believe.
These giants wandering far and wide
Their evil nature falsely hide,
And watching with malignant skill
Assail us when we fear no ill.
Well ponder every hope and fear
Until thy doubtful course be clear;
Then own his merit or detect
His guile, and welcome or reject."
Then Śarabha the bold and brave
In turn his prudent sentence gave:
"Yea, Ráma, send a skilful spy
With keenest tact to test and try.
Then let the stranger, as is just,
Obtain or be refused thy trust."
Then he whose heart was rich in store
Of scripture's life-directing lore,
King Jámbaván, stood forth and cried:
"Suspect, suspect a foe allied
With Rávaṇ lord of Lanká's isle,
And Rákshas sin and Rákshas guile."
Then Mainda, wisest chief, who knew
The wrong, the right, the false, the true,
Pondered a while, then silence broke,
And thus his sober counsel spoke:
"Let one with gracious speech draw near
And gently charm Vibhishaṇ's ear,
Till he the soothing witchery feel
And all his secret heart reveal.
So thou his aims and hopes shalt know,
And hail the friend or shun the foe."
"Not he," Hanúmán cried, "not he
Who taught the Gods 928 may rival thee,
Supreme in power of quickest sense,

First in the art of eloquence.
But hear me soothly speak, O King,
And learn the hope to which I cling.
Vibhishaṇ comes no crafty spy:
Urged by his brother's fault to fly.
With righteous soul that loathes the sin,
He fled from Lanká and his kin.
If strangers question, doubt will rise
And chill the heart of one so wise.
Marred by distrust the parle will end,
And thou wilt lose a faithful friend.
Nor let it seem so light a thing
To sound a stranger's heart, O King.
And he, I ween, whate'er he say,
Will ne'er an evil thought betray.
He comes a friend in happy time,
Loathing his brother for his crime.
His ear has heard thine old renown,
The might that struck King Báli down,
And set Sugríva on the throne.
And looking now to thee alone
He comes thy matchless aid to win
And punish Rávaṇ for his sin.
Thus have I tried thy heart to move,
And thus Vibhishaṇ's truth to prove.
Still in his friendship I confide;
But ponder, wisest, and decide."

Canto XVIII
Ráma's Speech

Then Ráma's rising doubt was stilled,
And friendly thoughts his bosom filled.
Thus, deep in Scripture's lore, he spake:
"The suppliant will I ne'er forsake,
Nor my protecting aid refuse
When one in name of friendship sues.
Though faults and folly blot his fame,
Pity and help he still may claim."
He ceased: Sugríva bowed his head
And pondered for a while, and said:
"Past number be his faults or few,
What think ye of the Rákshas who,
When threatening clouds of danger rise,
Deserts his brother's side and flies?
Say, Vánars, who may hope to find
True friendship in his faithless kind?"
The son of Raghu heard his speech:
He cast a hasty look on each
Of those brave Vánar chiefs, and while
Upon his lips there played a smile,
To Lakshman turned and thus expressed
The thoughts that moved his gallant breast:
"Well versed in Scripture's lore, and sage
And duly reverent to age,
Is he, with long experience stored,
Who counsels like this Vánar lord.
Yet here, methinks, for searching eyes

Some deeper, subtler matter lies.
To you and all the world are known
The perils of a monarch's throne,
While foe and stranger, kith and kin
By his misfortune trust to win.
By hope of such advantage led,
Vibhishan o'er the sea has fled.
He in his brother's stead would reign,
And our alliance seeks to gain;
And we his offer may embrace,
A stranger and of alien race.
But if he comes a spy and foe,
What power has he to strike a blow
In furtherance of his close design?
What is his strength compared with mine?
And can I, Vánar King, forget
The great, the universal debt,
Ever to aid and welcome those
Who pray for shelter, friends or foes?
Hast thou not heard the deathless praise
Won by the dove in olden days,
Who conquering his fear and hate
Welcomed the slayer of his mate,
And gave a banquet, to refresh
The weary fowler, of his flesh?
Now hear me, Vánar King, rehearse
What Kaṇḍu 929 spoke in ancient verse,
Saint Kaṇva's son who loved the truth
And clave to virtue from his youth:
"Strike not the suppliant when he stands
And asks thee with beseeching hands
For shelter: strike him not although
He were thy father's mortal foe.
No, yield him, be he proud or meek,

The shelter which he comes to seek,
And save thy foeman, if the deed
Should cost thy life, in desperate need."
And shall I hear the wretched cry,
And my protecting aid deny?
Shall I a suppliant's prayer refuse,
And heaven and glory basely lose?
No, I will do for honour sake
E'en as the holy Kaṇdu spake,
Preserve a hero's name from stain,
And bliss in heaven and glory gain.
Bound by a solemn vow I sware
That all my saving help should share
Who sought me in distress and cried,
"Thou art my hope, and none beside."
Then go, I pray thee, Vánar King,
Vibhishaṇ to my presence bring,
Yea, were he Rávaṇ's self, my vow
Forbids me to reject him now."
He ceased: the Vánar king approved;
And Ráma toward Vibhishaṇ moved.
So moves, a brother God to greet,
Lord Indra from his heavenly seat.

Canto XIX
Vibhishan's Counsel

When Raghu's son had owned his claim
Down from the air Vibhishan came,
And with his four attendants bent
At Ráma's feet most reverent.
"O Ráma," thus he cried, "in me
Vibhishan, Rávan's brother see.
By him disgraced thine aid I seek,
Sure refuge of the poor and weak.
From Lanká, friends, and wealth I fly,
And reft of all on thee rely.
On thee, the wretch's firmest friend,
My kingdom, joys, and life depend."
With glance of favour Ráma eyed
The Rákshas chief and thus replied:
"First from thy lips I fain would hear
Each brighter hope, each darker fear.
Speak, stranger, that I well may know
The strength and weakness of the foe."
He ceased: the Rákshas chief obeyed,
And thus in turn his answer made:
"O Prince, the Self-existent gave
This boon to Rávan; he may brave
All foes in fight; no fiend or snake,
Gandharva, God, his life may take.
His brother Kumbhakarna vies
In might with him who rules the skies.
The captain of his armies—fame

Perhaps has taught the warrior's name—
Is terrible Prahasta, who
King Maṇibhadra's 930 self o'erthrew.
Where is the warrior found to face
Young Indrajít, when armed with brace
And guard 931 and bow he stands in mail
And laughs at spear and arrowy hail?
Within his city Lanká dwell
Ten million giants fierce and fell,
Who wear each varied shape at will
And eat the flesh of those they kill.
These hosts against the Gods he led,
And heavenly might discomfited."
Then Ráma cried: "I little heed
Gigantic strength or doughty deed.
In spite of all their might has done
The king, the captain, and the son
Shall fall beneath my fury dead,
And thou shalt reign in Rávaṇ's stead.
He, though in depths of earth he dwell,
Or seek protection down in hell,
Or kneel before the Sire supreme,
His forfeit life shall ne'er redeem.
Yea, by my brothers' lives I swear,
I will not to my home repair
Till Rávaṇ and his kith and kin
Have paid in death the price of sin."
Vibhishaṇ bowed his head and cried:
"Thy conquering army will I guide
To storm the city of the foe,
And aid the tyrant's overthrow."
Thus spake Vibhishaṇ: Ráma pressed
The Rákshas chieftain to his breast,
And cried to Lakshmaṇ: "Haste and bring

Sea-water for the new-made king."
He spoke, and o'er Vibhishaṇ's head
The consecrating drops were shed
Mid shouts that hailed with one accord
The giants' king and Lanká's lord.
"Is there no way," Hanúmán cried,
"No passage o'er the boisterous tide?
How may we lead the Vánar host
In triumph to the farther coast?"
"Thus," said Vibhishaṇ, "I advise:
Let Raghu's son in suppliant guise
Entreat the mighty Sea to lend
His succour and this cause befriend.
His channels, as the wise have told,
By Sagar's sons were dug of old, 932
Nor will high-thoughted Ocean scorn
A prince of Sagar's lineage born."
He ceased; the prudent counsel won
The glad assent of Raghu's son.
Then on the ocean shore a bed
Of tender sacred grass was spread,
Where Ráma at the close of day
Like fire upon an altar lay.

Canto XX
The Spies

Śárdúla, Rávaṇ's spy, surveyed
The legions on the strand arrayed.
And bore, his bosom racked with fear,
These tidings to the monarch's ear:
"They come, they come. A rushing tide,
Ten leagues they spread from side to side,
And on to storm thy city press,
Fierce rovers of the wilderness.
Rich in each princely power and grace,
The pride of Daśaratha's race,
Ráma and Lakshmaṇ lead their bands,
And halt them on the ocean sands.
O Monarch, rise, this peril meet;
Risk not the danger of defeat.
First let each wiser art be tried;
Bribe them, or win them, or divide."
Such was the counsel of the spy:
And Rávaṇ called to Śuka: "Fly,
Sugríva lord of Vánars seek,
And thus my kingly message speak:
"Great power and might and fame are thine,
Brave scion of a royal line,
King Riksharajas' son, in thee
A brother and a friend I see.
How wronged by me canst thou complain?
What profit here pretend to gain?
If from the wood the wife I stole

Of Ráma of the prudent soul,
What cause hast thou to mourn the theft?
Thou art not injured or bereft.
Return, O King, thy steps retrace
And seek thy mountain dwelling-place.
No, never may thy hosts within
My Lanká's walls a footing win.
A mighty town whose strength defies
The gathered armies of the skies."
He ceased: obedient Śuka heard;
With wings and plumage of a bird
He rose in eager speed and through
The air upon his errand flew.
Borne o'er the sea with rapid wing
He stood above the Vánar king,
And spoke aloud, sublime in air,
The message he was charged to bear.
The Vánar heard the words he spoke,
And quick redoubling stroke on stroke
On head and pinions hemmed him round
And bore him struggling to the ground.
The Rákshas wounded and distressed
These words to Raghu's son addressed:
"Quick, quick! This Vánar host restrain,
For heralds never must be slain.
To him alone, a wretch untrue,
The punishment of death is due
Who leaves his master's speech unsaid
And speaks another in its stead."
Moved by the suppliant speech and prayer
Up sprang the prince and cried, forbear.
Saved from his wild assailant's blows
Again the Rákshas herald rose
And borne on light wings to the sky

Addressed Sugríva from on high:
"O Vánar Monarch, chief endued
With power and wonderous fortitude,
What answer is my king, the fear
And scourge of weeping worlds, to hear?"
"Go tell thy lord," Sugríva cried,
"Thou, Ráma's foe, art thus defied.
His arm the guilty Báli slew;
Thus, tyrant, shalt thou perish too.
Thy sons, thy friends, proud King, and all
Thy kith and kin with thee shall fall;
And, emptied of the giant's brood,
Burnt Lanká be a solitude.
Fly to the Sun-God's pathway, go
And hide thee deep in hell below:
In vain from Ráma shalt thou flee
Though heavenly warriors fight for thee.
Thine arm subdued, securely bold,
The Vulture-king infirm and old:
But will thy puny strength avail
When Raghu's wrathful sons assail?
A captive in thy palace lies
The lady of the lotus eyes:
Thou knowest not how fierce and strong
Is he whom thou hast dared to wrong.
The best of Raghu's lineage, he
Whose conquering hand shall punish thee."
He ceased: and Angad raised a cry;
"This is no herald but a spy.
Above thee from his airy post
His rapid eye surveyed our host,
Where with advantage he might scan
Our gathered strength from rear to van.
Bind him, Vánars, bind the spy,

Nor let him back to Lanká fly."
They hurled the Rákshas to the ground,
They grasped his neck, his pinions bound,
And firmly held him while in vain
His voice was lifted to complain.
But Ráma's heart inclined to spare,
He listened to his plaint and prayer,
And cried aloud: "O Vánars, cease;
The captive from his bonds release."

Canto XXI
Ocean Threatened

His hands in reverence Ráma raised
And southward o'er the ocean gazed;
Then on the sacred grass that made
His lowly couch his limbs he laid.
His head on that strong arm reclined
Which Sítá, best of womankind,
Had loved in happier days to hold
With soft arms decked with pearls and gold.
Then rising from his bed of grass,
"This day," he cried, "the host shall pass
Triumphant to the southern shore,
Or Ocean's self shall be no more."
Thus vowing in his constant breast
Again he turned him to his rest,
And there, his eyes in slumber closed,
Silent beside the sea reposed.
Thrice rose the Day-God thrice he set,
The lord of Ocean came not yet,
Thrice came the night, but Raghu's son
No answer by his service won.
To Lakshman thus the hero cried,
His eyes aflame with wrath and pride:
"In vain the softer gifts that grace
The good are offered to the base.
Long-suffering, patience, gentle speech
Their thankless hearts can never reach.
The world to him its honour pays

Whose ready tongue himself can praise,
Who scorns the true, and hates the right,
Whose hand is ever raised to smite.
Each milder art is tried in vain:
It wins no glory, but disdain.
And victory owns no softer charm
Than might which nerves a warrior's arm.
My humble suit is still denied
By Ocean's overweening pride.
This day the monsters of the deep
In throes of death shall wildly leap.
My shafts shall rend the serpents curled
In caverns of the watery world,
Disclose each sunless depth and bare
The tangled pearl and coral there.
Away with mercy! at a time
Like this compassion is a crime.
Welcome, the battle and the foe!
My bow! my arrows and my bow!
This day the Vánars' feet shall tread
The conquered Sea's exhausted bed,
And he who never feared before
Shall tremble to his farthest shore."
Red flashed his eyes with angry glow:
He stood and grasped his mighty bow,
Terrific as the fire of doom
Whose quenchless flames the world consume.
His clanging cord the archer drew,
And swift the fiery arrows flew
Fierce as the flashing levin sent
By him who rules the firmament.
Down through the startled waters sped
Each missile with its flaming head.
The foamy billows rose and sank,

And dashed upon the trembling bank.
Sea monsters of tremendous form
With crash and roar of thunder storm.
Still the wild waters rose and fell
Crowned with white foam and pearl and shell.
Each serpent, startled from his rest,
Raised his fierce eyes and glowing crest.
And prisoned Dánavs 933 where they dwelt
In depths below the terror felt.
Again upon his string he laid
A flaming shaft, but Lakshmaṇ stayed
His arm, with gentle reasoning tried
To soothe his angry mood, and cried:
"Brother, reflect: the wise control
The rising passions of the soul.
Let Ocean grant, without thy threat,
The boon on which thy heart is set.
That gracious lord will ne'er refuse
When Ráma son of Raghu sues."
He ceased: and voices from the air
Fell clear and loud, Spare, Ráma, spare.

Canto XXII
Ocean Threatened

With angry menace Ráma, best
Of Raghu's sons, the Sea addressed:
"With fiery flood of arrowy rain
Thy channels will I dry and drain.
And I and all the Vánar host
Will reach on foot the farther coast.
Thou shalt not from destruction save
The creatures of the teeming wave,
And lapse of time shall ne'er efface
The memory of the dire disgrace."
Thus spoke the warrior, and prepared
The mortal shaft which never spared,
Known mystic weapon, by the name
Of Brahmá, red with quenchless flame.
Great terror, as he strained the bow,
Struck heaven above and earth below.
Through echoing skies the thunder pealed,
And startled mountains rocked and reeled,
The earth was black with sudden night
And heaven was blotted from the sight.
Then ever and anon the glare
Of meteors shot through murky air,
And with a wild terrific sound
Red lightnings struck the trembling ground.
In furious gusts the fierce wind blew:
Tall trees it shattered and o'erthrew,
And, smiting with a giant's stroke,

Huge masses from the mountain broke.
A cry of terror long and shrill
Came from each valley, plain, and hill.
Each ruined dale, each riven peak
Re-echoed with a wail or shriek.
While Raghu's son undaunted gazed,
The waters of the deep were raised,
And, still uplifted more and more,
Leapt in wild flood upon the shore.
Still Ráma looked upon the tide
And kept his post unterrified.
Then from the seething flood upreared
Majestic Ocean's form appeared,
As rising from his eastern height
Springs through the sky the Lord of Light.
Attendant on their monarch came
Sea serpents with their eyes aflame.
Like lazulite mid burning gold
His form was wondrous to behold.
Bright with each fairest precious stone
A chain about his neck was thrown.
Calm shone his lotus eyes beneath
The blossoms of his heavenly wreath,
And many a pearl and sea-born gem
Flashed in the monarch's diadem.
There Gangá, tributary queen,
And Sindhu 934 by his lord, were seen,
And every stream and brook renowned
In ancient story girt him round.
Then, as the waters rose and swelled,
The king with suppliant hands upheld,
His glorious head to Ráma bent
And thus addressed him reverent:
"Air, ether, fire, earth, water, true

To nature's will, their course pursue;
And I, as ancient laws ordain,
Unfordable must still remain.
Yet, Raghu's son, my counsel hear:
I ne'er for love or hope or fear
Will pile my waters in a heap
And leave a pathway through the deep.
Still shall my care for thee provide
An easy passage o'er the tide,
And like a city's paven street
Shall be the road beneath thy feet."
He ceased: and Ráma spoke again:
"This spell is ne'er invoked in vain.
Where shall the magic shaft, to spend
The fury of its might, descend?"
"Shoot," Ocean cried, "thine arrow forth
With all its fury to the north,
Where sacred Drumakulya lies,
Whose glory with thy glory vies.
There dwells a wild Abhíra 935 race,
As vile in act as foul of face,
Fierce Dasyus 936 who delight in ill,
And drink my tributary rill.
My soul no longer may endure
Their neighbourhood and touch impure.
At these, O son of Raghu, aim
Thine arrow with the quenchless flame."
Swift from the bow, as Ráma drew
His cord, the fiery arrow flew.
Earth groaned to feel the wound, and sent
A rush of water through the rent;
And famed for ever is the well
Of Vraṇa 937 where the arrow fell.
Then every brook and lake beside

Throughout the region Ráma dried.
But yet he gave a boon to bless
And fertilize the wilderness:
No fell disease should taint the air,
And sheep and kine should prosper there:
Earth should produce each pleasant root,
The stately trees should bend with fruit;
Oil, milk, and honey should abound,
And fragrant herbs should clothe the ground.
Then spake the king of brooks and seas
To Raghu's son in words like these:
"Now let a wondrous task be done
By Nala, Viśvakarmá's son,
Who, born of one of Vánar race,
Inherits by his father's grace
A share of his celestial art.
Call Nala to perform his part,
And he, divinely taught and skilled,
A bridge athwart the sea shall build."
He spoke and vanished. Nala, best
Of Vánar chiefs, the king addressed:
"O'er the deep sea where monsters play
A bridge, O Ráma, will I lay;
For, sharer of my father's skill,
Mine is the power and mine the will.
'Tis vain to try each gentler art
To bribe and soothe the thankless heart;
In vain on such is mercy spent;
It yields to naught but punishment.
Through fear alone will Ocean now
A passage o'er his waves allow.
My mother, ere she bore her son,
This boon from Viśvakarmá won:
"O Mandarí, thy child shall be

In skill and glory next to me."
But why unbidden should I fill
Thine ear with praises of my skill?
Command the Vánar hosts to lay
Foundations for the bridge to-day."
He spoke: and swift at Ráma's hest
Up sprang the Vánars from their rest,
The mandate of the king obeyed
And sought the forest's mighty shade.
Unrooted trees to earth they threw,
And to the sea the timber drew.
The stately palm was bowed and bent,
Aśokas from the ground were rent,
And towering Sáls and light bamboos,
And trees with flowers of varied hues,
With loveliest creepers wreathed and crowned,
Shook, reeled, and fell upon the ground.
With mighty engines piles of stone
And seated hills were overthrown:
Unprisoned waters sprang on high,
In rain descending from the sky:
And ocean with a roar and swell
Heaved wildly when the mountains fell.
Then the great bridge of wondrous strength
Was built, a hundred leagues in length.
Rocks huge as autumn clouds bound fast
With cordage from the shore were cast,
And fragments of each riven hill,
And trees whose flowers adorned them still.
Wild was the tumult, loud the din
As ponderous rocks went thundering in.
Ere set of sun, so toiled each crew,
Ten leagues and four the structure grew;
The labours of the second day

Gave twenty more of ready way,
And on the fifth, when sank the sun,
The whole stupendous work was done.
O'er the broad way the Vánars sped,
Nor swayed it with their countless tread.
Exultant on the ocean strand
Vibhishaṇ stood, and, mace in hand,
Longed eager for the onward way,
And chafed impatient at delay.
Then thus to Ráma trained and tried
In battle King Sugríva cried:
"Come, Hanumán's broad back ascend;
Let Angad help to Lakshmaṇ lend.
These high above the sea shall bear
Their burthen through the ways of air."
So, with Sugríva, borne o'erhead
Ikshváku's sons the legions led.
Behind, the Vánar hosts pursued
Their march in endless multitude.
Some skimmed the surface of the wave,
To some the air a passage gave.
Amid their ceaseless roar the sound
Of Ocean's fearful voice was drowned,
As o'er the bridge by Nala planned
They hastened on to Lanká's strand,
Where, by the pleasant brooks, mid trees
Loaded with fruit, they took their ease.

Canto XXIII
The Omens

Then Ráma, peerless in the skill
That marks each sign of good and ill,
Strained his dear brother to his breast,
And thus with prudent words addressed:
"Now, Lakshman, by the water's side
In fruitful groves the host divide,
That warriors of each woodland race
May keep their own appointed place.
Dire is the danger: loss of friends,
Of Vánars and of bears, impends.
Distained with dust the breezes blow,
And earth is shaken from below.
The tall hills rock from foot to crown,
And stately trees come toppling down.
In threatening shape, with voice of fear,
The clouds like cannibals appear,
And rain in fitful torrents, red
With sanguinary drops, is shed.
Long streaks of lurid light invest
The evening skies from east to west.
And from the sun at times a ball
Of angry fire is seen to fall.
From every glen and brake is heard
The boding voice of beast and bird:
From den and lair night-prowlers run
And shriek against the falling sun.
Up springs the moon, but hot and red

Kills the sad night with woe and dread;
No gentle lustre, but the gloom
That heralds universal doom.
A cloud of dust and vapour mars
The beauty of the evening stars,
And wild and fearful is the sky
As though the wreck of worlds were nigh.
Around our heads in boding flight
Wheel hawk and vulture, crow and kite;
And every bird of happy note
Shrieks terror from his altered throat.
Sword, spear and shaft shall strew the plain
Dyed red with torrents of the slain.
To-day the Vánar troops shall close
Around the city of our foes."

Canto XXIV
The Spy's Return

As shine the heavens with autumn's moon
Refulgent in the height of noon,
So shone with light which Ráma gave
That army of the bold and brave,
As from the sea it marched away
In war's magnificent array,
And earth was shaken by the beat
And trampling of unnumbered feet.
Then to the giants' ears were borne,
The mingled notes of drum and horn,
And clash of tambours smote the sky,
And shouting and the battle cry.
The sound of martial strains inspired
Each chieftain, and his bosom fired:
While giants from their walls replied,
And answering shouts the foe defied,
Then Ráma looked on Lanká where
Bright banners floated in the air,
And, pierced with anguish at the view,
His loving thoughts to Sítá flew.
"There, prisoned by the giant, lies
My lady of the tender eyes,
Like Rohiṇí the queen of stars
O'erpowered by the fiery Mars."
Then turned he to his brother chief
And cried in agony of grief:
"See on the hill, divinely planned

And built by Viśvakarmá's hand,
The towers and domes of Lanká rise
In peerless beauty to the skies.
Bright from afar the city shines
With gleam of palaces and shrines,
Like pale clouds through the region spread
By Vishṇu's self inhabited.
Fair gardens grow, and woods between
The stately domes are fresh and green,
Where trees their bloom and fruit display,
And sweet birds sing on every spray.
Each bird is mad with joy, and bees
Sing labouring in the bloomy trees
On branches by the breezes bowed,
Where the gay Koïl's voice is loud."
This said, he ranged with warlike art
Each body of the host apart.
"There in the centre," Ráma cried,
"Be Angad's place by Níla's side.
Let Rishabh of impetuous might
Be lord and leader on the right,
And Gandhamádan, next in rank,
Be captain of the farther flank.
Lakshmaṇ and I the hosts will lead,
And Jámbaván of ursine breed,
With bold Susheṇ unused to fear,
And Vegadarśí, guide the rear."
Thus Ráma spoke: the chiefs obeyed;
And all the Vánar hosts arrayed
Showed awful as the autumn sky
When clouds embattled form on high.
Their arms were mighty trees o'erthrown,
And massy blocks of mountain stone.
One hope in every warlike breast,

One firm resolve, they onward pressed,
To die in fight or batter down
The walls and towers of Lanká's town.
Those marshalled legions Ráma eyed,
And thus to King Sugríva cried:
"Now, Monarch, ere the hosts proceed,
Let Śuka, Rávaṇ's spy, be freed."
He spoke: the Vánar gave consent
And loosed him from imprisonment:
And Śuka, trembling and afraid,
His homeward way to Rávaṇ made.
Loud laughed the lord of Lanká's isle:
"Where hast thou stayed this weary while?
Why is thy plumage marred, and why
Do twisted cords thy pinions tie?
Say, comest thou in evil plight
The victim of the Vánars' spite?"
He ceased: the spy his fear controlled,
And to the king his story told:
"I reached the ocean's distant shore,
Thy message to the king I bore.
In sudden wrath the Vánars rose,
They struck me down with furious blows;
They seized me helpless on the ground,
My plumage rent, my pinions bound.
They would not, headlong in their ire,
Consider, listen, or inquire;
So fickle, wrathful, rough and rude
Is the wild forest multitude.
There, marshalling the Vánar bands,
King Ráma with Sugríva stands,
Ráma the matchless warrior, who
Virádha and Kabandha slew,
Khara, and countless giants more,

And tracks his queen to Lanká's shore.
A bridge athwart the sea was cast,
And o'er it have his legions passed.
Hark! heralded by horns and drums
The terrible avenger comes.
E'en now the giants' isle he fills
With warriors huge as clouds and hills,
And burning with vindictive hate
Will thunder soon at Lanká's gate.
Yield or oppose him: choose between
Thy safety and the Maithil queen."
He ceased: the tyrant's eyeballs blazed
With fury as his voice he raised:
"No, if the dwellers of the sky,
Gandharvas, fiends assail me, I
Will keep the Maithil lady still,
Nor yield her back for fear of ill.
When shall my shafts with iron hail
My foeman, Raghu's son, assail,
Thick as the bees with eager wing
Beat on the flowery trees of spring?
O, let me meet my foe at length,
And strip him of his vaunted strength,
Fierce as the sun who shines afar
Stealing the light of every star.
Strong as the sea's impetuous might
My ways are like the tempest's flight;
But Ráma knows not this, or he
In terror from my face would flee."

Canto XXV
Rávan's Spies938

When Ráma and the host he led
Across the sea had safely sped,
Thus Rávaṇ, moved by wrath and pride,
To Śuka and to Sáraṇ cried:
"O counsellors, the Vánar host
Has passed the sea from coast to coast,
And Daśaratha's son has wrought
A wondrous deed surpassing thought.
And now in truth I needs must know
The strength and number of the foe.
Go ye, to Ráma's host repair
And count me all the legions there.
Learn well what power each captain leads
His name and fame for warlike deeds.
Learn by what artist's wondrous aid
That bridge athwart the sea was made;
Learn how the Vánar host came o'er
And halted on the island shore.
Mark Ráma son of Raghu well;
His valour, strength, and weapons tell.
Watch his advisers one by one,
And Lakshmaṇ, Raghu's younger son.
Learn with observant eyes, and bring
"Unerring tidings to your king.
He ceased: then swift in Vánar guise
Forth on their errand sped the spies.
They reached the Vánars, and, dismayed,

Their never-ending lines surveyd:
Nor would they try, in mere despair,
To count the countless legions there,
That crowded valley, plain and hill,
That pressed about each cave and rill.
Though sea-like o'er the land were spread
The endless hosts which Ráma led,
The bridge by thousands yet was lined,
And eager myriads pressed behind.
But sage Vibhishan's watchful eyes
Had marked the giants in disguise.
He gave command the pair to seize,
And told the tale in words like these:
"O Ráma these, well known erewhile,
Are giant sons of Lanká's isle,
Two counsellors of Rávan sent
To watch the invading armament."
Vibhishan ceased: at Ráma's look
The Rákshas envoys quailed and shook;
Then suppliant hand to hand they pressed
And thus Ikshváku's son addressed:
"O Ráma, bear the truth we speak:
Our monarch Rávan bade us seek
The Vánar legions and survey
Their numbers, strength, and vast array."
Then Ráma, friend and hope and guide
Of suffering creatures, thus replied:
"Now giants, if your eyes have scanned
Our armies, numbering every band,
Marked lord and chief, and gazed their fill,
Return to Rávan when ye will.
If aught remain, if aught anew
Ye fain would scan with closer view,
Vibhishan, ready at your call,

Will lead you forth and show you all.
Think not of bonds and capture; fear
No loss of life, no peril here:
For, captive, helpless and unarmed,
An envoy never should be harmed.
Again to Lanká's town repair,
Speed to the giant monarch there,
And be these words to Rávan told,
Fierce brother of the Lord of Gold:
"Now, tyrant, tremble for thy sin:
Call up thy friends, thy kith and kin,
And let the power and might be seen
Which made thee bold to steal my queen.
To-morrow shall thy mournful eye
Behold thy bravest warriors die,
And Lanká's city, tower and wall,
Struck by my fiery shafts, will fall.
Then shall my vengeful blow descend
Its rage on thee and thine to spend,
Fierce as the fiery bolt that flew
From heaven against the Dánav crew,
Mid those rebellious demons sent
By him who rules the firmament."
Thus spake Ikshváku's son, and ceased:
The giants from their bonds released
Lauded the King with glad accord,
And hasted homeward to their lord.
Before the tyrant side by side
Śuka and Sáran stood and cried:
"Vibhishan seized us, King, and fain
His helpless captives would have slain.
But glorious Ráma saw us; he,
Great-hearted hero, made us free.
There in one spot our eyes beheld

Four chiefs on earth unparalleled,
Who with the guardian Gods may vie
Who rule the regions of the sky.
There Ráma stood, the boast and pride
Of Raghu's race, by Lakshman's side.
There stood the sage Vibhishan, there
Sugríva strong beyond compare.
These four alone can batter down
Gate, rampart, wall, and Lanká's town.
Nay, Ráma matchless in his form,
A single foe, thy town would storm:
So wondrous are his weapons, he
Needs not the succour of the three.
Why speak we of the countless train
That fills the valley, hill and plain,
The millions of the Vánar breed
Whom Ráma and Sugríva lead?
O King, be wise, contend no more,
And Sítá to her lord restore."

Canto XXVI
The Vánar Chiefs

"Not if the Gods in heaven who dwell,
Gandharvas, and the fiends of hell
In banded opposition rise
Against me, will I yield my prize.
Still trembling from the ungentle touch
Of Vánar hands ye fear too much,
And bid me, heedless of the shame,
Give to her lord the Maithil dame."
Thus spoke the king in stern reproof;
Then mounted to his palace roof
Aloft o'er many a story raised,
And on the lands beneath him gazed.
There by his faithful spies he stood
And looked on sea and hill and wood.
There stretched before him far away
The Vánars' numberless array:
Scarce could the meadows' tender green
Beneath their trampling feet be seen.
He looked a while with furious eye,
Then questioned thus the nearer spy:
"Bend, Sáraṇ, bend thy gaze, and show
The leaders of the Vánar foe.
Tell me their heroes' names, and teach
The valour, power and might of each."
Obedient Sáraṇ eyed the van,
The leaders marked, and thus began:
"That chief conspicuous at the head

Of warriors in the forest bred,
Who hither bends his ruthless eye
And shouts his fearful battle cry:
Whose voice with pealing thunder shakes
All Lanká, with the groves and lakes
And hills that tremble at the sound,
Is Níla, for his might renowned:
First of the Vánar lords controlled
By King Sugríva lofty-souled.
He who his mighty arm extends,
And his fierce eye on Lanká bends,
In stature like a stately tower,
In colour like a lotus flower,
Who with his wild earth-shaking cries
Thee, Rávaṇ, to the field defies,
Is Angad, by Sugríva's care
Anointed his imperial heir:
In wondrous strength, in martial fire
Peer of King Báli's self, his sire;
For Ráma's sake in arms arrayed
Like Varuṇ called to Śakra's aid.
Behind him, girt by warlike bands,
Nala the mighty Vánar stands,
The son of Viśvakarmá, he
Who built the bridge athwart the sea.
Look farther yet, O King, and mark
That chieftain clothed in Sandal bark.
'Tis Śweta, famed among his peers,
A sage whom all his race reveres.
See, in Sugríva's ear he speaks,
Then, hasting back, his post reseeks,
And turns his practised eye to view
The squadrons he has formed anew.
Next Kumud stands who roamed of yore

On Gomatí's 939 delightful shore,
Feared where the waving woods invest
His seat on Mount Sanrochan's crest.
Next him a chieftain strong and dread,
Comes Chaṇḍa at his legions' head;
Exulting in his warrior might
He hastens, burning for the fight,
And boasts that his unaided powers
Shall cast to earth thy walls and towers.
Mark, mark that chief of lion gait,
Who views thee with a glance of hate
As though his very eyes would burn
The city walls to which they turn:
'Tis Rambha, Vánar king; he dwells
In Krishṇagiri's tangled dells,
Where Vindhya's pleasant slopes are spread
And fair Sudarśan lifts his head.
There, listening with erected ears,
Śarabha, mighty chief, appears.
His soul is burning for the strife,
Nor dreads the jeopardy of life.
He trembles as he moves, for ire,
And bends around his glance of fire.
Next, like a cloud that veils the skies,
A chieftain of terrific size,
Conspicuous mid the Vánars, comes
With battle shout like rolling drums,
'Tis Panas, trained in war and tried,
Who dwells on Páriyátra's side.
He, far away, the chief who throws
A glory o'er the marshalled rows
That ranged behind their captain stand
Exulting on the ocean strand,
Is Vinata the fierce in fight,

Preëminent like Dardur's height.
That chieftain bending down to drink
On lovely Veṇá's verdant brink,
Is Krathan; now he lifts his eyes
And thee to mortal fray defies.
Next Gavaya comes, whose haughty mind
Scorns all the warriors of his kind.
He comes to trample—such his boast—
On Lanká with his single host."

Canto XXVII
The Vánar Chiefs

"Yet more remain, brave chiefs who stake
Their noble lives for Ráma's sake.
See, glorious, golden-coated, one
Who glisters like the morning sun,
Whom thousands of his race surround,
'Tis Hara for his strength renowned.
Next comes a mighty chieftain, he
Whose legions, armed with rock and tree,
Press on, in numbers passing tale,
The ramparts of our town to scale.
O Rávaṇ, see the king advance
Terrific with his fiery glance,
Girt by the bravest of his train,
Majestic as the God of Rain,
Parjanya, when his host of clouds
About the king, embattled, crowds:
On Rikshaván's high mountain nursed,
In Narmadá 940 he slakes his thirst,
Dhúmra, proud ursine chief, who leads
Wild warriors whom the forest breeds.
His brother, next in strength and age,
In Jámbaván the famous sage.
Of yore his might and skill he lent
To him who rules the firmament,
And Indra's liberal boons repaid
The chieftain for the timely aid.
There like a gloomy cloud that flies

Borne by the tempest through the skies,
Pramáthí stands: he roamed of yore
The forest wilds on Gangá's shore,
Where elephants were struck with dread
And trembling at his coming fled.
There on his foes he loved to sate
The old hereditary hate. 941
Look, Gaja and Gaváksha show
Their lust of battle with the foe.
See Nala burning for the fray,
And Níla chafing at delay.
Behind the eager captains press
Wild hosts in numbers numberless,
And each for Ráma's sake would fall
Or force his way through Lanká's wall."

Canto XXVIII
The Chieftains

There Sáraṇ ceased: then Śuka broke
The silence and to Rávaṇ spoke:
"O Monarch, yonder chiefs survey:
Like elephants in size are they,
And tower like stately trees that grow
Where Gangá's nursing waters flow;
Yea, tall as mountain pines that fling
Long shadows o'er the snow-crowned king.
They all in wild Kishkindhá dwell
And serve their lord Sugríva well.
The Gods' and bright Gandharvas' seed,
They take each form that suits their need.
Now farther look, O Monarch, where
Those chieftains stand, a glorious pair,
Conspicuous for their godlike frames;
Dwivid and Mainda are their names.
Their lips the drink of heaven have known,
And Brahmá claims them for his own.
That chieftain whom thine eyes behold
Refulgent like a hill of gold,
Before whose wrathful might the sea
Roused from his rest would turn and flee,
The peerless Vánar, he who came
To Lanká for the Maithil dame,
The Wind-God's son Hanumán; thou
Hast seen him once, behold him now.
Still nearer let thy glance be bent,

And mark that prince preëminent
Mid chieftains for his strength and size
And splendour of his lotus eyes.
Far through the worlds his virtues shine,
The glory of Ikshváku's line.
The path of truth he never leaves,
And still through all to duty cleaves.
Deep in the Vedas, skilled to wield
The mystic shafts to him revealed:
Whose flaming darts to heaven ascend,
And through the earth a passage rend:
In might like him who rules the sky;
Like Yáma, when his wrath grows high:
Whose queen, the darling of his soul,
Thy magic art deceived and stole:
There royal Ráma stands and longs
For battle to avenge his wrongs.
Near on his right a prince, in hue
Like pure gold freshly burnished, view:
Broad is his chest, his eye is red,
His black hair curls about his head:
'Tis Lakshman, faithful friend, who shares
His brother's joys, his brother's cares.
By Ráma's side he loves to stand
And serve him as his better hand,
For whose dear sake without a sigh
The warrior youth would gladly die.
On Ráma's left Vibhishan view,
With giants for his retinue:
King-making drops have dewed his head,
Appointed monarch in thy stead.
Behold that chieftain sternly still,
High towering like a rooted hill,
Supreme in power and pride of place,

The monarch of the Vánar race.
Raised high above his woodland kind,
In might and glory, frame and mind,
His head above his host he shows
Conspicuous as the Lord of Snows.
His home is far from hostile eyes
Where deep in woods Kishkindhá lies.
A glistering chain which flowers bedeck
With burnished gold adorns his neck.
Queen Fortune, loved by Gods and kings,
To him her chosen favourite clings.
That chain he owes to Ráma's grace,
And Tárá and his kingly place.
In him the great Sugríva know,
Whom Ráma rescued from his foe." 942

Canto XXIX
Sárdúla Captured

The giant viewed with earnest ken
The Vánars and the lords of men;
Then thus, with grief and anger moved,
In bitter tone the spies reproved:
"Can faithful servants hope to please
Their master with such fates as these?
Or hope ye with wild words to wring
The bosom of your lord and king?
Such words were better said by those
Who come arrayed our mortal foes.
In vain your ears have heard the sage,
And listened to the lore of age,
Untaught, though lectured many a day,
The first great lesson, to obey,
'Tis marvel Rávan reigns and rules
Whose counsellors are blind and fools.
Has death no terrors that ye dare
To tempt your monarch to despair,
From whose imperial mandate flow
Disgrace and honour, weal and woe?
Yea, forest trees, when flames are fanned
About their scorching trunks, may stand;
But naught can set the sinner free
When kings the punishment decree.
I would not in mine anger spare
The traitorous foe-praising pair,
But years of faithful service plead

For pardon, and they shall not bleed.
Henceforth to me be dead: depart,
Far from my presence and my heart."
Thus spoke the angry king: the two
Cried, Long live Rávan, and withdrew,
The giant monarch turned and cried
To strong Mahodar at his side:
"Go thou, and spies more faithful bring.
More duteous to their lord the king."
Swift at his word Mahodar shed,
And came returning at the head
Of long tried messengers, who bent
Before their monarch reverent.
"Go quickly hence," said Rávan "scan
With keenest eyes the foeman's plan.
Learn who, as nearest friends, advise
And mould each secret enterprise.
Learn when he wakes and goes to rest,
Sound every purpose of his breast.
Learn what the prince intends to-day:
Watch keenly all, and come away."
With joy they heard the words he said:
Then with Śardúla at their head
About the giant king they went
With circling paces reverent.
By fair Suvela's grassy side
The chiefs of Raghu's race they spied,
Where, shaded by the waving wood,
Vibhishan and Sugríva stood.
A while they rested there and viewed
The Vánars' countless multitude.
Vibhishan with observant eyes
Knew at a glance the giant spies,
And bade the warriors of his train

Bind the rash foes with cord and chain:
"Śárdúla's is the sin," he cried.
He neath the Vánars' hands had died,
But Ráma from their fury freed
The captive in his utmost need,
And, merciful at sight of woe,
Loosed all the spies and bade them go.
Then home to Lanká's monarch fled
The giant chiefs discomfited.

Canto XXX
Sárdúla's Speech

They told their lord that Ráma still
Lay waiting by Suvela's hill.
The tyrant, flushed with angry glow,
Heard of the coming of the foe,
And thus with close inquiry pressed
Sárdúla spokesman for the rest:
"Why art thou sad, night-rover? speak:
Has grief or terror changed thy cheek?
Have the wild Vánars' hostile bands
Assailed thee with their mighty hands?"
Sárdúla heard, but scarce might speak;
His trembling tones were faint and weak:
"O Giant King, in vain we try
The purpose of the foe to spy.
Their strength and number none may tell,
And Ráma guards his legions well.
He leaves no hope to prying eyes,
And parley with the chiefs denies:
Each road and path a Vánar guard,
Of mountain size, has closed and barred.
Soon as my feet an entrance found
By giants was I seized and bound,
And wounded sore I fell beneath
Their fists and knees and hands and teeth.
Then trembling, bleeding, wellnigh dead
To Ráma's presence was I led.
He in his mercy stooped to save,

And freedom to the captive gave.
With rocks and shattered mountains he
Has bridged his way athwart the sea,
And he and all his legions wait
Embattled close to Lanká's gate.
Soon will the host thy wall assail,
And, swarming on, the rampart scale.
Now, O my King, his consort yield,
Or arm thee with the sword and shield.
This choice is left thee: choose between
Thy safety and the Maithil queen." 943

Canto XXXI
The Magic Head

The tyrant's troubled eye confessed
The secret fear that filled his breast.
With dread of coming woe dismayed
He called his counsellors to aid;
Then sternly silent, deep in thought,
His chamber in the palace sought.
Then, as the surest hope of all,
The monarch bade his servants call
Vidyujjihva, whom magic skill
Made master of the means of ill.
Then spake the lord of Lanká's isle:
"Come, Sítá with thine arts beguile.
With magic skill and deftest care
A head like Ráma's own prepare.
This head, long shafts and mighty bow,
To Janak's daughter will we show."
He ceased: Vidyujjihva obeyed,
And wondrous magic skill displayed;
And Rávaṇ for the art he showed
An ornament of price bestowed.
Then to the grove where Sítá lay
The lord of Lanká took his way.
Pale, wasted, weeping, on the ground
The melancholy queen he found,
Whose thoughts in utmost stress of ill
Were fixed upon her husband still.
The giant king approached the dame,

Declared in tones of joy his name;
Then heeding naught her wild distress
Bespake her, stern and pitiless:
"The prince to whom thy fancies cling
Though loved and wooed by Lanká's king,
Who slew the noble Khara,—he
Is slain by warriors sent by me.
Thy living root is hewn away,
Thy scornful pride is tamed to-day.
Thy lord in battle's front has died,
And Sítá shall be Rávan's bride.
Hence, idle thoughts: thy hope is fled;
What wilt thou, Sítá, with the dead?
Rise, child of Janak, rise and be
The queen of all my queens and me.
Incline thine ear, and I will tell,
Dear lady, how thy husband fell.
He bridged his way across the sea
With countless troops to fight with me.
The setting sun had flushed the west
When on the shore they took their rest.
Weary with toil no watch they kept,
Securely on the sands they slept.
Prahasta's troops assailed our foes,
And smote them in their deep repose.
Scarce could their bravest prove their might:
They perished in the dark of night.
Axe, spear, and sword, directed well,
Upon the sleeping myriads fell.
First in the fight Prahasta's sword
Reft of his head thy slumbering lord.
Roused at the din Vibhishan rose,
The captive of surrounding foes,
And Lakshman through the woods that spread

Around him with his Vánars fled.
Hanúmán fell: one deadly stroke
The neck of King Sugríva broke,
And Mainda sank, and Dwivid lay
Gasping in blood his life away.
The Vánars died, or fled dispersed
Like cloudlets when the storm has burst.
Some rose aloft in air, and more
Ran to the sea and filled the shore.
On shore, in woods, on hill and plain
Our conquering giants left the slain.
Thus my victorious host o'erthrew
The Vánars, and thy husband slew:
See, rudely stained with dust, and red
With dropping blood, the severed head."
Then, turning to a Rákshas slave,
The ruthless king his mandate gave,
And straight Vidyujjihva who bore
The head still wet with dripping gore,
The arrows and the mighty bow,
Bent down before his master low.
"Vidyujjihva," cried Rávaṇ, "place
The head before the lady's face,
And let her see with weeping eyes
That low in death her husband lies."
Before the queen the giant laid
The beauteous head his art had made.
And Rávaṇ cried: "Thine eyes will know
These arrows and the mighty bow.
With fame of this by Ráma strung
The earth and heaven and hell have rung.
Prahasta brought it hither when
His hand had slain thy prince of men.
Now, widowed Queen, thy hopes resign:

Forget thy husband and be mine."

Canto XXXII
Sítá's Lament

Again her eyes with tears o'erflowed:
She gazed upon the head he showed,
Gazed on the bow so famed of yore,
The glorious bow which Ráma bore.
She gazed upon his cheek and brows,
The eyes of her beloved spouse;
His lips, the lustre of his hair,
The priceless gem that glittered there.
The features of her lord she knew,
And, pierced with anguish at the view,
She lifted up her voice and cried:
"Kaikeyí, art thou satisfied?
Now all thy longings are fulfilled;
The joy of Raghu's race is killed,
And ruined is the ancient line,
Destroyer, by that fraud of thine.
Ah, what offence, O cruel dame,
What fault in Ráma couldst thou blame,
To drive him clad in hermit dress
With Sítá to the wilderness?"
Great trembling seized her frame, and she
Fell like a stricken plantain tree.
As lie the dead she lay; at length
Slowly regaining sense and strength,
On the dear head she fixed her eye
And cried with very bitter cry:
"Ah, when thy cold dead cheek I view,

My hero, I am murdered too.
Then first a faithful woman's eyes
See sorrow, when her husband dies.
When thou, my lord, wast nigh to save,
Some stealthy hand thy death wound gave.
Thou art not dead: rise, hero, rise;
Long life was thine, as spake the wise
Whose words, I ween, are ever true,
For faith lies open to their view.
Ah lord, and shall thy head recline
On earth's cold breast, forsaking mine,
Counting her chill lap dearer far
Than I and my caresses are?
Ah, is it thus these eyes behold
Thy famous bow adorned with gold,
Whereon of yore I loved to bind
Sweet garlands that my hands had twined?
And hast thou sought in heaven a place
Amid the founders of thy race,
Where in the home deserved so well
Thy sires and Daśaratha dwell?
Or dost thou shine a brighter star
In skies where blest immortals are,
Forsaking in thy lofty scorn
The race wherein thy sires were born?
Turn to my gaze, O turn thine eye:
Why are thy cold lips silent, why?
When first we met as youth and maid,
When in thy hand my hand was laid,
Thy promise was thy steps should be
Through life in duty's path with me.
Remember, faithful still, thy vow,
And take me with thee even now.
Is that broad bosom where I hung,

That neck to which I fondly clung,
Where flowery garlands breathed their scent
By hungry dogs and vultures rent?
Shall no funereal honours grace
The parted lord of Raghu's race,
Whose bounty liberal fees bestowed,
For whom the fires of worship glowed?
Kauśalyá wild with grief will see
One sole survivor of the three
Who in their hermit garments went
To the dark woods in banishment.
Then at her cry shall Lakshmaṇ tell
How, slain by night, the Vánars fell;
How to thy side the giants crept,
And slew the hero as he slept.
Thy fate and mine the queen will know,
And broken-hearted die of woe.
For my unworthy sake, for mine,
Ráma, the glory of his line,
Who bridged his way across the main,
Is basely in a puddle slain;
And I, the graceless wife he wed,
Have brought this ruin on his head.
Me, too, on him, O Rávaṇ, slay:
The wife beside her husband lay.
By his dear body let me rest,
Cheek close to cheek and breast to breast,
My happy eyes I then will close,
And follow whither Ráma goes."
Thus cried the miserable dame;
When to the king a warder came,
Before the giant monarch bowed
And said that, followed by a crowd
Of counsellors and lords of state,

Prahasta stood before the gate,
And, sent by some engrossing care,
Craved audience of his master there.
The anxious tyrant left his seat
And hastened forth the chief to meet:
Then summoning his nobles all,
Took counsel in his regal hall.
When Lanká's lord had left the queen,
The head and bow no more were seen.
The giant king his nobles eyed,
And, terrible as Yáma, cried:
"O faithful lords, the time is come:
Gather our hosts with beat of drum.
Nigh to the town our foeman draws:
Be prudent, nor reveal the cause."
The nobles listened and obeyed:
Swift were the gathered troops arrayed,
And countless rovers of the night
Stood burning for the hour of fight.

Canto XXXIII
Saramá

But Saramá, of gentler mood,
With pitying eyes the mourner viewed,
Stole to her side and softly told
Glad tidings that her heart consoled,
Revealing with sweet voice and smile
The secret of the giant's guile.
She, one of those who night and day
Watching in turns by Sítá lay,
Though Rákshas born felt pity's touch,
And loved the hapless lady much.
"I heard," she said, "thy bitter cry,
Heard Rávaṇ's speech and thy reply,
For, hiding in the thicket near,
No word or tone escaped mine ear.
When Rávaṇ hastened forth I bent
My steps to follow as he went,
And learnt the secret cause that drove
The monarch from the Aśoka grove.
Believe me, Queen, thou needst not weep
For Ráma slaughtered in his sleep.
Thy lion lord of men defies
By day attack, by night surprise.
Can even giants slay with ease
Vast hosts who fight with brandished trees,
For whom, with eye that never sleeps,
His constant watch thy Ráma keeps?
Lord of the mighty arm and chest,

Of earthly warriors first and best,
Whose fame through all the regions rings,
Proud scion of a hundred kings;
Who guards his life and loves to lend
His saving succour to a friend:
Whose bow no hand but his can strain, —
Thy lord, thy Ráma is not slain.
Obedient to his master's will,
A great magician, trained in ill,
With deftest art surpassing thought
That marvellous illusion wrought.
Let rising hope thy grief dispel:
Look up and smile, for all is well,
And gentle Lakshmí, Fortune's Queen,
Regards thee with a favouring mien.
Thy Ráma with his Vánar train
Has thrown a bridge athwart the main,
Has led his countless legions o'er,
And ranged them on this southern shore.
These eyes have seen the hero stand
Girt by his hosts on Lanká's strand,
And breathless spies each moment bring
Fresh tidings to the giant king;
And every peer and lord of state
Is called to counsel and debate."
She ceased: the sound, long loud and clear,
Of gathering armies smote her ear,
Where call of drum and shell rang out,
The tambour and the battle shout;
And, while the din the echoes woke,
Again to Janak's child she spoke:
"Hear, lady, hear the loud alarms
That call the Rákshas troops to arms,
From stable and from stall they lead

The elephant and neighing steed,
Brace harness on with deftest care,
And chariots for the fight prepare.
Swift o'er the trembling ground career
Mailed horsemen armed with axe and spear,
And here and there in road and street
The terrible battalions meet.
I hear the gathering near and far,
The snorting steed, the rattling car.
Bold chieftains, leaders of the brave,
Press densely on, like wave on wave,
And bright the evening sunbeams glance
On helm and shield, on sword and lance.
Hark, lady, to the ringing steel,
Hark to the rolling chariot wheel:
Hark to the mettled courser's neigh
And drums' loud thunder far away.
The Queen of Fortune holds thee dear,
For Lanká's troops are struck with fear,
And Ráma with the lotus eyes,
Like Indra monarch of the skies,
With conquering arm will slay his foe
And free his lady from her woe.
Soon will his breast support thy head,
And tears of joy thine eyes will shed.
Soon by his mighty arm embraced
The long-lost rapture wilt thou taste,
And Ráma, meet for highest bliss,
Will gain his guerdon in thy kiss."

Canto XXXIV
Saramá's Tidings

Thus Saramá her story told:
And Sítá's spirit was consoled,
As when the first fresh rain is shed
The parching earth is comforted.
Then, filled with zeal for Sítá's sake,
Again in gentle tones she spake,
And, skilled in arts that soothe and please,
Addressed the queen in words like these:
"Thy husband, lady, will I seek,
Say the fond words thy lips would speak,
And then, unseen of any eye,
Back to thy side will swiftly fly.
My airy flights are speedier far
Than Garuḍa's and the tempest are."
Then Sítá spake: her former woe
Still left her accents faint and low:
"I know thy steps, which naught can stay,
Can urge through heaven and hell their way.
Then if thy love and changeless will
Would serve the helpless captive still,
Go forth and learn each plot and guile
Planned by the lord of Lanká's isle.
With magic art like maddening wine
He cheats these weeping eyes of mine,
Torments me with his suit, nor spares
Reproof or flattery, threats or prayers.
These guards surround me night and day;

My heart is sad, my senses stray;
And helpless in my woe I fear
The tyrant Rávaṇ even here."
Then Saramá replied: "I go
To learn the purpose of thy foe,
Soon by thy side again to stand
And tell thee what the king has planned."
She sped, she heard with eager ears
The tyrant speak his hopes and fears,
Where, gathered at their master's call,
The nobles filled the council hall;
Then swiftly, to her promise true,
Back to the Aśoka grove she flew.
The lady on the grassy ground,
Longing for her return, she found;
Who with a gentle smile, to greet
The envoy, led her to a seat.
Through her worn frame a shiver ran
As Saramá her tale began:
"There stood the royal mother: she
Besought her son to set thee free,
And to her counsel, tears and prayers,
The elder nobles added theirs:
"O be the Maithil queen restored
With honour to her angry lord,
Let Janasthán's unhappy fight
Be witness of the hero's might.
Hanúmán o'er the waters came
And looked upon the guarded dame.
Let Lanká's chiefs who fought and fell
The prowess of the leader tell."
In vain they sued, in vain she wept,
His purpose still unchanged he kept,
As clings the miser to his gold,

He would not loose thee from his hold.
No, never till in death he lies,
Will Lanká's lord release his prize.
Soon slain by Ráma's arrows all
The giants with their king will fall,
And Ráma to his home will lead
His black-eyed queen from bondage freed."
An awful sound that moment rose
From Lanká's fast-approaching foes,
Where drum and shell in mingled peal
Made earth in terror rock and reel.
The hosts within the walls arrayed
Stood trembling, in their hearts dismayed;
Thought of the tempest soon to burst,
And Lanká's lord, their ruin, cursed.

Canto XXXV
Malyaván's Speech

The fearful notes of drum and shell
Upon the ear of Rávaṇ fell.
One moment quailed his haughty look,
One moment in his fear he shook,
But soon recalling wonted pride,
His counsellors he sternly eyed,
And with a voice that thundered through
The council hall began anew:
"Lords, I have heard—your tongues have told—
How Raghu's son is fierce and bold.
To Lanká's shore has bridged his way
And hither leads his wild array.
I know your might, in battle tried,
Fighting and conquering by my side.
Why now, when such a foe is near,
Looks eye to eye in silent fear?"
He ceased, his mother's sire well known
For wisdom in the council shown,
Malyaván, sage and faithful guide.
Thus to the monarch's speech replied:
"Long reigns the king in safe repose,
Unmoved by fear of vanquished foes,
Whose feet by saving knowledge led
In justice path delight to tread:
Who knows to sheath the sword or wield,
To order peace, to strike or yield:
Prefers, when foes are stronger, peace,

And bids a doubtful conflict cease.
Now, King, the choice before thee lies,
Make peace with Ráma, and be wise.
This day the captive queen restore
Who brings the foe to Lanká's shore.
The Sire by whom the worlds are swayed
Of yore the Gods and demons made.
With these Injustice sided; those
Fair Justice for her champions chose.
Still Justice dwells with Gods above;
Injustice, fiends and giants love.
Thou, through the worlds that fear thee, long
Hast scorned the right and loved the wrong,
And Justice, with thy foes allied,
Gives might resistless to their side.
Thou, guided by thy wicked will,
Hast found delight in deeds of ill,
And sages in their holy rest
Have trembled, by thy power oppressed.
But they, who check each vain desire,
Are clothed with might which burns like fire.
In them the power and glory live
Which zeal and saintly fervour give.
Their constant task, their sole delight
Is worship and each holy rite,
To chant aloud the Veda hymn,
Nor let the sacred fires grow dim.
Now through the air like thunder ring
The echoes of the chants they sing.
The vapours of their incense rise
And veil with cloudy pall the skies,
And Rákshas might grows weak and faint
Killed by the power of sage and saint.
By Brahmá's boon thy life was screened

From God, Gandharva, Yaksha, fiend;
But Vánars, men, and bears, arrayed
Against thee now, thy shores invade.
Red meteors, heralds of despair
Flash frequent through the lurid air,
Foretelling to my troubled mind
The ruin of the Rákshas kind.
With awful thundering overhead
Clouds black as night are densely spread,
And oozing from the gloomy pall
Great drops of blood on Lanká fall.
Dogs roam through house and shrine to steal
The sacred oil and curd and meal,
Cats pair with tigers, hounds with swine,
And asses' foals are born of kine.
In these and countless signs I trace
The ruin of the giant race.
'Tis Vishṇu's self who comes to storm
Thy city, clothed in Ráma's form;
For, well I ween, no mortal hand
The ocean with a bridge has spanned.
O giant King, the dame release,
And sue to Raghu's son for peace"

Canto XXXVI
Rávan's Reply

But Rávaṇ's breast with fury swelled,
And thus he spake by Death impelled,
While, under brows in anger bent,
Fierce glances from his eyes were sent:
"The bitter words which thou, misled
By friendly thought, hast fondly said,
Which praise the foe and counsel fear,
Unheeded fall upon mine ear.
How canst thou deem a mighty foe
This Ráma who, in stress of woe,
Seeks, banished as his sire decreed,
Assistance from the Vánar breed?
Am I so feeble in thine eyes,
Though feared by dwellers of the skies,—
Whose might in many a battle shown
The glorious race of giants own?
Shall I for fear of him restore
The lady whom I hither bore,
Exceeding fair like Beauty's Queen 944
Without her well-loved lotus seen?
Around the chief let Lakshmaṇ stand,
Sugríva, and each Vánar band,
Soon, Malyaván, thine eyes will see
This boasted Ráma slain by me.
I in the brunt of war defy
The mightiest warriors of the sky;
And if I stoop to combat men,

Shall I be weak and tremble then?
This mangled trunk the foe may rend,
But Rávan ne'er can yield or bend,
And be it vice or virtue, I
This nature never will belie.
What marvel if he bridged the sea?
Why should this deed disquiet thee?
This, only this, I surely know,
Back with his life he shall not go."
Thus in loud tones the king exclaimed,
And mute stood Malyaván ashamed,
His reverend head he humbly bent,
And slowly to his mansion went.
But Rávan stayed, and deep in care
Held counsel with his nobles there,
All entrance to secure and close,
And guard the city from their foes.
He bade the chief Prahasta wait,
Commander at the eastern gate,
To fierce Mahodar, strong and brave,
To keep the southern gate, he gave,
Where Mahápársva's might should aid
The chieftain with his hosts arrayed.
To guard the west—no chief more fit—
He placed the warrior Indrajít,
His son, the giant's joy and boast,
Surrounded by a Rákshas host:
And mighty Sáran hastened forth
With Śuka to protect the north. 945
"I will myself," the monarch cried,
"Be present on the northern side."
These orders for the walls' defence
The tyrant gave, then parted thence,
And, by the hope of victory fired,

To chambers far within, retired.

Canto XXXVII
Preparations

Lords of the legions of the wood,
The chieftains with Vibhishaṇ stood,
And, strangers in the foeman's land,
Their hopes and fears in council scanned:
"See, see where Lanká's towers ascend,
Which Rávaṇ's power and might defend,
Which Gods, Gandharvas, fiends would fail
To conquer, if they durst assail.
How shall our legions pass within,
The city of the foe to win,
With massive walls and portals barred
Which Rávaṇ keeps with surest guard?"
With anxious looks the walls they eyed:
And sage Vibhishaṇ thus replied:
"These lords of mine 946 can answer: they
Within the walls have found their way,
The foeman's plan and order learned,
And hither to my side returned.
Now, Ráma, let my tongue declare
How Rávaṇ's hosts are stationed there.
Prahasta heads, in warlike state,
His legions at the eastern gate.
To guard the southern portal stands
Mahodar, girt by Rákshas bands,
Where mighty Mahápárśva, sent
By Rávaṇ's hest, his aid has lent.
Guard of the gate that fronts the west

Is valiant Indrajít, the best
Of warriors, Rávan's joy and pride;
And by the youthful chieftain's side
Are giants, armed for fierce attacks
With sword and mace and battle-axe.
North, where approach is dreaded most,
The king, encompassed with a host
Of giants trained in war, whose hands
Wield maces, swords and lances, stands.
All these are chiefs whom Rávan chose
As mightiest to resist his foes;
And each a countless army 947 leads
With elephants and cars and steeds."
Then Ráma, while his spirit burned
For battle, words like these returned:
"The eastern gate be Níla's care,
Opponent of Prahasta there.
The southern gate, with troops arrayed
Let Angad, Báli's son, invade.
The gate that fronts the falling sun
Shall be by brave Hanúmán won;
Soon through its portals shall he lead
His myriads of Vánar breed.
The gate that fronts the north shall be
Assailed by Lakshman and by me,
For I myself have sworn to kill
The tyrant who delights in ill.
Armed with the boon which Brahmá gave,
The Gods of heaven he loves to brave,
And through the trembling worlds he flies,
Oppressor of the just and wise.
Thou, Jámbaván, and thou, O King
Of Vánars, all your bravest bring,
And with your hosts in dense array

Straight to the centre force your way.
But let no Vánar in the storm
Disguise him in a human form,
Ye chiefs who change your shapes at will,
Retain your Vánar semblance still.
Thus, when we battle with the foe,
Both men and Vánars will ye know,
In human form will seven appear;
Myself, my brother Lakshman here;
Vibhishan, and the four he led
From Lanká's city when he fled."
Thus Raghu's son the chiefs addressed:
Then, gazing on Suvela's crest,
Transported by the lovely sight,
He longed to climb the mountain height.

Canto XXXVIII
The Ascent Of Suvela

"Come let us scale," the hero cried,
"This hill with various metals dyed.
This night upon the breezy crest
Sugríva, Lakshman, I, will rest,
With sage Vibhishan, faithful friend,
His counsel and his lore to lend.
From those tall peaks each eager eye
The foeman's city shall espy,
Who from the wood my darling stole
And brought long anguish on my soul."
Thus spake the lord of men, and bent
His footsteps to the steep ascent,
And Lakshman, true in weal and woe,
Next followed with his shafts and bow.
Vibhishan followed, next in place,
The sovereign of the Vánar race,
And hundreds of the forest kind
Thronged with impetuous feet, behind.
The chiefs in woods and mountains bred
Fast followed to Suvela's head,
And gazed on Lanká bright and fair
As some gay city in the air.
On glittering gates, on ramparts raised
By giant hands, the chieftains gazed.
They saw the mighty hosts that, skilled
In arts of war, the city filled,
And ramparts with new ramparts lined,

The swarthy hosts that stood behind.
With spirits burning for the fight
They saw the giants from the height,
And from a hundred throats rang out
Defiance and the battle shout.
Then sank the sun with dying flame,
And soft the shades of twilight came,
And the full moon's delicious light
Was shed upon the tranquil night.

Canto XXXIX
Lanká

They slept secure: the sun arose
And called the chieftains from repose.
Before the wondering Vánars, gay
With grove and garden, Lanká lay,
Where golden buds the Champak showed,
And bright with bloom Aśoka glowed,
And palm and Sál and many a tree
With leaf and flower were fair to see.
They looked on wood and lawn and glade,
On emerald grass and dusky shade,
Where creepers filled the air with scent,
And luscious fruit the branches bent,
Where bees inebriate loved to throng,
And each sweet bird was loud in song.
The wondering Vánars passed the bound
That circled that enchanting ground,
And as they came a sweet breeze through
The odorous alleys softly blew.
Some Vánars, at their king's behest,
Onward to bannered Lanká pressed,
While, startled by the strangers' tread,
The birds and deer before them fled.
Earth trembled at each step they took,
And Lanká at their shouting shook.
Bright rose before their wondering eyes
Trikúṭa's peak that kissed the skies,
And, clothed with flowers of every hue,

Afar its golden radiance threw.
Most fair to see the mountain's head
A hundred leagues in length was spread.
There Rávan's town, securely placed,
The summit of Trikúṭa graced.
O'er leagues of land she stretched in pride,
A hundred long and twenty wide.
They saw a lofty wall enfold
The city, built of blocks of gold,
They saw the beams of morning fall
On dome and fane within the wall,
Bright with the shine that mansion gives
Where Vishṇu in his glory lives.
White-crested like the Lord of Snows
Before them Rávan's palace rose.
High on a thousand pillars raised
With gold and precious stone it blazed,
Guarded by giant warders, crown
And ornament of Lanká's town.

Canto XL
Rávan Attacked

Still stood the son of Raghu where
Suvela's peak rose high in air,
And with Sugríva turned his eye
To scan each quarter of the sky.
There on Trikúṭa, nobly planned
And built by Viśvakarmá's hand,
He saw the lovely Lanká, dressed
In all her varied beauty, rest.
High on a tower above the gate
The tyrant stood in kingly state.
The royal canopy displayed
Above him lent its grateful shade,
And servants, from the giant band,
His cheek with jewelled chowries fanned.
Red sandal o'er his breast was spread,
His ornaments and robe were red:
Thus shows a cloud of darksome hue
With golden sunbeams flashing through.
While Ráma and the chiefs intent
Upon the king their glances bent,
Up sprang Sugríva from the ground
And reached the turret at a bound.
Unterrified the Vánar stood,
And wroth, with wondrous hardihood,
The king in bitter words addressed,
And thus his scorn and hate expressed:
"King of the giant race, in me

The friend and slave of Ráma see.
Lord of the world, he gives me power
To smite thee in thy fenced tower."
While through the air his challenge rang,
At Rávan's face the Vánar sprang.
Snatched from his head the kingly crown
And dashed it in his fury down.
Straight at his foe the giant flew,
His mighty arms about him threw.
With strength resistless swung him round
And dashed him panting to the ground.
Unharmed amid the storm of blows
Swift to his feet Sugríva rose.
Again in furious fight they met:
With streams of blood their limbs were wet,
Each grasping his opponent's waist.
Thus with their branches interlaced,
Which, crimson with the flowers of spring,
From side to side the breezes swing,
In furious wrestle you may see
The Kinśuk and the Seemal tree. 948
They fought with fists and hands, alike
Prepared to parry and to strike.
Long time the doubtful combat, waged
With matchless strength and fury, raged.
Each fiercely struck, each guarded well,
Till, closing, from the tower they fell,
And, grasping each the other's throat,
Lay for an instant in the moat.
They rose, and each in fiercer mood
The sanguinary strife renewed.
Well matched in size and strength and skill
They fought the dubious battle still.
While sweat and blood their limbs bedewed

They met, retreated, and pursued:
Each stratagem and art they tried,
Stood front to front and swerved aside.
His hand a while the giant stayed
And called his magic to his aid.
But brave Sugríva, swift to know
The guileful purpose of the foe,
Gained with light leap the upper air,
And breath and strength and spirit there;
Then, joyous as for victory won,
Returned to Raghu's royal son.

Canto XLI
Ráma's Envoy

When Ráma saw each bloody trace
On King Sugríva's limbs and face,
He cried, while, sorrowing at the view,
His arms about his friend he threw:
"Too venturous chieftain, kings like us
Bring not their lives in peril thus;
Nor, save when counsel shows the need,
Attempt so bold, so rash a deed.
Remember, I, Vibhishaṇ all
Have sorrowed fearing for thy fall.
O do not—for us all I speak—
These desperate adventures seek."
"I could not," cried Sugríva, "brook
Upon the giant king to look,
Nor challenge to the deadly strife
The fiend who robbed thee of thy wife."
"Now Lakshmaṇ, marshal," Ráma cried,
"Our legions where the woods are wide,
And stand we ready to oppose
The fury of our giant foes.
This day our armies shall ascend
The walls which Rávaṇ's powers defend,
And floods of Rákshas blood shall stain
The streets encumbered with the slain."
Down from the peak he came, and viewed
The Vánars' ordered multitude.
Each captain there for battle burned,

Each fiery eye to Lanká turned.
On, where the royal brothers led
To Lanká's walls the legions sped.
The northern gate, where giant foes
Swarmed round their monarch, Ráma chose
Where he in person might direct
The battle, and his troops protect.
What arm but his the post might keep
Where, strong as he who sways the deep, 949
Mid thousands armed with bow and mace,
Stood Rávaṇ mightiest of his race?
The eastern gate was Níla's post,
Where marshalled stood his Vánar host,
And Mainda with his troops arrayed,
And Dwivid stood to lend him aid.
The southern gate was Angad's care,
Who ranged his bold battalions there.
Hanúmán by the port that faced
The setting sun his legions placed,
And King Sugríva held the wood
East of the gate where Rávaṇ stood.
On every side the myriads met,
And Lanká's walls of close beset
That scarce the roving gale could win
A passage to the hosts within.
Loud as the angry ocean's roar
When wild waves lash the rocky shore,
Ten thousand thousand throats upsent
A shout that tore the firmament,
And Lanká with each grove and brook
And tower and wall and rampart shook.
The giants heard, and were appalled:
Then Raghu's son to Angad called,
And, led by kingly duty, 950 gave

This order merciful as brave:
"Go, Angad, Rávaṇ's presence seek,
And thus my words of warning speak:
"How art thou changed and fallen now,
O Monarch of the giants, thou
Whose impious fury would not spare
Saint, nymph, or spirit of the air;
Whose foot in haughty triumph trod
On Yaksha, king, and Serpent God:
How art thou fallen from thy pride
Which Brahmá's favour fortified!
With myriads at thy Lanká's gate
I stand my righteous ire to sate,
And punish thee with sword and flame,
The tyrant fiend who stole my dame.
Now show the might, employ the guile,
O Monarch of the giants' isle,
Which stole a helpless dame away:
Call up thy power and strength to-day.
Once more I warn thee, Rákshas King,
This hour the Maithil lady bring,
And, yielding while there yet is time,
Seek, suppliant, pardon for the crime,
Or I will leave beneath the sun
No living Rákshas, no, not one.
In vain from battle wilt thou fly,
Or borne on pinions seek the sky;
The hand of Ráma shall not spare;
His fiery shaft shall smite thee there.' "
He ceased: and Angad bowed his head;
Thence like embodied flame he sped,
And lighted from his airy road
Within the Rákshas king's abode.
There sate, the centre of a ring

Of counsellors, the giant king.
Swift through the circle Angad pressed,
And spoke with fury in his breast:
"Sent by the lord of Kośal's land,
His envoy here, O King, I stand,
Angad the son of Báli: fame
Has haply taught thine ears my name.
Thus in the words of Ráma I
Am come to warn thee or defy:
Come forth, and fighting in the van
Display the spirit of a man.
This arm shall slay thee, tyrant: all
Thy nobles, kith and kin shall fall:
And earth and heaven, from terror freed,
Shall joy to see the oppressor bleed.
Vibhishaṇ, when his foe is slain,
Anointed king in peace shall reign.
Once more I counsel thee: repent,
Avoid the mortal punishment,
With honour due the dame restore,
And pardon for thy sin implore."
Loud rose the king's infuriate cry:
"Seize, seize the Vánar, let him die."
Four of his band their lord obeyed,
And eager hands on Angad laid.
He purposing his strength to show
Gave no resistance to the foe,
But swiftly round his captors cast
His mighty arms and held them fast.
Fierce shout and cry around him rang:
Light to the palace roof he sprang,
There his detaining arms unwound,
And hurled the giants to the ground.
Then, smiting with a fearful stroke,

A turret from the roof he broke,—
As when the fiery levin sent
By Indra from the clouds has rent
The proud peak of the Lord of Snow,—
And flung the stony mass below.
Again with loud terrific cry
He sprang exulting to the sky,
And, joyous for his errand done,
Stood by the side of Raghu's son.

Canto XLII
The Sally

Still was the cry, "The Vánar foes
Around the leaguered city close."
King Rávan from the terrace gazed
And saw, with eyes where fury blazed,
The Vánar host in serried ranks
Press to the moat and line the banks,
And, first in splendour and in place,
The lion lord of Raghu's race.
And Ráma looked on Lanká where
Gay flags were streaming to the air,
And, while keen sorrow pierced him through,
His loving thoughts to Sítá flew:
"There, there in deep affliction lies
My darling with the fawn-like eyes.
There on the cold bare ground she keeps
Sad vigil and for Ráma weeps."
Mad with the thought, "Charge, charge," he cried.
"Let earth with Rákshas blood be dyed."
Responsive to his call rang out
A loud, a universal shout,
As myriads filled the moat with stone,
Trees, rocks, and mountains overthrown,
And charging at their leader's call
Pressed forward furious to the wall.
Some in their headlong ardour scaled
The rampart's height, the guard assailed,
And many a ponderous fragment rent

From portal, tower, and battlement.
Huge gates adorned with burnished gold
Were loosed and lifted from their hold;
And post and pillar, with a sound
Like thunder, fell upon the ground.
At every portal, east and west
And north and south, the chieftains pressed
Each in his post appointed led
His myriads in the forest bred.
"Charge, let the gates be opened wide:
Charge, charge, my giants," Rávan cried.
They heard his voice, and loud and long
Rang the wild clamour of the throng,
And shell and drum their notes upsent,
And every martial instrument.
Forth, at the bidding of their lord
From every gate the giants poured,
As, when the waters rise and swell,
Huge waves preceding waves impel.
Again from every Vánar throat
A scream of fierce defiance smote
The welkin: earth and sea and sky
Reëchoed with the awful cry.
The roar of elephants, the neigh
Of horses eager for the fray.
The frequent clash of warriors' steel,
The rattling of the chariot wheel.
Fierce was the deadly fight: opposed
In terrible array they closed,
As when the Gods of heaven enraged
With rebel fiends wild battle waged.
Axe, spear, and mace were wielded well:
At every blow a Vánar fell.
But shivered rock and brandished tree

Brought many a giant on his knee,
To perish in his turn beneath
The deadly wounds of nails and teeth.

Canto XLIII
The Single Combats

Brave chiefs of each opposing side
Their strength in single combat tried.
Fierce Indrajít the fight began
With Angad in the battle's van.
Sampáti, strongest of his race,
Stood with Prajangha face to face.
Hanúmán, Jambumáli met
In mortal opposition set.
Vibhishaṇ, brother of the lord
Of Lanká, raised his threatening sword
And singled out, with eyes aglow
With wrath, Śatrughna for his foe.
The mighty Gaja Tapan sought,
And Níla with Nikumbha fought.
Sugríva, Vánar king, defied
Fierce Praghas long in battle tried,
And Lakshmaṇ fearless in the fight
Encountered Vírúpáksha's might.
To meet the royal Ráma came
Wild Agniketu fierce as flame;
Mitraghana, he who loved to strike
His foeman and his friend alike:
With Raśmiketu, known and feared
Where'er his ponderous flag was reared;
And Yajnakopa whose delight
Was ruin of the sacred rite.
These met and fought, with thousands more,

And trampled earth was red with gore.
Swift as the bolt which Indra sends
When fire from heaven the mountain rends
Smote Indrajít with furious blows
On Angad queller of his foes.
But Angad from his foeman tore
The murderous mace the warrior bore,
And low in dust his coursers rolled,
His driver, and his car of gold.
Struck by the shafts Prajangha sped,
The Vánar chief Sampáti bled,
But, heedless of his gashes he
Crushed down the giant with a tree.
Then car-borne Jambumáli smote
Hanumán on the chest and throat;
But at the car the Vánar rushed,
And chariot, steeds, and rider crushed.
Sugríva whirled a huge tree round,
And struck fierce Praghas to the ground.
One arrow shot from Lakshman's bow
Laid mighty Vírúpáksha low.
His giant foes round Ráma pressed
And shot their shafts at head and breast;
But, when the iron shower was spent,
Four arrows from his bow he sent,
And every missile, deftly sped;
Cleft from the trunk a giant head. 951

Canto XLIV
The Night

The lord of Light had sunk and set:
Night came; the foeman struggled yet;
And fiercer for the gloom of night
Grew the wild fury of the fight.
Scarce could each warrior's eager eye
The foeman from the friend descry.
"Rákshas or Vánar? say;" cried each,
And foe knew foeman by his speech.
"Why wilt thou fly? O warrior, stay:
Turn on the foe, and rend and slay:"
Such were the cries, such words of fear
Smote through the gloom each listening ear.
Each swarthy rover of the night
Whose golden armour flashed with light,
Showed like a towering hill embraced
By burning woods about his waist.
The giants at the Vánars flew,
And ravening ate the foes they slew:
With mortal bite like serpent's fang,
The Vánars at the giants sprang,
And car and steeds and they who bore
The pennons fell bedewed with gore.
No serried band, no firm array
The fury of their charge could stay.
Down went the horse and rider, down
Went giant lords of high renown.
Though midnight's shade was dense and dark,

With skill that swerved not from the mark
Their bows the sons of Raghu drew,
And each keen shaft a chieftain slew.
Uprose the blinding dust from meads
Ploughed by the cars and trampling steeds,
And where the warriors fell the flood
Was dark and terrible with blood.
Six giants 952 singled Ráma out,
And charged him with a furious shout
Loud as the roaring of the sea
When every wind is raging free.
Six times he shot: six heads were cleft;
Six giants dead on earth were left.
Nor ceased he yet: his bow he strained,
And from the sounding weapon rained
A storm of shafts whose fiery glare
Filled all the region of the air;
And chieftains dropped before his aim
Like moths that perish in the flame.
Earth glistened where the arrows fell,
As shines in autumn nights a dell
Which fireflies, flashing through the gloom,
With momentary light illume.
But Indrajít, when Báli's son 953
The victory o'er the foe had won,
Saw with a fury-kindled eye
His mangled steeds and driver die;
Then, lost in air, he fled the fight,
And vanished from the victor's sight.
The Gods and saints glad voices raised,
And Angad for his virtue praised;
And Raghu's sons bestowed the meed
Of honour due to valorous deed.
Compelled his shattered car to quit,

Rage filled the soul of Indrajít,
Who brooked not, strong by Brahmá's grace
Defeat from one of Vánar race.
In magic mist concealed from view
His bow the treacherous warrior drew,
And Raghu's sons were first to feel
The tempest of his winged steel.
Then when his arrows failed to kill
The princes who defied him still,
He bound them with the serpent noose, 954
The magic bond which none might loose.

Canto XLV
Indrajít's Victory

Brave Ráma, burning still to know
The station of his artful foe,
Gave to ten chieftains, mid the best
Of all the host, his high behest.
Swift rose in air the Vánar band:
Each region of the sky they scanned:
But Rávaṇ's son by magic skill
Checked them with arrows swifter still,
When streams of blood from chest and side
The dauntless Vánars' limbs had dyed,
The giant in his misty shroud
Showed like the sun obscured by cloud.
Like serpents hissing through the air,
His arrows smote the princely pair;
And from their limbs at every rent
A stream of rushing blood was sent.
Like Kinśuk trees they stood, that show
In spring their blossoms' crimson glow.
Then Indrajít with fury eyed
Ikshváku's royal sons, and cried:
"Not mighty Indra can assail
Or see me when I choose to veil
My form in battle: and can ye,
Children of earth, contend with me?
The arrowy noose this hand has shot
Has bound you with a hopeless knot;
And, slaughtered by my shafts and bow,

To Yáma's hall this hour ye go."
He spoke, and shouted. Then anew
The arrows from his bowstring flew,
And pierced, well aimed with perfect art,
Each limb and joint and vital part.
Transfixed with shafts in every limb,
Their strength relaxed, their eyes grew dim.
As two tall standards side by side,
With each sustaining rope untied,
Fall levelled by the howling blast,
So earth's majestic lords at last
Beneath the arrowy tempest reeled,
And prostrate pressed the battle field.

Canto XLVI
Indrajít's Triumph

The Vánar chiefs whose piercing eyes
Scanned eagerly the earth and skies,
Saw the brave brothers wounded sore
Transfixed with darts and stained with gore.
The monarch of the Vánar race,
With wise Vibhishaṇ, reached the place;
Angad and Níla came behind,
And others of the forest kind,
And standing with Hanúmán there
Lamented for the fallen pair.
Their melancholy eyes they raised;
In fruitless search a while they gazed.
But magic arts Vibhishaṇ knew;
Not hidden from his keener view,
Though veiled by magic from the rest,
The son of Rávaṇ stood confessed.
Fierce Indrajít with savage pride
The fallen sons of Raghu eyed,
And every giant heart was proud
As thus the warrior cried aloud:
"Slain by mine arrows Ráma lies,
And closed in death are Lakshmaṇ's eyes.
Dead are the mighty princes who
Dúshaṇ and Khara smote and slew.
The Gods and fiends may toil in vain
To free them from the binding chain.
The haughty chief, my father's dread,

Who drove him sleepless from his bed,
While Lanká, troubled like a brook
In rain time, heard his name and shook:
He whose fierce hate our lives pursued
Lies helpless by my shafts subdued.
Now fruitless is each wondrous deed
Wrought by the race the forests breed,
And fruitless every toil at last
Like cloudlets when the rains are past."
Then rose the shout of giants loud
As thunder from a bursting cloud,
When, deeming Ráma, dead, they raised
Their voices and the conqueror praised.
Still motionless, as lie the slain,
The brothers pressed the bloody plain,
No sigh they drew, no breath they heaved,
And lay as though of life bereaved.
Proud of the deed his art had done,
To Lanká's town went Rávaṇ's son,
Where, as he passed, all fear was stilled,
And every heart with triumph filled.
Sugríva trembled as he viewed
Each fallen prince with blood bedewed,
And in his eyes which overflowed
With tears the flame of anger glowed.
"Calm," cried Vibhishaṇ, "calm thy fears,
And stay the torrent of thy tears.
Still must the chance of battle change,
And victory still delight to range.
Our cause again will she befriend
And bring us triumph in the end.
This is not death: each prince will break
The spell that holds him, and awake;
Nor long shall numbing magic bind

The mighty arm, the lofty mind."
He ceased: his finger bathed in dew
Across Sugríva's eyes he drew;
From dulling mist his vision freed,
And spoke these words to suit the need:
"No time is this for fear: away
With fainting heart and weak delay.
Now, e'en the tear which sorrow wrings
From loving eyes destruction brings.
Up, on to battle at the head
Of those brave troops which Ráma led.
Or guardian by his side remain
Till sense and strength the prince regain.
Soon shall the trance-bound pair revive,
And from our hearts all sorrow drive.
Though prostrate on the earth he lie,
Deem not that Ráma's death is nigh;
Deem not that Lakshmí will forget
Or leave her darling champion yet.
Rest here and be thy heart consoled;
Ponder my words, be firm and bold.
I, foremost in the battlefield,
Will rally all who faint or yield.
Their staring eyes betray their fear;
They whisper each in other's ear.
They, when they hear my cheering cry
And see the friend of Ráma nigh,
Will cast their gloom and fears away
Like faded wreaths of yesterday."
Thus calmed he King Sugríva's dread;
Then gave new heart to those who fled.
Fierce Indrajít, his soul on fire
With pride of conquest, sought his sire,
Raised reverent hands, and told him all,

The battle and the princes' fall.
Rejoicing at his foes' defeat
Upsprang the monarch from his seat,
Girt by his giant courtiers: round
His warrior son his arms he wound,
Close kisses on his head applied,
And heard again how Ráma died.

Canto XLVII
Sítá

Still on the ground where Ráma slept
Their faithful watch the Vánars kept.
There Angad stood o'erwhelmed with grief
And many a lord and warrior chief;
And, ranged in densest mass around,
Their tree-armed legions held the ground.
Far ranged each Vánar's eager eye,
Now swept the land, now sought the sky,
All fearing, if a leaf was stirred,
A Rákshas in the sound they heard.
The lord of Lanká in his hall,
Rejoicing at his foeman's fall,
Commanded and the warders came
Who ever watched the Maithil dame.
"Go," cried the Rákshas king, "relate
To Janak's child her husband's fate.
Low on the earth her Ráma lies,
And dark in death are Lakshman's eyes.
Bring forth my car and let her ride
To view the chieftains side by side.
The lord to whom her fancy turned
For whose dear sake my love she spurned,
Lies smitten, as he fiercely led
The battle, with his brother dead.
Lead forth the royal lady: go
Her husband's lifeless body show.
Then from all doubt and terror free

Her softening heart will turn to me."
They heard his speech: the car was brought;
That shady grove the warders sought
Where, mourning Ráma night and day,
The melancholy lady lay.
They placed her in the car and through
The yielding air they swiftly flew.
The lady looked upon the plain,
Looked on the heaps of Vánar slain,
Saw where, triumphant in the fight,
Thronged the fierce rovers of the night,
And Vánar chieftains, mournful-eyed,
Watched by the fallen brothers' side.
There stretched upon his gory bed
Each brother lay as lie the dead,
With shattered mail and splintered bow
Pierced by the arrows of the foe.
When on the pair her eyes she bent,
Burst from her lips a wild lament
Her eyes o'erflowed, she groaned and sighed
And thus in trembling accents cried:

Canto XLVIII
Sítá's Lament

"False are they all, proved false to-day,
The prophets of my fortune, they
Who in the tranquil time of old
A blessed life for me foretold,
Predicting I should never know
A childless dame's, a widow's woe,
False are they all, their words are vain,
For thou, my lord and life, art slain.
False was the priest and vain his lore
Who blessed me in those days of yore
By Ráma's side in bliss to reign:
For thou, my lord and life, art slain.
They hailed me happy from my birth,
Proud empress of the lord of earth.
They blessed me—but the thought is pain—
For thou, my lord and life, art slain.
Ah, fruitless hope! each glorious sign
That stamps the future queen is mine,
With no ill-omened mark to show
A widow's crushing hour of woe.
They say my hair is black and fine,
They praise my brows' continuous line;
My even teeth divided well,
My bosom for its graceful swell.
They praise my feet and fingers oft;

They say my skin is smooth and soft,
And call me happy to possess
The twelve fair marks that bring success. 955
But ah, what profit shall I gain?
Thou, O my lord and life, art slain.
The flattering seer in former days
My gentle girlish smile would praise,
And swear that holy water shed
By Bráhman hands upon my head
Should make me queen, a monarch's bride:
How is the promise verified?
Matchless in might the brothers slew
In Janasthán the giant crew.
And forced the indomitable sea
To let them pass to rescue me.
Theirs was the fiery weapon hurled
By him who rules the watery world; 956
Theirs the dire shaft by Indra sped;
Theirs was the mystic Brahmá's Head. 957
In vain they fought, the bold and brave:
A coward's hand their death-wounds gave.
By secret shafts and magic spell
The brothers, peers of Indra, fell.
That foe, if seen by Ráma's eye
One moment, had not lived to fly.
Though swift as thought, his utmost speed
Had failed him in the hour of need.
No might, no tear, no prayer may stay
Fate's dark inevitable day.
Nor could their matchless valour shield
These heroes on the battle field.
I sorrow for the noble dead,
I mourn my hopes for ever fled;
But chief my weeping eyes o'erflow

For Queen Kauśalyá's hopeless woe.
The widowed queen is counting now
Each hour prescribed by Ráma's vow,
And lives because she longs to see
Once more her princely sons and me."
Then Trijatá, 958 of gentler mould
Though Rákshas born, her grief consoled:
"Dear Queen, thy causeless woe dispel:
Thy husband lives, and all is well.
Look round: in every Vánar face
The light of joyful hope I trace.
Not thus, believe me, shine the eyes
Of warriors when their leader dies.
An Army, when the chief is dead,
Flies from the field dispirited.
Here, undisturbed in firm array,
The Vánars by the brothers stay.
Love prompts my speech; no longer grieve;
Ponder my counsel, and believe.
These lips of mine from earliest youth
Have spoken, and shall speak, the truth.
Deep in my heart thy gentle grace
And patient virtues hold their place.
Turn, lady, turn once more thine eye:
Though pierced with shafts the heroes lie,
On brows and cheeks with blood-drops wet
The light of beauty lingers yet.
Such beauty ne'er is found in death,
But vanishes with parting breath.
O, trust the hope these tokens give:
The heroes are not dead, but live."
Then Sítá joined her hands, and sighed,
"O, may thy words be verified!"
The car was turned, which fleet as thought

The mourning queen to Lanká brought.
They led her to the garden, where
Again she yielded to despair,
Lamenting for the chiefs who bled
On earth's cold bosom with the dead.

Canto XLIX
Ráma's Lament

Ranged round the spot where Ráma fell
Each Vánar chief stood sentinel.
At length the mighty hero broke
The trance that held him, and awoke.
He saw his senseless brother, dyed
With blood from head to foot, and cried:
"What have I now to do with life
Or rescue of my prisoned wife,
When thus before my weeping eyes,
Slain in the fight, my brother lies?
A queen like Sítá I may find
Among the best of womankind,
But never such a brother, tried
In war, my guardian, friend, and guide.
If he be dead, the brave and true,
I will not live but perish too.
How, reft of Lakshmaṇ, shall I meet
My mother, and Kaikeyí greet?
My brother's eager question brook,
And fond Sumitrá's longing look?
What shall I say, o'erwhelmed with shame
To cheer the miserable dame?
How, when she hears her son is dead,
Will her sad heart be comforted?
Ah me, for longer life unfit

This mortal body will I quit;

For Lakshman slaughtered for my sake,

From sleep of death will never wake.

Ah when I sank oppressed with care,

Thy gentle voice could soothe despair.

And art thou, O my brother, killed?

Is that dear voice for ever stilled?

Cold are those lips, my brother, whence

Came never word to breed offence?

Ah stretched upon the gory plain

My brother lies untimely slain:

Numbed is the mighty arm that slew

The leaders of the giant crew.

Transfixed with shafts, with blood-streams red,

Thou liest on thy lowly bed:

So sinks to rest, his journey done,

Mid arrowy rays the crimson sun.

Thou, when from home and sire I fled,

The wood's wild ways with me wouldst tread:

Now close to thine my steps shall be,

For I in death will follow thee.

Vibhishan now will curse my name,

And Ráma as a braggart blame,

Who promised—but his word is vain—

That he in Lanká's isle should reign.

Return, Sugríva: reft of me

Lead back thy Vánars o'er the sea,

Nor hope to battle face to face

With him who rules the giant race.

Well have ye done and nobly fought,

And death in desperate combat sought.

All that heroic might can do,

Brave Vánars, has been done by you.

My faithful friends I now dismiss:
Return: my last farewell is this."
Bedewed with tears was every cheek
As thus the Vánars heard him speak.
Vibhishan on the field had stayed
The Vánar hosts who fled dismayed.
Now lifting up his mace on high
With martial step the chief drew nigh.
The hosts who watched by Ráma's side
Beheld his shape and giant stride.
'Tis he, 'tis Rávan's son, they thought:
And all in flight their safety sought.

Canto L
The Broken Spell

Sugríva viewed the flying crowd,
And thus to Angad cried aloud:
"Why run the trembling hosts, as flee
Storm-scattered barks across the sea?"
"Dost thou not mark," the chief replied,
"Transfixed with shafts, with bloodstreams dyed,
With arrowy toils about them wound,
The sons of Raghu on the ground?"
That moment brought Vibhishan near.
Sugríva knew the cause of fear,
And ordered Jámbaván, who led
The bears, to check the hosts that fled.
The king of bears his hest obeyed:
The Vánars' headlong flight was stayed.
A little while Vibhishan eyed
The brothers fallen side by side.
His giant fingers wet with dew
Across the heroes' eyes he drew,
Still on the pair his sad look bent,
And spoke these word in wild lament:
"Ah for the mighty chiefs brought low
By coward hand and stealthy blow!
Brave pair who loved the open fight,
Slain by that rover of the night.
Dishonest is the victory won
By Indrajít my brother's son.
I on their might for aid relied,

And in my cause they fought and died.
Lost is the hope that soothed each pain:
I live, but live no more to reign,
While Lanká's lord, untouched by ill,
Exults in safe defiance still."
"Not thus," Sugríva said, "repine,
For Lanká's isle shall still be thine.
Nor let the tyrant and his son
Exult before the fight be done.
These royal chiefs, though now dismayed,
Freed from the spell by Garuḍ's aid,
Triumphant yet the foe shall meet
And lay the robber at their feet."
His hope the Vánar monarch told,
And thus Vibhishaṇ's grief consoled.
Then to Susheṇ who at his side
Expectant stood, Sugríva cried:
"When these regain their strength and sense,
Fly, bear them to Kishkindhá hence.
Here with my legions will I stay,
The tyrant and his kinsmen slay,
And, rescued from the giant king,
The Maithil lady will I bring,
Like Glory lost of old, restored
By Śakra, heaven's almighty lord."
Susheṇ made answer: "Hear me yet:
When Gods and fiends in battle met,
So fiercely fought the demon crew,
So wild a storm of arrows flew,
That heavenly warriors faint with pain,
Sank smitten by the ceaseless rain.
Vṛihaspati, 959 with herb and spell,
Cured the sore wounds of those who fell.
And, skilled in arts that heal and save,

New life and sense and vigour gave.
Far, on the Milky Ocean's shore,
Still grow those herbs in boundless store;
Let swiftest Vánars thither speed
And bring them for our utmost need.
Those herbs that on the mountain spring
Let Panas and Sampáti bring,
For well the wondrous leaves they know,
That heal each wound and life bestow.
Beside that sea which, churned of yore,
The amrit on its surface bore,
Where the white billows lash the land,
Chandra's fair height and Droṇa stand.
Planted by Gods each glittering steep
Looks down upon the milky deep.
Let fleet Hanúmán bring us thence
Those herbs of wondrous influence."
Meanwhile the rushing wind grew loud,
Red lightnings flashed from banks of cloud.
The mountains shook, the wild waves rose,
And smitten with resistless blows
Unrooted fell each stately tree
That fringed the margin of the sea.
All life within the waters feared
Then, as the Vánars gazed, appeared
King Garuḍ's self, a wondrous sight,
Disclosed in flames of fiery light.
From his fierce eye in sudden dread
All serpents in a moment fled.
And those transformed to shaft that bound
The princes vanished in the ground.
On Raghu's sons his eyes he bent,
And hailed the lords armipotent.
Then o'er them stooped the feathered king,

And touched their faces with his wing.
His healing touch their pangs allayed,
And closed each rent the shafts had made.
Again their eyes were bright and bold,
Again the smooth skin shone like gold.
Again within their shell enshrined
Came memory and each power of mind:
And, from those numbing bonds released,
Their spirit, zeal, and strength increased.
Firm on their feet they stood, and then
Thus Ráma spake, the lord of men:
"By thy dear grace in sorest need
From deadly bonds we both are freed.
To these glad eyes as welcome now
As Aja 960 or my sire art thou.
Who art thou, mighty being? say,
Thus glorious in thy bright array."
He ceased: the king of birds replied,
While flashed his eye with joy and pride:
"In me, O Raghu's son, behold
One who has loved thee from of old:
Garuḍ, the lord of all that fly,
Thy guardian and thy friend am I.
Not all the Gods in heaven could loose
These numbing bonds, this serpent noose,
Wherewith fierce Rávaṇ's son, renowned
For magic arts, your limbs had bound.
Those arrows fixed in every limb
Were mighty snakes, transformed by him.
Blood thirsty race, they live beneath
The earth, and slay with venomed teeth.
On, smite the lord of Lanká's isle,
But guard you from the giants' guile
Who each dishonest art employ

And by deceit brave foes destroy.
So shall the tyrant Rávaṇ bleed,
And Sítá from his power be freed."
Thus Garuḍ spake: then, swift as thought,
The region of the sky he sought,
Where in the distance like a blaze
Of fire he vanished from the gaze.
Then the glad Vánars' joy rang out
In many a wild tumultuous shout,
And the loud roar of drum and shell
Startled each distant sentinel.

Canto LI
Dhúmráksha's Sally

King Rávaṇ, where he sat within,
Heard from his hall the deafening din,
And with a spirit ill at ease
Addressed his lords in words like these:
"That warlike shout, those joyous cries,
Loud as the thunder of the skies,
Upsent from every Vánar throat,
Some new-born confidence denote.
Hark, how the sea and trembling shore
Re-echo with the Vánars' roar.
Though arrowy chains, securely twined
Both Ráma and his brother bind,
Still must the fierce triumphant shout
Disturb my soul with rising doubt.
Swift envoys to the army send,
And learn what change these cries portend."
Obedient, at their master's call,
Fleet giants clomb the circling wall.
They saw the Vánars formed and led:
They saw Sugríva at their head,
The brothers from their bonds released:
And hope grew faint and fear increased.
Their faces pale with doubt and dread,
Back to the giant king they sped,
And to his startled ear revealed
The tidings of the battle field.
The flush of rage a while gave place

To chilling fear that changed his face:
"What?" cried the tyrant, "are my foes
Freed from the binding snakes that close
With venomed clasp round head and limb,
Bright as the sun and fierce like him:
The spell a God bestowed of yore,
The spell that never failed before?
If arts like these be useless, how
Shall giant strength avail us now?
Go forth, Dhúmráksha, good at need,
The bravest of my warriors lead:
Force through the foe thy conquering way,
And Ráma and the Vánars slay."
Before his king with reverence due
Dhúmráksha bowed him, and withdrew.
Around him at his summons came
Fierce legions led by chiefs of fame.
Well armed with sword and spear and mace,
They hurried to the gathering place,
And rushed to battle, borne at speed
By elephant and car and steed.

Canto LII
Dhúmráksha's Death

The Vánars saw the giant foe
Pour from the gate in gallant show,
Rejoiced with warriors' fierce delight
And shouted, longing for the fight.
Near came the hosts and nearer yet:
Dire was the tumult as they met,
As, serried line to line opposed,
The Vánars and the giants closed.
Fierce on the foe the Vánars rushed,
And, wielding trees, the foremost crushed;
But, feathered from the heron's wing,
With eager flight from sounding string,
Against them shot with surest aim
A ceaseless storm of arrows came:
And, pierced in head and chest and side,
Full many a Vánar fell and died.
They perished slain in fierce attacks
With sword and pike and battle-axe;
But myriads following undismayed
Their valour in the fight displayed.
Unnumbered Vánars rent and torn
With shaft and spear to earth were borne.
But crushed by branchy trees and blocks
Of jagged stone and shivered rocks
Which the wild Vánars wielded well
The bravest of the giants fell.
Their trampled banners strewed the fields,

And broken swords and spears and shields;
And, crushed by blows which none might stay,
Cars, elephants, and riders lay.
Dhúmráksha turned his furious eye
And saw his routed legions fly.
Still dauntless, with terrific blows,
He struck and slew his foremost foes.
At every blow, at every thrust,
He laid a Vánar in the dust.
So fell they neath the sword and lance
In battle's wild Gandharva 961 dance,
Where clang of bow and clash of sword
Did duty for the silvery chord,
And hoofs that rang and steeds that neighed
Loud concert for the dancers made.
So fiercely from Dhúmráksha's bow
His arrows rained in ceaseless flow,
The Vánar legions turned and fled
To all the winds discomfited.
Hanúmán saw the Vánars fly;
He heaved a mighty rock on high.
His keen eyes flashed with wrathful fire,
And, rapid as the Wind his sire,
Strong as the rushing tempests are,
He hurled it at the advancing car.
Swift through the air the missile sang:
The giant from the chariot sprang,
Ere crushed by that terrific blow
Lay pole and wheel and flag and bow.
Hanúmán's eyes with fury blazed:
A mountain's rocky peak he raised,
Poised it on high in act to throw,
And rushed upon his giant foe.
Dhúmráksha saw: he raised his mace

And smote Hanúmán on the face,
Who maddened by the wound's keen pang
Again upon his foeman sprang;
And on the giant's head the rock
Descended with resistless shock.
Crushed was each limb: a shapeless mass
He lay upon the blood-stained grass.

Canto LIII
Vajradanshtra's Sally

When Rávaṇ in his palace heard
The mournful news, his wrath was stirred;
And, gasping like a furious snake,
To Vajradanshṭra thus he spake:
"Go forth, my fiercest captain, lead
The bravest of the giants' breed.
Go forth, the sons of Raghu slay
And by their side Sugríva lay."
He ceased: the chieftain bowed his head
And forth with gathered troops he sped.
Cars, camels, steeds were well arrayed,
And coloured banners o'er them played.
Rings decked his arms: about his waist
The life-protecting mail was braced,
And on the chieftain's forehead set
Glittered his cap and coronet.
Borne on a bannered car that glowed
With golden sheen the warrior rode,
And footmen marched with spear and sword
And bow and mace behind their lord.
In pomp and pride of warlike state
They sallied from the southern gate,
But saw, as on their way they sped,
Dread signs around and overhead.
For there were meteors falling fast,
Though not a cloud its shadow cast;
And each ill-omened bird and beast,

Forboding death, the fear increased,
While many a giant slipped and reeled,
Falling before he reached the field.
They met in mortal strife engaged,
And long and fierce the battle raged.
Spears, swords uplifted, gleamed and flashed,
And many a chief to earth was dashed.
A ceaseless storm of arrows rained,
And limbs were pierced and blood-distained.
Terrific was the sound that filled
The air, and every heart was chilled,
As hurtling o'er the giants flew
The rocks and trees which Vánars threw.
Fierce as a hungry lion when
Unwary deer approach his den,
Angad, his eyes with fury red,
Waving a tree above his head,
Rushed with wild charge which none could stay
Where stood the giants' dense array.
Like tall trees levelled by the blast
Before him fell the giants fast,
And earth that streamed with blood was strown
With warriors, steeds, and cars o'erthrown.

Canto LIV
Vajradanshtra's Death

The giant leader fiercely rained
His arrows and the fight maintained.
Each time the clanging cord he drew
His certain shaft a Vánar slew.
Then, as the creatures he has made
Fly to the Lord of Life for aid,
To Angad for protection fled
The Vánar hosts dispirited.
Then raged the battle fiercer yet
When Angad and the giant met.
A hundred thousand arrows, hot
With flames of fire, the giant shot;
And every shaft he deftly sent
His foeman's body pierced and rent.
From Angad's limbs ran floods of gore:
A stately tree from earth he tore,
Which, maddened as his gashes bled,
He hurled at his opponent's head.
His bow the dauntless giant drew;
To meet the tree swift arrows flew,
Checked the huge missile's onward way,
And harmless on the earth it lay.
A while the Vánar chieftain gazed,
Then from the earth a rock he raised
Rent from a thunder-splitten height,
And cast it with resistless might.
The giant marked, and, mace in hand,

Leapt from his chariot to the sand,
Ere the rough mass descending broke
The seat, the wheel, the pole and yoke.
Then Angad seized a shattered hill,
Whereon the trees were flowering still,
And with full force the jagged peak
Fell crashing on the giant's cheek.
He staggered, reeled, and fell: the blood
Gushed from the giant in a flood.
Reft of his might, each sense astray,
A while upon the sand he lay.
But strength and wandering sense returned
Again his eyes with fury burned,
And with his mace upraised on high
He wounded Angad on the thigh.
Then from his hand his mace he threw,
And closer to his foeman drew.
Then with their fists they fought, and smote
On brow and cheek and chest and throat.
Worn out with toil, their limbs bedewed,
With blood, the strife they still renewed,
Like Mercury and fiery Mars
Met in fierce battle mid the stars.
A while the deadly fight was stayed:
Each armed him with his trusty blade
Whose sheath with tinkling bells supplied,
And golden net, adorned his side;
And grasped his ponderous leather shield
To fight till one should fall or yield.
Unnumbered wounds they gave and took:
Their wearied bodies reeled and shook.
At length upon the sand that drank
Streams of their blood the warriors sank,
But as a serpent rears his head

Sore wounded by a peasant's tread,

So Angad, fallen on his knees,

Yet gathered strength his sword to seize;

And, severed by the glittering blade,

The giant's head on earth was laid.

[I omit Cantos LV, LVI, LVII, and LVIII, which relate how Akampan and Prahasta sally out and fall. There is little novelty of incident in these Cantos and the results are exactly the same as before. In Canto LV, Akampan, at the command of Rávaṇ, leads forth his troops. Evil omens are seen and heard. The enemies meet, and many fall on each side, the Vánars transfixed with arrows, the Rákshases crushed with rocks and trees.

In Canto LVI Akampan sees that the Rákshases are worsted, and fights with redoubled rage and vigour. The Vánars fall fast under his "nets of arrows." Hanumán comes to the rescue. He throws mountain peaks at the giant which are dexterously stopped with flights of arrows; and at last beats him down and kills him with a tree.

In Canto LVII, Rávaṇ is seriously alarmed. He declares that he himself, Kumbhakarṇa or Prahasta, must go forth. Prahasta sallies out vaunting that the fowls of the air shall eat their fill of Vánar flesh.

In Canto LVIII, the two armies meet. Dire is the conflict; ceaseless is the rain of stones and arrows. At last Níla meets Prahasta and breaks his bow. Prahasta leaps from his car, and the giant and the Vánar fight on foot. Níla with a huge tree crushes his opponent who falls like a tree when its roots are cut.]

Canto LIX
Rávan's Sally

They told him that the chief was killed,
And Rávan's breast with rage was filled.
Then, fiercely moved by wrath and pride,
Thus to his lords the tyrant cried:
"No longer, nobles, may we show
This lofty scorn for such a foe
By whom our bravest, with his train
Of steeds and elephants, is slain.
Myself this day will take the field,
And Raghu's sons their lives shall yield."
High on the royal car, that glowed
With glory from his face, he rode;
And tambour shell and drum pealed out,
And joyful was each giant's shout.
A mighty host, with eyeballs red
Like flames of kindled fire, he led.
He passed the city gate, and viewed,
Arrayed, the Vánar multitude,
Those wielding massy rocks, and these
Armed with the stems of uptorn trees,
And Ráma with his eyes aglow
With warlike ardour viewed the foe,
And thus the brave Vibhishaṇ, best
Of weapon-wielding chiefs, addressed:
"What captain leads this bright array
Where lances gleam and banners play,
And thousands armed with spear and sword

Await the bidding of their lord?"
"Seest, thou," Vibhishan answered, "one
Whose face is as the morning sun,
Preëminent for hugest frame?
Akampan 962 is the giant's name.
Behold that chieftain, chariot-borne,
Whom Brahmá's chosen gifts adorn.
He wields a bow like Indra's own;
A lion on his flag is shown,
His eyes with baleful fire are lit:
'Tis Rávan's son, 'tis Indrajít.
There, brandishing in mighty hands
His huge bow, Atikáya stands.
And that proud warrior o'er whose head
A moon-bright canopy is spread:
Whose might, in many a battle tried,
Has tamed imperial Indra's pride;
Who wears a crown of burnished gold,
Is Lanká's lord the lofty-souled."
He ceased: and Ráma knew his foe,
And laid an arrow on his bow:
"Woe to the wretch," he cried, "whom fate
Abandons to my deadly hate."
He spoke, and, firm by Lakshman's side,
The giant to the fray defied.
The lord of Lanká bade his train
Of warriors by the gates remain,
To guard the city from surprise
By Ráma's forest born allies.
Then as some monster of the sea
Cleaves swift-advancing billows, he
Charged with impetuous onset through
The foe, and cleft the host in two.
Sugríva ran, the king to meet:

A hill uprooted from its seat
He hurled, with trees that graced the height
Against the rover of the night:
But cleft with shafts that checked its way
Harmless upon the earth it lay.
Then fiercer Rávan's fury grew,
An arrow from his side he drew,
Swift as a thunderbolt, aglow
With fire, and launched it at the foe.
Through flesh and bone a way it found,
And stretched Sugríva on the ground.
Sushen and Nala saw him fall,
Gaváksha, Gavaya heard their call,
And, poising hills, in act to fling
They charged amain the giant king.
They charged, they hurled the hills in vain,
He checked them with his arrowy rain,
And every brave assailant felt
The piercing wounds his missiles dealt,
Then smitten by the shafts that came
Keen, fleet, and thick, with certain aim,
They fled to Ráma, sure defence
Against the oppressor's violence,
Then, reverent palm to palm applied,
Thus Lakshman to his brother cried:
"To me, my lord, the task entrust
To lay this giant in the dust."
"Go, then," said Ráma, "bravely fight;
Beat down this rover of the night.
But he, unmatched in bold emprise,
Fears not the Lord of earth and skies,
Keep on thy guard: with keenest eye
Thy moments of attack espy.
Let hand and eye in due accord

Protect thee with the bow and sword."
Then Lakshmaṇ round his brother threw
His mighty arms in honour due,
Bent lowly down his reverent head,
And onward to the battle sped.
Hanúmán from afar beheld
How Rávaṇ's shafts the Vánars quelled:
To meet the giant's car he ran,
Raised his right arm and thus began:
"If Brahmá's boon thy life has screened
From Yaksha, God, Gandharva, fiend,
With these contending fear no ill,
But tremble at a Vánar still."
With fury flashing from his eye
The lord of Lanká made reply:
"Strike, Vánar, strike: the fray begin,
And hope eternal fame to win.
This arm shall prove thee in the strife
And end thy glory and thy life."
"Remember," cried the Wind-God's son,
"Remember all that I have done,
My prowess, King, thou knowest well,
Shown in the fight when Aksha 963 fell."
With heavy hand the giant smote
Hanúmán on the chest and throat,
Who reeled and staggered to and fro,
Stunned for a moment by the blow.
Till, mustering strength, his hand he reared
And struck the foe whom Indra feared.
His huge limbs bent beneath the shock,
As mountains, in an earthquake, rock,
And from the Gods and sages pealed
Shouts of loud triumph as he reeled.
But strength returning nerved his frame:

His eyeballs flashed with fiercer flame.
No living creature might resist
That blow of his tremendous fist
Which fell upon Hanúmán's flank:
And to the ground the Vánar sank,
No sign of life his body showed:
And Rávan in his chariot rode
At Níla; and his arrowy rain
Fell on the captain and his train.
Fierce Níla stayed his Vánar band,
And, heaving with his single hand
A mountain peak, with vigorous swing
Hurled the huge missile at the king.
Hanúmán life and strength regained,
Burned for the fight and thus complained:
"Why, coward giant, didst thou flee
And leave the doubtful fight with me?"
Seven mighty arrows keen and fleet
The giant launched, the hill to meet;
And, all its force and fury stayed,
The harmless mass on earth was laid.
Enraged the Vánar chief beheld
The mountain peak by force repelled,
And rained upon the foe a shower
Of trees uptorn with branch and flower.
Still his keen shafts which pierced and rent
Each flying tree the giant sent:
Still was the Vánar doomed to feel
The tempest of the winged steel.
Then, smarting from that arrowy storm,
The Vánar chief condensed his form, 964
And lightly leaping from the ground
On Rávan's standard footing found;
Then springing unimpeded down

Stood on his bow and golden crown.
The Vánar's nimble leaps amazed
Ikshváku's son who stood and gazed.
The giant, raging in his heart,
Laid on his bow a fiery dart;
The Vánar on his flagstaff eyed,
And thus in tones of fury cried:
"Well skilled in magic lore art thou:
But will thine art avail thee now?
See if thy magic will defend
Thy life against the dart I send."
Thus Rávan spake, the giant king,
And loosed the arrow from the string.
It pierced, with direst fury sped,
The Vánar with its flaming head.
His father's might, his power innate
Preserved him from the threatened fate.
Upon his knees he fell, distained
With streams of blood, but life remained.
Still Rávan for the battle burned:
At Lakshman next his car he turned,
And charged amain with furious show,
Straining in mighty hands his bow.
"Come," Lakshman cried, "assay the fight:
Leave foes unworthy of thy might."
Thus Lakshman spoke: and Lanká's lord
Heard the dread thunder of the cord.
And mad with burning rage and pride
In hasty words like these replied:
"Joy, joy is mine, O Raghu's son:
Thy fate to-day thou canst not shun.
Slain by mine arrows thou shalt tread
The gloomy pathway of the dead."
Thus as he spoke his bow he drew,

And seven keen shafts at Lakshman flew,
But Raghu's son with surest aim
Cleft every arrow as it came.
Thus with fleet shafts each warrior shot
Against his foe, and rested not.
Then one choice weapon from his store,
By Brahmá's self bestowed of yore,
Fierce as the flames that end the world,
The giant king at Lakshman hurled.
The hero fell, and racked with pain,
Scarce could his hand his bow retain.
But sense and strength resumed their seat
And, lightly springing to his feet,
He struck with one tremendous stroke
And Rávan's bow in splinters broke.
From Lakshman's cord three arrows flew
And pierced the giant monarch through.
Sore wounded Rávan closed, and round
Ikshváku's son his strong arms wound.
With strength unrivalled, Brahmá's gift,
He strove from earth his foe to lift.
"Shall I," he cried, "who overthrow
Mount Meru and the Lord of Snow,
And heaven and all who dwell therein,
Be foiled by one of Ráma's kin?"
But though he heaved, and toiled, and strained,
Unmoved Ikshváku's son remained.
His frame by those huge arms compressed
The giant's God-given force confessed,
But conscious that himself was part
Of Vishnu, he was firm in heart.
The Wind-God's son the fight beheld,
And rushed at Rávan, rage-impelled.

Down crashed his mighty hand; the foe
Full in the chest received the blow.
His eyes grew dim, his knees gave way,
And senseless on the earth he lay.
The Wind-God's son to Ráma bore
Deep-wounded Lakshmaṇ stained with gore.
He whom no foe might lift or bend
Was light as air to such a friend.
The dart that Lakshmaṇ's side had cleft,
Untouched, the hero's body left,
And flashing through the air afar
Resumed its place in Rávaṇ's car;
And, waxing well though wounded sore,
He felt the deadly pain no more.
And Rávaṇ, though with deep wounds pained,
Slowly his sense and strength regained,
And furious still and undismayed
On bow and shaft his hand he laid.
Then Hanumán to Ráma cried:
"Ascend my back, great chief, and ride
Like Vishṇu borne on Garuḍ's wing,
To battle with the giant king."
So, burning for the dire attack,
Rode Ráma on the Vánar's back,
And with fierce accents loud and slow
Thus gave defiance to the foe,
While his strained bowstring made a sound
Like thunder when it shakes the ground:
"Stay, Monarch of the giants, stay,
The penalty of sin to pay.
Stay! whither wilt thou fly, and how
Escape the death that waits thee now?"
No word the giant king returned:
His eyes with flames of fury burned.

His arm was stretched, his bow was bent,
And swift his fiery shafts were sent.
Red torrents from the Vánar flowed:
Then Ráma near to Rávan strode,
And with keen darts that never failed,
The chariot of the king assailed.
With surest aim his arrows flew:
The driver and the steeds he slew.
And shattered with the pointed steel
Car, flag, and pole and yoke and wheel.
As Indra hurls his bolt to smite
Mount Meru's heaven-ascending height,
So Ráma with a flaming dart
Struck Lanká's monarch near the heart,
Who reeled and fell beneath the blow
And from loose fingers dropped his bow.
Bright as the sun, with crescent head,
From Ráma's bow an arrow sped,
And from his forehead, proud no more,
Cleft the bright coronet he wore.
Then Ráma stood by Rávan's side
And to the conquered giant cried:
"Well hast thou fought: thine arm has slain
Strong heroes of the Vánar train.
I will not strike or slay thee now,
For weary, faint with fight art thou.
To Lanká's town thy footsteps bend,
And there the night securely spend.
To-morrow come with car and bow,
And then my prowess shalt thou know."
He ceased: the king in humbled pride
Rose from the earth and naught replied.

With wounded limbs and shattered crown
He sought again his royal town.

Canto LX
Kumbhakarna Roused

With humbled heart and broken pride
Through Lanká's gate the giant hied,
Crushed, like an elephant beneath
A lion's spring and murderous teeth,
Or like a serpent 'neath the wing
And talons of the Feathered King.
Such was the giant's wild alarm
At arrows shot by Ráma's arm;
Shafts with red lightning round them curled,
Like Brahmá's bolts that end the world.
Supported on his golden throne,
With failing eye and humbled tone,
"Giants," he cried, "the toil is vain,
Fruitless the penance and the pain,
If I whom Indra owned his peer,
Secure from Gods, a mortal fear.
My soul remembers, now too late,
Lord Brahmá's words who spoke my fate:
"Tremble, proud Giant," thus they ran,
"And dread thy death from slighted man.
Secure from Gods and demons live,
And serpents, by the boon I give.
Against their power thy life is charmed,
But against man is still unarmed."
This Ráma is the man foretold
By Anaraṇya's 965 lips of old:
"Fear, Rávaṇ, basest of the base:

For of mine own imperial race
A prince in after time shall spring
And thee and thine to ruin bring.
And Vedavatí, 966 ere she died
Slain by my ruthless insult, cried:
"A scion of my royal line
Shall slay, vile wretch, both thee and thine."
She in a later birth became
King Janak's child, now Ráma's dame.
Nandíśvara 967 foretold this fate,
And Umá 968 when I moved her hate,
And Rambhá, 969 and the lovely child
Of Varuṇ 970 by my touch defiled.
I know the fated hour is nigh:
Hence, captains, to your stations fly.
Let warders on the rampart stand:
Place at each gate a watchful band;
And, terror of immortal eyes,
Let mightiest Kumbhakarṇa rise.
He, slumbering, free from care and pain,
By Brahmá's curse, for months has lain.
But when Prahasta's death he hears,
Mine own defeat and doubts and fears,
The chief will rise to smite the foe
And his unrivalled valour show.
Then Raghu's royal sons and all
The Vánars neath his might will fall."
The giant lords his hest obeyed,
They left him, trembling and afraid,
And from the royal palace strode
To Kumbhakarṇa's vast abode.
They carried garlands sweet and fresh,
And reeking loads of blood and flesh.
They reached the dwelling where he lay,

A cave that reached a league each way,
Sweet with fair blooms of lovely scent
And bright with golden ornament.
His breathings came so fierce and fast,
Scarce could the giants brook the blast.
They found him on a golden bed
With his huge limbs at length outspread.
They piled their heaps of venison near,
Fat buffaloes and boars and deer.
With wreaths of flowers they fanned his face,
And incense sweetened all the place.
Each raised his mighty voice as loud
As thunders of an angry cloud,
And conchs their stirring summons gave
That echoed through the giant's cave.
Then on his breast they rained their blows,
And high the wild commotion rose
When cymbal vied with drum and horn.
And war cries on the gale upborne.
Through all the air loud discord spread,
And, struck with fear, the birds fell dead.
But still he slept and took his rest.
Then dashed they on his shaggy chest
Clubs, maces, fragments of the rock:
He moved not once, nor felt the shock.
The giants made one effort more
With shell and drum and shout and roar.
Club, mallet, mace, in fury plied,
Rained blows upon his breast and side.
And elephants were urged to aid,
And camels groaned and horses neighed.
They drenched him with a hundred pails,
They tore his ears with teeth and nails.
They bound together many a mace

And beat him on the head and face;
And elephants with ponderous tread
Stamped on his limbs and chest and head.
The unusual weight his slumber broke:
He started, shook his sides, and woke;
And, heedless of the wounds and blows,
Yawning with thirst and hunger rose,
His jaws like hell gaped fierce and wide,
Dire as the flame neath ocean's tide.
Red as the sun on Meru's crest
The giant's face his wrath expressed,
And every burning breath he drew
Was like the blast that rushes through
The mountain cedars. Up he raised
His awful head with eyes that blazed
Like comets, dire as Death in form
Who threats the worlds with fire and storm.
The giants pointed to their stores
Of buffaloes and deer and boars,
And straight he gorged him with a flood
Of wine, with marrow, flesh, and blood.
He ceased: the giants ventured near
And bent their lowly heads in fear.
Then Kumbhakar[n.]a glared with eyes
Still heavy in their first surprise,
Still drowsy from his troubled rest,
And thus the giant band addressed.
"How have ye dared my sleep to break?
No trifling cause should bid me wake.
Say, is all well? or tell the need
That drives you with unruly speed
To wake me. Mark the words I say,
The king shall tremble in dismay,
The fire be quenched and Indra slain

Ere ye shall break my rest in vain."
Yúpáksha answered: "Chieftain, hear;
No God or fiend excites our fear.
But men in arms our walls assail:
We tremble lest their might prevail.
For vengeful Ráma vows to slay
The foe who stole his queen away,
And, matchless for his warlike deeds,
A host of mighty Vánars leads.
Ere now a monstrous Vánar came,
Laid Lanká waste with ruthless flame,
And Aksha, Rávan's offspring, slew
With all his warrior retinue.
Our king who never trembled yet
For heavenly hosts in battle met,
At length the general dread has shared,
O'erthrown by Ráma's arm and spared."
He ceased: and Kumbhakarna spake:
"I will go forth and vengeance take;
Will tread their hosts beneath my feet,
Then triumph-flushed our king will meet.
Our giant bands shall eat their fill
Of Vánars whom this arm shall kill.
The princes' blood shall be my draught,
The chieftains' shall by you be quaffed."
He spake, and, with an eager stride
That shook the earth, to Rávan hied.

Canto LXI
The Vánars' Alarm

The son of Raghu near the wall
Saw, proudly towering over all,
The mighty giant stride along
Attended by the warrior throng;
Heard Kumbhakarṇa's heavy feet
Awake the echoes of the street;
And, with the lust of battle fired,
Turned to Vibhishaṇ and inquired:
"Vibhishaṇ, tell that chieftain's name
Who rears so high his mountain frame;
With glittering helm and lion eyes,
Preëminent in might and size
Above the rest of giant birth,
He towers the standard of the earth;
And all the Vánars when they see
The mighty warrior turn and flee."
"In him," Vibhishaṇ answered, "know
Viśravas' son, the Immortals' foe,
Fierce Kumbhakarṇa, mightier far
Than Gods and fiends and giants are.
He conquered Yáma in the fight,
And Indra trembling owned his might.
His arm the Gods and fiends subdued,
Gandharvas and the serpent brood.
The rest of his gigantic race
Are wondrous strong by God-giving grace;
But nature at his birth to him

Gave matchless power and strength of limb.
Scarce was he born, fierce monster, when
He killed and ate a thousand men.
The trembling race of men, appalled,
On Indra for protection called;
And he, to save the suffering world,
His bolt at Kumbhakarṇa hurled.
So awful was the monster's yell
That fear on all the nations fell,
He, rushing on with furious roar,
A tusk from huge Airávat tore,
And dealt the God so dire a blow
That Indra reeling left his foe,
And with the Gods and mortals fled
To Brahmá's throne dispirited.
"O Brahmá," thus the suppliants cried,
"Some refuge for this woe provide.
If thus his maw the giant sate
Soon will the world be desolate."
The Self-existent calmed their woe,
And spake in anger to their foe:
"As thou wast born, Pulastya's son,
That worlds might weep by thee undone,
Thou like the dead henceforth shalt be:
Such is the curse I lay on thee."
Senseless he lay, nor spoke nor stirred;
Such was the power of Brahmá's word.
But Rávaṇ, troubled for his sake,
Thus to the Self-existent spake:
"Who lops the tree his care has reared
When golden fruit has first appeared?
Not thus, O Brahmá, deal with one
Descended from thine own dear son. 971
Still thou, O Lord, thy word must keep,

He may not die, but let him sleep.
Yet fix a time for him to break
The chains of slumber and awake."
He ceased: and Brahmá made reply;
"Six months in slumber shall he lie
And then arising for a day
Shall cast the numbing bonds away."
Now Rávan in his doubt and dread
Has roused the monster from his bed,
Who comes in this the hour of need
On slaughtered Vánars flesh to feed.
Each Vánar, when his awe-struck eyes
Behold the monstrous chieftain, flies.
With hopeful words their minds deceive,
And let our trembling hosts believe
They see no giant, but, displayed,
A lifeless engine deftly made."
Then Ráma called to Níla: "Haste,
Let troops near every gate be placed,
And, armed with fragments of the rock
And trees, each lane and alley block."
Thus Ráma spoke: the chief obeyed,
And swift the Vánars stood arrayed,
As when the black clouds their battle form,
The summit of a hill to storm.

Canto LXII
Rávan's Request

Along bright Lanká's royal road
The giant, roused from slumber, strode,
While from the houses on his head
A rain of fragrant flowers was shed.
He reached the monarch's gate whereon
Rich gems and golden fretwork shone.
Through court and corridor that shook
Beneath his tread his way he took,
And stood within the chamber where
His brother sat in dark despair.
But sudden, at the grateful sight
The monarch's eye again grew bright.
He started up, forgot his fear,
And drew his giant brother near.
The younger pressed the elder's feet
And paid the King observance meet,
Then cried: "O Monarch, speak thy will,
And let my care thy word fulfil.
What sudden terror and dismay
Have burst the bonds in which I lay?"
Fierce flashed the flame from Rávan's eye,
As thus in wrath he made reply:
"Fair time, I ween, for sleep is this,
To lull thy soul in tranquil bliss,
Unheeding, in oblivion drowned,
The dangers that our lives surround.
Brave Ráma, Daśaratha's son,

A passage o'er the sea has won,
And, with the Vánar monarch's aid,
Round Lanká's walls his hosts arrayed.
Though never in the deadly field
My Rákshas troops were known to yield,
The bravest of the giant train
Have fallen by the Vánars slain.
Hence comes my fear. O fierce and brave,
Go forth, our threatened Lanká save.
Go forth, a dreadful vengeance take:
For this, O chief, I bade thee wake.
The Gods and trembling fiends have felt
The furious blows thine arm has dealt.
Earth has no warrior, heaven has none
To match thy might, Paulastya's son."

Canto LXIII
Kumbhakarna's Boast

Then Kumbhakarṇa laughed aloud
And cried; "O Monarch, once so proud,
We warned thee, but thou wouldst not hear;
And now the fruits of sin appear.
We warned thee, I, thy nobles, all
Who loved thee, in thy council hall.
Those sovereigns who with blinded eyes
Neglect the foe their hearts despise,
Soon, falling from their high estate
Bring on themselves the stroke of fate.
Accept at length, thy life to save,
The counsel sage Vibhishaṇ gave,
The prudent counsel spurned before,
And Sítá to her lord restore." 972
The monarch frowned, by passion moved
And thus in angry words reproved:
"Wilt thou thine elder brother school,
Forgetful of the ancient rule
That bids thee treat him as the sage
Who guides thee with the lore of age?
Think on the dangers of the day,
Nor idly throw thy words away:
If, led astray, by passion stirred,
I in the pride of power have erred;
If deeds of old were done amiss,
No time for vain reproach is this.
Up, brother; let thy loving care

The errors of thy king repair."
To calm his wrath, his soul to ease,
The younger spake in words like these:
"Yea, from our bosoms let us cast
All idle sorrow for the past.
Let grief and anger be repressed:
Again be firm and self-possessed.
This day, O Monarch, shalt thou see
The Vánar legions turn and flee,
And Ráma and his brother slain
With their hearts' blood shall dye the plain.
Yea, if the God who rules the dead,
And Varuṇ their battalions led;
If Indra with the Storm-Gods came
Against me, and the Lord of Flame,
Still would I fight with all and slay
Thy banded foes, my King, to-day.
If Raghu's son this day withstand
The blow of mine uplifted hand,
Deep in his breast my darts shall sink,
And torrents of his life-blood drink.
O fear not, in my promise trust:
This arm shall lay him in the dust,
Shall leave the fierce Sugríva dyed
With gore, and Lakshmaṇ by his side,
And strike the great Hanúmán down,
The spoiler of our glorious town." 973

Canto LXIV
Mahodar's Speech

He ceased: and when his lips were closed
Mahodar thus his rede opposed:
"Why wilt thou shame thy noble birth
And speak like one of little worth?
Why boast thee thus in youthful pride
Rejecting wisdom for thy guide?
How will thy single arm oppose
The victor of a thousand foes,
Who proved in Janasthán his might
And slew the rovers of the night?
The remnant of those legions, they
Who saw his power that fatal day,
Now in this leaguered city dread
The mighty chief from whom they fled.
And wouldst thou meet the lord of men,
Beard the great lion in his den,
And, when thine eyes are open, break
The slumber of a deadly snake?
Who may an equal battle wage
With him, so awful in his rage,
Fierce as the God of Death whom none
May vanquish, Daśaratha's son?
But, Rávaṇ, shall the lady still
Refuse compliance with thy will?
No, listen, King, to this design
Which soon shall make the captive thine.
This day through Lanká's streets proclaim

That four of us 974 of highest fame
With Kumbhakarṇa at our head
Will strike the son of Raghu dead.
Forth to the battle will we go
And prove our prowess on the foe.
Then, if our bold attempt succeed,
No further plans thy hopes will need.
But if in vain our warriors strive,
And Raghu's son be left alive,
We will return, and, wounded sore,
Our armour stained with gouts of gore,
Will show the shafts that rent each frame,
Keen arrows marked with Ráma's name,
And say we giants have devoured
The princes whom our might o'erpowered.
Then let the joyful tidings spread
That Raghu's royal sons are dead.
To all around thy pleasure show,
Gold, pearls, and precious robes, bestow.
Gay garlands round the portals twine,
Enjoy the banquet and the wine.
Then go, the scornful lady seek,
And woo her when her heart is weak.
Rich robes and gold and gems display,
And gently wile her grief away.
Then will she feel her hopeless state,
Widowed, forlorn, and desolate;
Know that on thee her bliss depends,
Far from her country and her friends;
Then, her proud spirit overthrown,
The lady will be all thine own."

Canto LXV
Kumbhakarna's Speech

But haughty Kumbhakarṇa spurned
His counsel, and to Rávaṇ turned:
"Thy life from peril will I free
And slay the foe who threatens thee.
A hero never vaunts in vain,
Like bellowing clouds devoid of rain,
Nor, Monarch, be thine ear inclined
To counsellors of slavish kind,
Who with mean arts their king mislead
And mar each gallant plan and deed.
O, let not words like his beguile
The glorious king of Lanká's isle."
Thus scornful Kumbhakarṇa cried,
And Rávaṇ with a laugh replied:
"Mahodar fears and fain would shun
The battle with Ikshváku's son.
Of all my giant warriors, who
Is strong as thou, and brave and true?
Ride, conqueror, to the battle ride,
And tame the foeman's senseless pride.
Go forth like Yáma to the field,
And let thine arm thy trident wield.
Scared by the lightning of thine eye
The Vánar hosts will turn and fly;
And Ráma, when he sees thee near,
With trembling heart will own his fear."
The champion heard, and, well content,

Forth from the hall his footsteps bent.
He grasped his spear, the foeman's dread,
Black iron all, both shaft and head,
Which, dyed in many a battle, bore
Great spots of slaughtered victims' gore.
The king upon his neck had thrown
The jewelled chain which graced his own.
And garlands of delicious scent
About his limbs for ornament.
Around his arms gay bracelets clung,
And pendants in his ears were hung.
Adorned with gold, about his waist
His coat of mail was firmly braced,
And like Náráyaṇ 975 or the God
Who rules the sky he proudly trod.
Behind him went a mighty throng
Of giant warriors tall and strong,
On elephants of noblest breeds.
With cars, with camels, and with steeds:
And, armed with spear and axe and sword
Were fain to battle for their lord. 976

Canto LXVI
Kumbhakarna's Sally

In pomp and pride of warlike state
The giant passed the city gate.
He raised his voice: the hills, the shore
Of Lanká's sea returned the roar.
The Vánars saw the chief draw nigh
Whom not the ruler of the sky,
Nor Yáma, monarch of the dead,
Might vanquish, and affrighted fled.
When royal Angad, Báli's son,
Saw the scared Vánars turn and run,
Undaunted still he kept his ground,
And shouted as he gazed around:
"O Nala, Níla, stay nor let
Your souls your generous worth forget,
O Kumud and Gaváksha, why
Like base-born Vánars will ye fly?
Turn, turn, nor shame your order thus:
This giant is no match for us"
They heard his voice: the flight was stayed;
Again for war they stood arrayed,
And hurled upon the foe a shower
Of mountain peaks and trees in flower.
Still on his limbs their missiles rained:
Unmoved, their blows he still sustained,
And seemed unconscious of the stroke
When rocks against his body broke.
Fierce as the flame when woods are dry

He charged with fury in his eye.
Like trees consumed with fervent heat
They fell beneath the giant's feet.
Some o'er the ground, dyed red with gore,
Fled wild with terror to the shore,
And, deeming that all hope was lost,
Ran to the bridge they erst had crossed.
Some clomb the trees their lives to save,
Some sought the mountain and the cave;
Some hid them in the bosky dell,
And there in deathlike slumber fell.
When Angad saw the chieftains fly
He called them with a mighty cry:
"Once more, O Vánars, charge once more,
On to the battle as before.
In all her compass earth has not,
To hide you safe, one secret spot.
What! leave your arms? each nobler dame
Will scorn her consort for the shame.
This blot upon your names efface,
And keep your valour from disgrace.
Stay, chieftains; wherefore will ye run,
A band of warriors scared by one?"
Scarce would they hear: they would not stay,
And basely spoke in wild dismay:
"Have we not fought, and fought in vain
Have we not seen our mightiest slain?
The giant's matchless force we fear,
And fly because our lives are dear."
But Báli's son with gentle art
Dispelled their dread and cheered each heart.
They turned and formed and waited still
Obedient to the prince's will.

Canto LXVII
Kumbhakarna's Death

Thus from their flight the Vánars turned,
And every heart for battle burned,
Determined on the spot to die
Or gain a warrior's meed on high.
Again the Vánars stooped to seize
Their weapons, rocks and fallen trees;
Again the deadly fight began,
And fiercely at the giant ran.
Unmoved the monster kept his place:
He raised on high his awful mace,
Whirled the huge weapon round his head
And laid the foremost Vánars dead.
Eight thousand fell bedewed with gore,
Then sank and died seven hundred more.
Then thirty, twenty, ten, or eight
At each fierce onset met their fate,
And fast the fallen were devoured
Like snakes by Garuḍ's beak o'erpowered.
Then Dwivid from the Vánar van,
Armed with an uptorn mountain, ran,
Like a huge cloud when fierce winds blow,
And charged amain the mountain foe.
With wondrous force the hill he threw:
O'er Kumbhakarṇa's head it flew,
And falling on his host afar
Crushed many a giant, steed, and car.
Rocks, trees, by fierce Hanúmán sped,

Rained fast on Kumbhakarṇa's head.
Whose spear each deadlier missile stopped,
And harmless on the plain it dropped.
Then with his furious eyes aglow
The giant rushed upon the foe,
Where, with a woody hill upheaved,
Hanúmán's might his charge received.
Through his vast frame the giant felt
The angry blow Hanúmán dealt.
He reeled a moment, sore distressed,
Then smote the Vánar on the breast,
As when the War-God's furious stroke
Through Krauncha's hill a passage broke. 977
Fierce was the blow, and deep and wide
The rent: with crimson torrents dyed,
Hanúmán, maddened by the pain,
Roared like a cloud that brings the rain,
And from each Rákshas throat rang out
Loud clamour and exultant shout.
Then Níla hurled with mustered might
The fragment of a mountain height;
Nor would the rock the foe have missed,
But Kumbhakarṇa raised his fist
And smote so fiercely that the mass
Fell crushed to powder on the grass.
Five chieftains of the Vánar race 978
Charged Kumbhakarṇa face to face,
And his huge frame they wildly beat
With rocks and trees and hands and feet.
Round Rishabh first the giant wound
His arms and hurled him to the ground,
Where speechless, senseless, wounded sore,
He lay his face besmeared with gore.
Then Níla with his fist he slew,

And Śarabh with his knee o'erthrew,
Nor could Gaváksha's strength withstand
The force of his terrific hand.
At Gandhamádan's eager call
Rushed thousands to avenge their fall,
Nor ceased those Vánars to assail
With knee and fist and tooth and nail.
Around his foes the giant threw
His mighty arms, and nearer drew
The captives subject to his will:
Then snatched them up and ate his fill.
There was no respite then, no pause:
Fast gaped and closed his hell-like jaws:
Yet, prisoned in that gloomy cave,
Some Vánars still their lives could save:
Some through his nostrils found a way,
Some through his ears resought the day.
Like Indra with his thunder, like
The God of Death in act to strike,
The giant seized his ponderous spear,
And charged the foe in swift career.
Before his might the Vánars fell,
Nor could their hosts his charge repel.
Then trembling, nor ashamed to run,
They turned and fled to Raghu's son.
When Báli's warrior son 979 beheld
Their flight, his heart with fury swelled.
He rushed, with his terrific shout,
To meet the foe and stay the rout.
He came, he hurled a mountain peak,
And smote the giant on the cheek.
His ponderous spear the giant threw:
Fierce was the cast, the aim was true;
But Angad, trained in war and tried,

Saw ere it came, and leapt aside.
Then with his open hand he smote
The giant on the chest and throat.
That blow the giant scarce sustained;
But sense and strength were soon regained.
With force which nothing might resist
He caught the Vánar by the wrist,
Whirled him, as if in pastime, round,
And dashed him senseless on the ground.
There low on earth his foe lay crushed:
At King Sugríva next he rushed,
Who, waiting for the charge, stood still,
And heaved on high a shattered hill,
He looked on Kumbhakarṇa dyed
With streams of blood, and fiercely cried:
"Great glory has thine arm achieved,
And thousands of their lives bereaved.
Now leave a while thy meaner foes,
And brook the hill Sugríva throws."
He spoke, and hurled the mass he held:
The giant's chest the stroke repelled,
Then on the Vánars fell despair,
And Rákshas clamour filled the air.
The giant raised his arm, and fast
Came the tremendous 980 spear he cast.
Hanúmán caught it as it flew,
And knapped it on his knee in two.
The giant saw the broken spear:
His clouded eye confessed his fear;
Yet at Sugríva's head he sent
A peak from Lanká's mountain rent.
The rushing mass no might could stay:
Sugríva fell and senseless lay.
The giant stooped his foe to seize,

And bore him thence, as bears the breeze
A cloud in autumn through the sky.
He heard the sad Immortals sigh,
And shouts of triumph long and loud
Went up from all the Rákshas crowd.
Through Lanká's gate the giant passed
Holding his struggling captive fast,
While from each terrace, house, and tower
Fell on his haughty head a shower
Of fragrant scent and flowery rain,
Blossoms and leaves and scattered grain. 981
By slow degrees the Vánars' lord
Felt life and sense and strength restored.
He heard the giants' joyful boast:
He thought upon his Vánar host.
His teeth and feet he fiercely plied,
And bit and rent the giant's side,
Who, mad with pain and smeared with gore,
Hurled to the ground the load he bore.
Regardless of a storm of blows
Swift to the sky the Vánar rose,
Then lightly like a flying ball
High overleapt the city wall,
And joyous for deliverance won
Regained the side of Raghu's son.
And Kumbhakarṇa, mad with hate
And fury, sallied from the gate,
The carnage of the foe renewed
And filled his maw with gory food.
Slaying, with headlong frenzy blind,
Both Vánar foes and giant kind.
Nor would Sumitrá's valiant son 982
The might of Kumbhakarṇa shun,
Who through his harness felt the sting

Of keen shafts loosened from the string.
His heart confessed the warrior's power,
And, bleeding from the ceaseless shower
That smote him on the chest and side,
With words like these the giant cried:
"Well fought, well fought, Sumitrá's son;
Eternal glory hast thou won,
For thou in desperate fight hast met
The victor never conquered yet,
Whom, borne on huge Airávat's back,
E'en Indra trembles to attack.
Go, son of Queen Sumitrá, go:
Thy valour and thy strength I know.
Now all my hope and earnest will
Is Ráma in the fight to kill.
Let him beneath my weapons fall,
And I will meet and conquer all."
The chieftain, of Sumitrá born,
Made answer as he laughed in scorn:
"Yea, thou hast won a victor's fame
From trembling Gods and Indra's shame.
There waits thee now a mightier foe
Whose prowess thou hast yet to know.
There, famous in a hundred lands,
Ráma the son of Raghu stands."
Straight at the king the giant sped,
And earth was shaken at his tread.
His bow the hero grasped and strained,
And deadly shafts in torrents rained.
As Kumbhakarṇa felt each stroke
From his huge mouth burst fire and smoke;
His hands were loosed in mortal pain
And dropped his weapons on the plain.
Though reft of spear and sword and mace

No terror changed his haughty face.
With heavy hands he rained his blows
And smote to death a thousand foes.
Where'er the furious monster strode
While down his limbs the red blood flowed
Like torrents down a mountain's side,
Vánars and bears and giants died.
High o'er his head a rock he swung,
And the huge mass at Ráma flung.
But Ráma's arrows bright as flame
Shattered the mountain as it came.
Then Raghu's son, his eyes aglow
With burning anger, charged the foe,
And as his bow he strained and tried
With fearful clang the cord replied.
Wroth at the bowstring's threatening clang
To meet his foe the giant sprang.
High towering with enormous frame
Huge as a wood-crowned hill he came.
But Ráma firm and self-possessed
In words like these the foe addressed:
"Draw near, O Rákshas lord, draw near,
Nor turn thee from the fight in fear.
Thou meetest Ráma face to face,
Destroyer of the giant race.
Come, fight, and thou shalt feel this hour,
Laid low in death, thy conqueror's power."
He ceased: and mad with wrath and pride
The giant champion thus replied:
"Come thou to me and thou shalt find
A foeman of a different kind.
No Khara, no Virádha,—thou
Hast met a mightier warrior now.
The strength of Kumbhakarṇa fear,

And dread the iron mace I rear
This mace in days of yore subdued
The Gods and Dánav multitude.
Prove, lion of Ikshváku's line,
Thy power upon these limbs of mine.
Then, after trial, shalt thou bleed,
And with thy flesh my hunger feed."
He ceased: and Ráma, undismayed,
Upon his cord those arrows laid
Which pierced the stately Sál trees through,
And Báli king of Vánars slew.
They flew, they smote, but smote in vain
Those mighty limbs that felt no pain.
Then Ráma sent with surest aim
The dart that bore the Wind-God's name.
The missile from the giant tore
His huge arm and the mace it bore,
Which crushed the Vánars where it fell:
And dire was Kumbhakarṇa's yell.
The giant seized a tree, and then
Rushed madly at the lord of men.
Another dart, Lord Indra's own,
To meet his furious onset thrown,
His left arm from the shoulder lopped,
And like a mountain peak it dropped.
Then from the bow of Ráma sped
Two arrows, each with crescent head;
And, winged with might which naught could stay,
They cut the giant's legs away.
They fell, and awful was the sound
As those vast columns shook the ground;
And sky and sea and hill and cave
In echoing roars their answer gave.
Then from his side the hero drew

A dart that like the tempest flew—
No deadlier shaft has ever flown
Than that which Indra called his own—
Nor could the giant's mail-armed neck
The fury of the missile check.
Through skin and flesh and bone it smote
And rent asunder head and throat.
Down with the sound of thunder rolled
The head adorned with rings of gold,
And crushed to pieces in its fall
A gate, a tower, a massive wall.
Hurled to the sea the body fell:
Terrific was the ocean's swell,
Nor could swift fin and nimble leap
Save the crushed creatures of the deep.
Thus he who plagued in impious pride
The Gods and Bráhmans fought and died.
Glad were the hosts of heaven, and long
The air re-echoed with their song. 983

Canto LXVIII
Rávan's Lament

They ran to Rávaṇ in his hall
And told him of his brother's fall:
"Fierce as the God who rules the dead,
Upon the routed foe he fed;
And, victor for a while, at length
Fell slain by Ráma's matchless strength.
Now like a mighty hill in size
His mangled trunk extended lies,
And where he fell, a bleeding mass,
Blocks Lanká's gate that none may pass."
The monarch heard: his strength gave way;
And fainting on the ground he lay.
Grieved at the giants' mournful tale,
Long, shrill was Atikáya's wail;
And Triśirás in sorrow bowed
His triple head, and wept aloud.
Mahodar, Mahápárśva shed
Hot tears and mourned their brother dead.
At length, his wandering sense restored,
In loud lament cried Lanká's lord:
"Ah chief, for might and valour famed,
Whose arm the haughty foeman tamed,
Forsaking me, thy friends and all,
Why hast thou fled to Yáma's hall?
Why hast thou fled to taste no more
The slaughtered foeman's flesh and gore?
Ah me, my life is done to-day:

My better arm is lopped away.
Whereon in danger I relied,
And, fearless, Gods and fiends defied.
How could a shaft from Ráma's bow
The matchless giant overthrow,
Whose iron frame so strong of yore
The crushing bolt of Indra bore?
This day the Gods and sages meet
And triumph at their foe's defeat.
This day the Vánar chiefs will boast
And, with new ardour fired, their host
In fiercer onset will assail
Our city, and the ramparts scale.
What care I for a monarch's name,
For empire, or the Maithil dame?
What joy can power and riches give,
Or life that I should care to live,
Unless this arm in mortal fray
The slayer of my brother slay?
For me, of Kumbhakarṇa reft,
Death is the only solace left;
And I will seek, o'erwhelmed with woes,
The realm to which my brother goes.
Ah me ill-minded, not to take
His counsel when Vibhishaṇ spake
When he this evil day foretold
My foolish heart was overbold:
I drove my sage adviser hence,
And reap the fruits of mine offence."

Canto LXIX
Narántak's Death

Pierced to the soul by sorrow's sting
Thus wailed the evil-hearted king.
Then Triśirás stood forth and cried:
"Yea, father, he has fought and died,
Our bravest: and the loss is sore:
But rouse thee, and lament no more.
Hast thou not still thy coat of mail,
Thy bow and shafts which never fail?
A thousand asses draw thy car
Which roars like thunder heard afar.
Thy valour and thy warrior skill,
Thy God-given strength, are left thee still.
Unarmed, thy matchless might subdued
The Gods and Dánav multitude.
Armed with thy glorious weapons, how
Shall Raghu's son oppose thee now?
Or, sire, within thy palace stay;
And I myself will sweep away
Thy foes, like Garuḍ when he makes
A banquet of the writhing snakes.
Soon Raghu's son shall press the plain,
As Narak 984 fell by Vishṇu slain,
Or Śambar 985 in rebellious pride
Who met the King of Gods 986 and died."
The monarch heard: his courage grew,
And life and spirit came anew.
Devántak and Narántak heard,

And their fierce souls with joy were stirred;
And Atikáya 987 burned to fight,
And heard the summons with delight;
While from the rest loud rang the cry,
"I too will fight," "and I," "and I."
The joyous king his sons embraced,
With gold and chains and jewels graced,
And sent them forth with stirring speech
Of benison and praise to each.
Forth from the gate the princes sped
And ranged for war the troops they led.
The Vánar legions charged anew,
And trees and rocks for missiles flew.
They saw Narántak's mighty form
Borne on a steed that mocked the storm.
To check his charge in vain they strove:
Straight through their host his way he clove,
As springs a dolphin through the tide:
And countless Vánars fell and died,
And mangled limbs and corpses lay
To mark the chief's ensanguined way,
Sugríva saw them fall or fly
When fierce Narántak's steed was nigh,
And marked the giant where he sped
O'er heaps of dying or of dead.
He bade the royal Angad face
That bravest chief of giant race.
As springs the sun from clouds dispersed,
So Angad from the Vánars burst.
No weapon for the fight he bore
Save nails and teeth, and sought no more.
"Leave, giant chieftain," thus he spoke,
"Leave foes unworthy of thy stroke,
And bend against a nobler heart

The terrors of thy deadly dart."
Narántak heard the words he spake:
Fast breathing, like an angry snake,
With bloody teeth his lips he pressed
And hurled his dart at Angad's breast.
True was the aim and fierce the stroke,
Yet on his breast the missile broke.
Then Angad at the giant flew,
And with a blow his courser slew:
The fierce hand crushed through flesh and bone,
And steed and rider fell o'erthrown.
Narántak's eyes with fury blazed:
His heavy hand on high he raised
And struck in savage wrath the head
Of Báli's son, who reeled and bled,
Fainted a moment and no more:
Then stronger, fiercer than before
Smote with that fist which naught could stay,
And crushed to death the giant lay.

Canto LXX
The Death Of Trisirás

Then raged the Rákshas chiefs, and all
Burned to avenge Narántak's fall.
Devántak raised his club on high
And rushed at Angad with a cry.
Behind came Triśirás, and near
Mahodar charged with levelled spear.
There Angad stood to fight with three:
High o'er his head he waved a tree,
And at Devántak, swift and true
As Indra's flaming bolt, it flew.
But, cut by giant shafts in twain,
With minished force it flew in vain.
A shower of trees and blocks of stone
From Angad's hand was fiercely thrown;
But well his club Devántak plied
And turned each rock and tree aside.
Nor yet, by three such foes assailed,
The heart of Angad sank or quailed.
He slew the mighty beast that bore
Mahodar: from his head he tore
A bleeding tusk, and blow on blow
Fell fiercely on his Rákshas foe.
The giant reeled, but strength regained,
And furious strokes on Angad rained,
Who, wounded by the storm of blows,
Sank on his knees, but swiftly rose.
Then Triśirás, as up he sprang,

Drew his great bow with awful clang,
And fixed three arrows from his sheaf
Full in the forehead of the chief.
Hanúmán saw, nor long delayed
To speed with Níla to his aid,
Who at the three-faced giant sent
A peak from Lanká's mountain rent.
But Trisirás with certain aim
Shot rapid arrows as it came:
And shivered by their force it broke
And fell to earth with flash and smoke.
Then as the Wind-God's son came nigh,
Devántak reared his mace on high.
Hanúmán smote him on the head
And stretched the monstrous giant dead.
Fierce Trisirás with fury strained
His bow, and showers of arrows rained
That smote on Níla's side and chest:
He sank a moment, sore distressed;
But quickly gathered strength to seize
A mountain with its crown of trees.
Crushed by the hill, distained with gore,
Mahodar fell to rise no more.
Then Trisirás raised high his spear
Which chilled the trembling foe with fear
And, like a flashing meteor through
The air at Hanúmán it flew.
The Vánar shunned the threatened stroke,
And with strong hands the weapon broke.
The giant drew his glittering blade:
Dire was the wound the weapon made
Deep in the Vánar's ample chest,
Who, for a moment sore oppressed,
Raised his broad hand, regaining might,

And struck the rover of the night.
Fierce was the blow: with one wild yell
Low on the earth the monster fell.
Hanúmán seized his fallen sword
Which served no more its senseless lord,
And from the monster triple-necked
Smote his huge heads with crowns bedecked.
Then Mahápárśva burned with ire;
Fierce flashed his eyes with vengeful fire.
A moment on the dead he gazed,
Then his black mace aloft was raised,
And down the mass of iron came
That struck and shook the Vánar's frame.
Hanúmán's chest was wellnigh crushed,
And from his mouth red torrents gushed:
Yet served one instant to restore
His spirit: from the foe he tore
His awful mace, and smote, and laid
The giant in the dust dismayed.
Crushed were his jaws and teeth and eyes:
Breathless and still he lay as lies
A summit from a mountain rent
By him who rules the firmament.

Canto LXXI
Atikáya's Death

But Atikáya's wrath grew high
To see his noblest kinsmen die.
He, fiercest of the giant race,
Presuming still on Brahmá's grace;
Proud tamer of the Immortals' pride,
Whose power and might with Indra's vied,
For blood and vengeful carnage burned,
And on the foe his fury turned.
High on a car that flashed and glowed
Bright as a thousand suns he rode.
Around his princely brows was set
A rich bejewelled coronet.
Gold pendants in his ears he wore;
He strained and tried the bow he bore,
And ever, as a shaft he aimed,
His name and royal race proclaimed.
Scarce might the Vánars brook to hear
His clanging bow and voice of fear:
To Raghu's elder son they fled,
Their sure defence in woe and dread.
Then Ráma bent his eyes afar
And saw the giant in his car
Fast following the flying crowd
And roaring like a rainy cloud.
He, with the lust of battle fired,
Turned to Vibhishaṇ and inquired:
"Say, who is this, of mountain size,

This archer with the lion eyes?
His car, which strikes our host with awe,
A thousand eager coursers draw.
Surrounded by the flashing spears
Which line his car, the chief appears
Like some huge cloud when lightnings play
About it on a stormy day;
And the great bow he joys to hold
Whose bended back is bright with gold,
As Indra's bow makes glad the skies,
That best of chariots glorifies.
O see the sunlike splendour flung
From the great flag above him hung,
Where, blazoned with refulgent lines,
Ráhu 988 the dreadful Dragon shines.
Full thirty quivers near his side,
His car with shafts is well supplied:
And flashing like the light of stars
Gleam his two mighty scimitars.
Say, best of giants, who is he
Before whose face the Vánars flee?"
Thus Ráma spake. Vibhishaṇ eyed
The giants' chief, and thus replied:
"This Ráma, this is Rávaṇ's son:
High fame his youthful might has won.
He, best of warriors, bows his ear
The wisdom of the wise to hear.
Supreme is he mid those who know
The mastery of sword and bow.
Unrivalled in the bold attack
On elephant's or courser's back,
He knows, beside, each subtler art,
To win the foe, to bribe, or part.
On him the giant hosts rely,

And fear no ill when he is nigh.
This peerless chieftain bears the name
Of Atikáya huge of frame,
Whom Dhanyamáliní of yore
To Rávaṇ lord of Lanká bore."
Roused by his bow-string's awful clang,
To meet their foes the Vánars sprang.
Armed with tall trees from Lanká's wood,
And rocks and mountain peaks, they stood.
The giant's arrows, gold-bedecked,
The storm of hurtling missiles checked;
And ever on his foemen poured
Fierce tempest from his clanging cord;
Nor could the Vánar chiefs sustain
His shafts' intolerable rain.
They fled: the victor gained the place
Where stood the lord of Raghu's race,
And cried with voice of thunder: "Lo,
Borne on my car, with shaft and bow,
I, champion of the giants, scorn
To fight with weaklings humbly born.
Come forth your bravest, if he dare,
And fight with one who will not spare."
Forth sprang Sumitrá's noble child, 989
And strained his ready bow, and smiled;
And giants trembled as the clang
Through heaven and earth reëchoing rang.
The giant to his string applied
A pointed shaft, and proudly cried;
"Turn, turn, Sumitrá's son and fly,
For terrible as Death am I.
Fly, nor that youthful form oppose,
Untrained in war, to warriors' blows.
What! wilt thou waste thy childish breath

And wake the dormant fire of death?
Cast down, rash boy, that useless bow:
Preserve thy life, uninjured go."
He ceased: and stirred by wrath & pride
Sumitrá's noble son replied:
"By warlike deed, not words alone,
The valour of the brave is shown.
Cease with vain boasts my scorn to move,
And with thine arm thy prowess prove.
Borne on thy car, with sword and bow,
With all thine arms, thy valour show.
Fight, and my deadly shafts this day
Low in the dust thy head shall lay,
And, rushing fast in ceaseless flood,
Shall rend thy flesh and drink thy blood."
His giant foe no answer made,
But on his string an arrow laid.
He raised his arm, the cord he drew,
At Lakshman's breast the arrow flew.
Sumitrá's son, his foemen's dread,
Shot a fleet shaft with crescent head,
Which cleft that arrow pointed well,
And harmless to the earth it fell.
A shower of shafts from Lakshman's bow
Fell fast and furious on the foe
Who quailed not as the missiles smote
With idle force his iron coat.
Then came the friendly Wind-God near,
And whispered thus in Lakshman's ear:
"Such shafts as these in vain assail
Thy foe's impenetrable mail.
A more tremendous missile try,
Or never may the giant die.
Employ the mighty spell, and aim

The weapon known by Brahmá's name."
He ceased; Sumitrá's son obeyed:
On his great bow the shaft was laid,
And with a roar like thunder, true
As Indra's flashing bolt, it flew.
The giant poured his shafts like rain
To check its course, but all in vain.
With spear and mace and sword he tried
To turn the fiery dart aside.
Winged with a force which naught could check,
It smote the monster in the neck,
And, sundered from his shoulders, rolled
To earth his head and helm of gold.

Canto LXXII
Rávan's Speech

The giants bent, in rage and grief,
Their eyes upon the fallen chief:
Then flying wild with fear and pale
To Rávan bore the mournful tale.
He heard how Atikáya died,
Then turned him to his lords, and cried:
"Where are they now—my bravest—where,
Wise to consult and prompt to dare?
Where is Dhúmráksha, skilled to wield
All weapons in the battle field?
Akampan, and Prahasta's might,
And Kumbhakarṇa bold in fight?
These, these and many a Rákshas more,
Each master of the arms he bore,
Who every foe in fight o'erthrew,
The victors none could e'er subdue,
Have perished by the might of one,
The vengeful arm of Raghu's son.
In vain I cast mine eyes around,
No match for Ráma here is found,
No chief to stand before that bow
Whose deadly shafts have caused our woe.
Now, warriors, to your stations hence;
Provide ye for the wall's defence,
And be the Aśoka garden, where
The lady lies, your special care.
Be every lane and passage barred,

Set at each gate a chosen guard.
And with your troops, where danger calls,
Be ready to defend the walls.
Each movement of the Vánars mark;
Observe them when the skies grow dark;
Be ready in the dead of night,
And ere the morning bring the light.
Taught by our loss we may not scorn
These legions of the forest-born."
He ceased: the Rákshas lords obeyed;
Each at his post his troops arrayed:
And, torn with pangs that pierced him through
The monarch from the hall withdrew.

Canto LXXIII
Indrajít's Victory

But Indrajít the fierce and bold
With words like these his sire consoled:
"Dismiss, O King, thy grief and dread,
And be not thus disquieted.
Against this numbing sorrow strive,
For Indrajít is yet alive;
And none in battle may withstand
The fury of his strong right hand.
This day, O sire, thine eyes shall see
The sons of Raghu slain by me."
He ceased: he bade the king farewell:
Clear, mid the roar of drum and shell,
The clash of sword and harness rang
As to his car the warrior sprang.
Close followed by his Rákshas train
Through Lanká's gate he reached the plain.
Then down he leapt, and bade a band
Of giants by the chariot stand:
Then with due rites, as rules require,
Did worship to the Lord of Fire.
The sacred oil, as texts ordain,
With wreaths of scented flowers and grain,
Within the flame in order due,
That mightiest of the giants threw.
There on the ground were spear and blade,
And arrowy leaves and fuel laid;
An iron ladle deep and wide,

And robes with sanguine colours dyed.
Beside him stood a sable goat:
The giant seized it by the throat,
And straight from the consuming flame
Auspicious signs of victory came.
For swiftly, curling to the right,
The fire leapt up with willing light
Undimmed by smoky cloud, and, red
Like gold, upon the offering fed.
They brought him, while the flame yet glowed,
The dart by Brahmá's grace bestowed,
And all the arms he wielded well
Were charmed with text and holy spell.
Then fiercer for the fight he burned,
And at the foe his chariot turned,
While all his followers lifting high
Their maces charged with furious cry.
Dire, yet more dire the battle grew,
As rocks and trees and arrows flew.
The giant shot his shafts like rain,
And Vánars fell in myriads slain,
Sugríva, Angad, Níla felt
The wounds his hurtling arrows dealt.
His shafts the blood of Gaya drank;
Hanúmán reeled and Mainda sank.
Bright as the glances of the sun
Came the swift darts they could not shun.
Caught in the arrowy nets he wove,
In vain the sons of Raghu strove;
And Ráma, by the darts oppressed,
His brother chieftain thus addressed:
"See, first this giant warrior sends
Destruction, mid our Vánar friends,
And now his arrows thick and fast

Their binding net around us cast.
To Brahmá's grace the chieftain owes
The matchless power and might he shows;
And mortal strength in vain contends
With him whom Brahmá's self befriends.
Then let us still with dauntless hearts
Endure this storm of pelting darts.
Soon must we sink bereaved of sense;
And then the victor, hurrying hence,
Will seek his father in his hall
And tell him of his foemen's fall."
He ceased: o'erpowered by shaft and spell
The sons of Raghu reeled and fell.
The Rákshas on their bodies gazed;
And, mid the shouts his followers raised,
Sped back to Lanká to relate
In Rávaṇ's hall the princes' fate.

Canto LXXIV
The Medicinal Herbs

The shades of falling night concealed
The carnage of the battle field,
Which, bearing each a blazing brand,
Hanúmán and Vibhishan scanned,
Moving with slow and anxious tread
Among the dying and the dead.
Sad was the scene of slaughter shown
Where'er the torches' light was thrown.
Here mountain forms of Vánars lay
Whose heads and limbs were lopped away,
Arms, legs and fingers strewed the ground,
And severed heads lay thick around.
The earth was moist with sanguine streams,
And sighs were heard and groans and screams.
There lay Sugríva still and cold,
There Angad, once so brave and bold.
There Jámbaván his might reposed,
There Vegadarśí's eyes were closed;
There in the dust was Nala's pride,
And Dwivid lay by Mainda's side.
Where'er they looked the ensanguined plain
Was strewn with myriads of the slain; 990
They sought with keenly searching eyes
King Jámbaván supremely wise.
His strength had failed by slow decay,
And pierced with countless shafts he lay.
They saw, and hastened to his side,

And thus the sage Vibhishaṇ cried:
"Thee, monarch of the bears, we seek:
Speak if thou yet art living, speak."
Slow came the aged chief's reply;
Scarce could he say with many a sigh:
"Torn with keen shafts which pierce each limb,
My strength is gone, my sight is dim;
Yet though I scarce can raise mine eyes,
Thy voice, O chief, I recognize.
O, while these ears can hear thee, say,
Has Hanúmán survived this day?"
"Why ask," Vibhishaṇ cried, "for one
Of lower rank, the Wind-God's son?
Hast thou forgotten, first in place,
The princely chief of Raghu's race?
Can King Sugríva claim no care,
And Angad, his imperial heir?"
"Yea, dearer than my noblest friends
Is he on whom our hope depends.
For if the Wind-God's son survive,
All we though dead are yet alive.
But if his precious life be fled
Though living still we are but dead:
He is our hope and sure relief."
Thus slowly spoke the aged chief:
Then to his side Hanúmán came,
And with low reverence named his name.
Cheered by the face he longed to view
The wounded chieftain lived anew.
"Go forth," he cried, "O strong and brave,
And in their woe the Vánars save.
No might but thine, supremely great,
May help us in our lost estate.
The trembling bears and Vánars cheer,

Calm their sad hearts, dispel their fear.
Save Raghu's noble sons, and heal
The deep wounds of the winged steel.
High o'er the waters of the sea
To far Himálaya's summits flee.
Kailása there wilt thou behold,
And Rishabh, with his peaks of gold.
Between them see a mountain rise
Whose splendour will enchant thine eyes;
His sides are clothed above, below,
With all the rarest herbs that grow.
Upon that mountain's lofty crest
Four plants, of sovereign powers possessed,
Spring from the soil, and flashing there
Shed radiance through the neighbouring air.
One draws the shaft: one brings again
The breath of life to warm the slain;
One heals each wound; one gives anew
To faded cheeks their wonted hue.
Fly, chieftain, to that mountain's brow
And bring those herbs to save us now."
Hanúmán heard, and springing through
The air like Vishṇu's discus 991 flew.
The sea was passed: beneath him, gay
With bright-winged birds, the mountains lay,
And brook and lake and lonely glen,
And fertile lands with toiling men.
On, on he sped: before him rose
The mansion of perennial snows.
There soared the glorious peaks as fair
As white clouds in the summer air.
Here, bursting from the leafy shade,
In thunder leapt the wild cascade.
He looked on many a pure retreat

Dear to the Gods' and sages' feet:
The spot where Brahmá dwells apart,
The place whence Rudra launched his dart; 992
Vishṇu's high seat and Indra's home,
And slopes where Yáma's servants roam.
There was Kuvera's bright abode;
There Brahmá's mystic weapon glowed.
There was the noble hill whereon
Those herbs with wondrous lustre shone,
And, ravished by the glorious sight,
Hanúmán rested on the height.
He, moving down the glittering peak,
The healing herbs began to seek:
But, when he thought to seize the prize,
They hid them from his eager eyes.
Then to the hill in wrath he spake:
"Mine arm this day shall vengeance take,
If thou wilt feel no pity, none,
In this great need of Raghu's son."
He ceased: his mighty arms he bent
And from the trembling mountain rent
His huge head with the life it bore,
Snakes, elephants, and golden ore.
O'er hill and plain and watery waste
His rapid way again he traced.
And mid the wondering Vánars laid
His burthen through the air conveyed,
The wondrous herbs' delightful scent
To all the host new vigour lent.
Free from all darts and wounds and pain
The sons of Raghu lived again,
And dead and dying Vánars healed
Rose vigorous from the battle field.

Canto LXXV
The Night Attack

Sugríva spake in words like these:
"Now, Vánar lords, the occasion seize.
For now, of sons and brothers reft,
To Rávaṇ little hope is left:
And if our host his gates assail
His weak defence will surely fail."
At dead of night the Vánar bands
Rushed on with torches in their hands.
Scared by the coming of the host
Each giant warder left his post.
Where'er the Vánar legions came
Their way was marked with hostile flame
That spread in fury to devour
Palace and temple, gate and tower.
Down came the walls and porches, down
Came stately piles that graced the town.
In many a house the fire was red,
On sandal wood and aloe fed.
And scorching flames in billows rolled
O'er diamonds and pearls and gold.
On cloth of wool, on silk brocade,
On linen robes their fury preyed.
Wheels, poles and yokes were burned, and all
The coursers' harness in the stall;
And elephants' and chariots' gear,
The sword, the buckler, and the spear.
Scared by the crash of falling beams,

Mid lamentations, groans and screams,
Forth rushed the giants through the flames
And with them dragged bewildered dames,
Each, with o'erwhelming terror wild,
Still clasping to her breast a child.
The swift fire from a cloud of smoke
Through many a gilded lattice broke,
And, melting pearl and coral, rose
O'er balconies and porticoes.
The startled crane and peacock screamed
As with strange light the courtyard gleamed,
And fierce unusual glare was thrown
On shrinking wood and heated stone.
From burning stall and stable freed
Rushed frantic elephant and steed,
And goaded by the driving blaze
Fled wildly through the crowded ways.
As earth with fervent heat will glow
When comes her final overthrow;
From gate to gate, from court to spire
Proud Lanká was one blaze of fire,
And every headland, rock and bay
Shone bright a hundred leagues away.
Forth, blinded by the heat and flame
Ran countless giants huge of frame;
And, mustering for fierce attack,
The Vánars charged to drive them back,
While shout and scream and roar and cry
Reëchoed through the earth and sky.
There Ráma stood with strength renewed,
And ever, as the foe he viewed,
Shaking the distant regions rang
His mighty bow's tremendous clang.
Then through the gates Nikumbha hied,

And Kumbha by his brother's side,
Sent forth—the bravest and the best—
To battle by the king's behest.
There fought the chiefs in open field,
And Angad fell and Dwivid reeled.
Sugríva saw: by rage impelled
He crushed the bow which Kumbha held.
About his foe Sugríva wound
His arms, and, heaving from the ground
The giant hurled him o'er the bank;
And deep beneath the sea he sank.
Like mandar hill with furious swell
Up leapt the waters where he fell.
Again he rose: he sprang to land
And raised on high his threatening hand:
Full on Sugríva's chest it came
And shook the Vánar's massy frame,
But on the wounded bone he broke
His wrist—so furious was the stroke.
With force that naught could stay or check,
Sugríva smote him neath the neck.
The fierce blow crashed through flesh and bone
And Kumbha lay in death o'erthrown.
Nikumbha saw his brother die,
And red with fury flashed his eye.
He dashed with mighty sway and swing
His axe against the Vánar king;
But shattered on that living rock
It split in fragments at the shock.
Sugríva, rising to the blow,
Raised his huge hand and smote his foe.
And in the dust the giant lay
Gasping in blood his soul away.

[I have briefly despatched Kumbha and Nikumbha, each of whom has in the text a long Canto to himself. When they fall Rávaṇ sends forth Makaráksha or Crocodile-Eye, the son of Khara who was slain by Ráma in the forest before the abduction of Sítá. The account of his sallying forth, of his battle with Ráma and of his death by the fiery dart of that hero occupies two Cantos which I entirely pass over. Indrajít again comes forth and, rendered invisible by his magic art slays countless Vánars with his unerring arrows. He retires to the city and returns bearing in his chariot an effigy of Sítá, the work of magic, weeping and wailing by his side. He grasps the lovely image by the hair and cuts it down with his scimitar in the sight of the enraged Hanúmán and all the Vánar host. At last after much fighting of the usual kind Indrajít's chariot is broken in pieces, his charioteer is slain, and he himself falls by Lakshmaṇ's hand, to the inexpressible delight of the high-souled saints, the nymphs of heaven and other celestial beings.]

Canto XCIII
Rávan's Lament

They sought the king, a mournful train,
And cried, "My lord, thy son is slain.
By Lakshmaṇ's hand, before these eyes,
The warrior fell no more to rise.
No time is this for vain regret:
Thy hero son a hero met;
And he whose might in battle pressed
Lord Indra and the Gods confessed,
Whose power was stranger to defeat,
Has gained in heaven a blissful seat."
The monarch heard the mournful tale:
His heart was faint, his cheek was pale;
His fleeting sense at length regained,
In trembling tones he thus complained:
"Ah me, my son, my pride: the boast
And glory of the giant host.
Could Lakshmaṇ's puny might defeat
The foe whom Indra feared to meet?
Could not thy deadly arrows split
Proud Mandar's peaks, O Indrajít,
And the Destroyer's self destroy?
And wast thou conquered by a boy?
I will not weep: thy noble deed
Has blessed thee with immortal meed
Gained by each hero in the skies
Who fighting for his sovereign dies.
Now, fearless of all meaner foes,

The guardian Gods 993 will taste repose:
But earth to me, with hill and plain,
Is desolate, for thou art slain.
Ah, whither hast thou fled, and left
Thy mother, Lanká, me bereft;
Left pride and state and wives behind,
And lordship over all thy kind?
I fondly hoped thy hand should pay
Due honours on my dying day:
And couldst thou, O beloved, flee
And leave thy funeral rites to me?
Life has no comfort left me, none,
O Indrajít my son, my son."
Thus wailed he broken by his woes:
But swift the thought of vengeance rose.
In awful wrath his teeth he gnashed,
And from his eyes red lightning flashed.
Hot from his mouth came fire and smoke,
As thus the king in fury spoke:
"Through many a thousand years of yore
The penance and the pain I bore,
And by fierce torment well sustained
The highest grace of Brahmá gained,
His plighted word my life assured,
From Gods of heaven and fiends secured.
He armed my limbs with burnished mail
Whose lustre turns the sunbeams pale,
In battle proof gainst heavenly bands
With thunder in their threatening hands.
Armed in this mail myself will go
With Brahmá's gift my deadly bow,
And, cleaving through the foes my way,
The slayers of my son will slay."
Then, by his grief to frenzy wrought,

The captive in the grove he sought.
Swift through the shady path he sped:
Earth trembled at his furious tread.
Fierce were his eyes: his monstrous hand
Held drawn for death his glittering brand.
There weeping stood the Maithil dame:
She shuddered as the giant came.
Near drew the rover of the night
And raised his sword in act to smite;
But, by his nobler heart impelled,
One Rákshas lord his arm withheld:
"Wilt thou, great Monarch," thus he cried,
"Wilt thou, to heavenly Gods allied,
Blot for all time thy glorious fame,
The slayer of a gentle dame?
What! shall a woman's blood be spilt
To stain thee with eternal guilt,
Thee deep in all the Veda's lore?
Far be the thought for evermore.
Ah look, and let her lovely face
This fury from thy bosom chase."
He ceased: the prudent counsel pleased
The monarch, and his wrath appeased;
Then to his council hall in haste
The giant lord his steps retraced.

[I omit two Cantos in the first of which Ráma with an enchanted Gandharva weapon deals destruction among the Rákshases sent out by Rávaṇ, and in the second the Rákshas dames lament the slain and mourn over the madness of Rávaṇ.]

Canto XCVI
Rávan's Sally

The groans and cries of dames who wailed
The ears of Lanká's lord assailed,
For from each house and home was sent
The voice of weeping and lament.
In troubled thought his head he bowed,
Then fiercely loosing on the crowd
Of nobles near his throne he broke
The silence, and in fury spoke:
"This day my deadly shafts shall fly,
And Raghu's sons shall surely die.
This day shall countless Vánars bleed
And dogs and kites and vultures feed.
Go, bid them swift my car prepare,
Bring the great bow I long to bear:
And let my host with sword and shield
And spear be ready for the field."
From street to street the captains passed
And Rákshas warriors gathered fast.
With spear and sword to pierce and strike,
And axe and club and mace and pike.

[I omit several weapons for which I cannot find distinctive names, and among them the *Sataghní* or *Centicide*, supposed by some to be a kind of fire-arms or rocket, but described by a commentator on the Mahábhárata as a stone or cylindrical piece of wood studded with iron spikes.]

Then Rávaṇ's warrior chariot 994 wrought
With gold and rich inlay was brought.
Mid tinkling bells and weapons' clang
The monarch on the chariot sprang,

Which, decked with gems of every hue,
Eight steeds of noble lineage drew.
Mid roars of drum and shell rang out
From countless throats a joyful shout.
As, girt with hosts in warlike pride,
Through Lanká's streets the tyrant hied.
Still, louder than the roar of drums,
Went up the cry "He comes, he comes,
Our ever conquering lord who trod
Beneath his feet both fiend and God."
On to the gate the warriors swept
Where Raghu's sons their station kept.
When Rávaṇ's car the portal passed
The sun in heaven was overcast.
Earth rocked and reeled from side to side
And birds with boding voices cried.
Against the standard of the king
A vulture flapped his horrid wing.
Big gouts of blood before him dropped,
His trembling steeds in terror stopped.
The hue of death was on his cheek,
And scarce his flattering tongue could speak,
When, terrible with flash and flame,
Through murky air a meteor came.
Still by the hand of Death impelled
His onward way the giant held.
The Vánars in the field afar
Heard the loud thunder of his car.
And turned with warriors' fierce delight
To meet the giant in the fight.
He came: his clanging bow he drew
And myriads of the Vánars slew.
Some through the side and heart he cleft,
Some headless on the plain were left.

Some struggling groaned with mangled thighs,

Or broken arms or blinded eyes.

[I omit Cantos XCVII, XCVIII, and XCIX, which describe in the usual way three single combats between Sugríva and Angad on the Vánar side and Virúpáksha, Mahodar, and Mahápárśva on the side of the giants. The weapons of the Vánars are trees and rocks; the giants fight with swords, axes, and bows and arrows. The details are generally the same as those of preceding duels. The giants fall, one in each Canto.]

Canto C
Rávan In The Field

The plain with bleeding limbs was spread,
And heaps of dying and of dead.
His mighty bow still Ráma strained,
And shafts upon the giants rained.
Still Angad and Sugríva, wrought
To fury, for the Vánars fought.
Crushed with huge rocks through chest and side
Mahodar, Mahápársva died,
And Virúpáksha stained with gore
Dropped on the plain to rise no more.
When Rávan saw the three o'erthrown
He cried aloud in furious tone:
"Urge, urge the car, my charioteer,
The haughty Vánars' death is near.
This very day shall end our griefs
For leaguered town and slaughtered chiefs.
Ráma the tree whose lovely fruit
Is Sítá, shall this arm uproot, —
Whose branches with protecting shade
Are Vánar lords who lend him aid."
Thus cried the king: the welkin rang
As forth the eager coursers sprang,
And earth beneath the chariot shook
With flowery grove and hill and brook.
Fast rained his shafts: where'er he sped
The conquered Vánars fell or fled,
On rolled the car in swift career

Till Raghu's noble sons were near.

Then Ráma looked upon the foe

And strained and tried his sounding bow,

Till earth and all the region rang

Re-echoing to the awful clang.

His bow the younger chieftain bent,

And shaft on shaft at Rávaṇ sent.

He shot: but Rávaṇ little recked;

Each arrow with his own he checked,

And headless, baffled of its aim,

To earth the harmless missile came;

And Lakshmaṇ stayed his arm o'erpowered

By the thick darts the giant showered.

Fierce waxed the fight and fiercer yet,

For Rávaṇ now and Ráma met,

And each on other poured amain

The tempest of his arrowy rain.

While all the sky above was dark

With missiles speeding to their mark

Like clouds, with flashing lightning twined

About them, hurried by the wind.

Not fiercer was the wondrous fight

When Vritra fell by Indra's might.

All arts of war each foeman knew,

And trained alike, his bowstring drew.

Red-eyed with fury Lanká's king

Pressed his huge fingers on the string,

And fixed in Ráma's brows a flight

Of arrows winged with matchless flight.

Still Raghu's son endured, and bore

That crown of shafts though wounded sore.

O'er a dire dart a spell he spoke

With mystic power to aid the stroke.

In vain upon the foe it smote

Rebounding from the steelproof coat.
The giant armed his bow anew,
And wondrous weapons hissed and flew,
Terrific, deadly, swift of flight,
Beaked like the vulture and the kite,
Or bearing heads of fearful make,
Of lion, tiger, wolf and snake. 995
Then Ráma, troubled by the storm
Of flying darts in every form
Shot by an arm that naught could tire,
Launched at the foe his dart of fire,
Which, sacred to the Lord of Flame,
Burnt and consumed where'er it came.
And many a blazing shaft beside
The hero to his string applied.
With fiery course of dazzling hue
Swift to the mark each missile flew,
Some flashing like a shooting star,
Some as the tongues of lightning are;
One like a brilliant plant, one
In splendour like the morning sun.
Where'er the shafts of Ráma burned
The giant's darts were foiled and turned.
Far into space his weapons fled,
But as they flew struck thousands dead.

Canto CI
Lakshman's Fall

When Rávan saw his darts repelled,
With double rage his bosom swelled.
He summoned, wroth but undismayed,
A mightier charm to lend its aid.
And, fierce as fire before the blast,
A storm of missiles thick and fast,
Spear, pike and javelin, mace and brand,
Came hurtling from the giant's hand.
But, mightier still, the arms employed
By Raghu's son their force destroyed,
And every dart fell dulled and spent
By powers the bards of heaven had lent.
With his huge mace Vibhishan slew
The steeds that Rávan's chariot drew.
Then Rávan hurled in deadly ire
A ponderous spear that flashed like fire:
But Ráma's arrows checked its way,
And harmless on the earth it lay,
The giant seized a mightier spear,
Which Death himself would shun with fear.
Vibhishan with the stroke had died,
But Lakshman's hand his bowstring plied,
And flying arrows thick as hail
Smote fiercely on the giant's mail.
Then Rávan turned his aim aside,
On Lakshman looked and fiercely cried:
"Thou, thou again my wrath hast braved,

And from his death Vibhishan saved.
Now in his stead this spear receive
Whose deadly point thy heart shall cleave."
He ceased: he hurled the mortal dart
By Maya forged with magic art.
The spear, with all his fury flung,
Swift, flickering like a serpent's tongue,
Adorned with many a tinkling bell,
Smote Lakshman, and the hero fell.
When Ráma saw, he heaved a sigh,
A tear one moment dimmed his eye.
But tender grief was soon repressed
And thoughts of vengeance filled his breast.
The air around him flashed and gleamed
As from his bow the arrows streamed;
And Lanká's lord, the foeman's dread,
O'erwhelmed with terror turned and fled.

Canto CII
Lakshman Healed

But Ráma, pride of Raghu's race,
Gazed tenderly on Lakshman's face,
And, as the sight his spirit broke,
Turned to Sushen and sadly spoke:
"Where is my power and valour? how
Shall I have heart for battle now,
When dead before my weeping eyes
My brother, noblest Lakshman, lies?
My tears in blinding torrents flow,
My hand unnerved has dropped my bow.
The pangs of woe have blanched my cheek,
My heart is sick, my strength is weak.
Ah me, my brother! Ah, that I
By Lakshman's side might sink and die:
Life, war and conquest, all are vain
If Lakshman lies in battle slain.
Why will those eyes my glances shun?
Hast thou no word of answer, none?
Ah, is thy noble spirit flown
And gone to other worlds alone?
Couldst thou not let thy brother seek
Those worlds with thee? O speak, O speak!
Rise up once more, my brother, rise,
Look on me with thy loving eyes.
Were not thy steps beside me still

In gloomy wood, on breezy hill?
Did not thy gentle care assuage
Thy brother's grief and fitful rage?
Didst thou not all his troubles share,
His guide and comfort in despair?"
As Ráma, vanquished, wept and sighed
The Vánar chieftain thus replied:
"Great Prince, unmanly thoughts dismiss,
Nor yield thy soul to grief like this.
In vain those burning tears are shed:
Our glory Lakshman is not dead.
Death on his brow no mark has set,
Where beauty's lustre lingers yet.
Clear is the skin, and tender hues
Of lotus flowers his palms suffuse.
O Ráma, cheer thy trembling heart;
Not thus do life and body part.
Now, Hanumán, to thee I speak:
Hie hence to tall Mahodaya's 996 peak
Where herbs of sovereign virtue grow
Which life and health and strength bestow
Bring thou the leaves to balm his pain,
And Lakshman shall be well again."
He ceased: the Wind-God's son obeyed
Swift through the clouds his way he made.
He reached the hill, nor stayed to find
The wondrous herbs of healing kind,
From its broad base the mount he tore
With all the shrubs and trees it bore,
Sped through the clouds again and showed
To wise Sushen his woody load. 997
Sushen in wonder viewed the hill,
And culled the sovereign salve of ill.

Soon as the healing herb he found,
The fragrant leaves he crushed and ground.
Then over Lakshman's face he bent,
Who, healed and strengthened by the scent
Of that blest herb divinely sweet,
Rose fresh and lusty on his feet.

Canto CIII
Indra's Car

Then Raghu's son forgot his woe:
Again he grasped his fallen bow
And hurled at Lanká's lord amain
The tempest of his arrowy rain.
Drawn by the steeds his lords had brought,
Again the giant turned and fought.
And drove his glittering chariot nigh
As springs the Day-God through the sky.
Then, as his sounding bow he bent,
Like thunderbolts his shafts were sent,
As when dark clouds in rain time shed
Fierce torrents on a mountain's head.
High on his car the giant rode,
On foot the son of Raghu strode.
The Gods from their celestial height
Indignant saw the unequal fight.
Then he whom heavenly hosts revere,
Lord Indra, called his charioteer:
"Haste, Mátali," he cried, "descend;
To Raghu's son my chariot lend.
With cheering words the chief address;
And all the Gods thy deed will bless."
He bowed; he brought the glorious car
Whose tinkling bells were heard afar;
Fair as the sun of morning, bright
With gold and pearl and lazulite.
He yoked the steeds of tawny hue

That swifter than the tempest flew.
Then down the slope of heaven he hied
And stayed the car by Ráma's side.
"Ascend, O Chief," he humbly cried,
"The chariot which the Gods provide.
The mighty bow of Indra see,
Sent by the Gods who favour thee;
Behold this coat of glittering mail,
And spear and shafts which never fail."
Cheered by the grace the Immortals showed
The chieftain on the chariot rode.
Then as the car-borne warriors met
The awful fight raged fiercer yet.
Each shaft that Rávaṇ shot became
A serpent red with kindled flame,
And round the limbs of Ráma hung
With fiery jaws and quivering tongue.
But every serpent fled dismayed
When Raghu's valiant son displayed
The weapon of the Feathered King, 998
And loosed his arrows from the string.
But Rávaṇ armed his bow anew,
And showers of shafts at Ráma flew,
While the fierce king in swift career
Smote with a dart the charioteer.
An arrow shot by Rávaṇ's hand
Laid the proud banner on the sand,
And Indra's steeds of heavenly strain
Fell by the iron tempest slain.
On Gods and spirits of the air
Fell terror, trembling, and despair.
The sea's white billows mounted high
With froth and foam to drench the sky.
The sun by lurid clouds was veiled,

The friendly lights of heaven were paled;
And, fiercely gleaming, fiery Mars
Opposed the beams of gentler stars.
Then Ráma's eyes with fury blazed
As Indra's heavenly spear he raised.
Loud rang the bells: the glistering head
Bright flashes through the region shed.
Down came the spear in swift descent:
The giant's lance was crushed and bent.
Then Rávan's horses brave and fleet
Fell dead beneath his arrowy sleet.
Fierce on his foeman Ráma pressed,
And gored with shafts his mighty breast.
And spouting streams of crimson dyed
The weary giant's limbs and side.

[I omit Cantos CIV and CV in which the fight is renewed and Rávan severely reprimands his charioteer for timidity and want of confidence in his master's prowess, and orders him to charge straight at Ráma on the next occasion.]

Canto CVI
Glory To The Sun

There faint and bleeding fast, apart
Stood Rávaṇ raging in his heart.
Then, moved with ruth for Ráma's sake,
Agastya 999 came and gently spake:
"Bend, Ráma, bend thy heart and ear
The everlasting truth to hear
Which all thy hopes through life will bless
And crown thine arms with full success.
The rising sun with golden rays,
Light of the worlds, adore and praise:
The universal king, the lord
By hosts of heaven and fiends adored.
He tempers all with soft control,
He is the Gods' diviner soul;
And Gods above and fiends below
And men to him their safety owe.
He Brahmá, Vishṇu, Śiva, he
Each person of the glorious Three,
Is every God whose praise we tell,
The King of Heaven, 1000 the Lord of Hell: 1001
Each God revered from times of old,
The Lord of War, 1002 the King of Gold: 1003
Mahendra, Time and Death is he,
The Moon, the Ruler of the Sea. 1004

He hears our praise in every form, —
The manes, 1005 Gods who ride the storm, 1006
The Aśvins, 1007 Manu, 1008 they who stand
Round Indra, 1009 and the Sádhyas' 1010 band
He is the air, and life and fire,
The universal source and sire:
He brings the seasons at his call,
Creator, light, and nurse of all.
His heavenly course he joys to run,
Maker of Day, the golden sun.
The steeds that whirl his car are seven, 1011
The flaming steeds that flash through heaven.
Lord of the sky, the conqueror parts
The clouds of night with glistering darts.
He, master of the Vedas' lore,
Commands the clouds' collected store:
He is the rivers' surest friend;
He bids the rains, and they descend.
Stars, planets, constellations own
Their monarch of the golden throne.
Lord of twelve forms, 1012 to thee I bow,
Most glorious King of heaven art thou.
O Ráma, he who pays aright
Due worship to the Lord of Light
Shall never fall oppressed by ill,
But find a stay and comfort still.
Adore with all thy heart and mind
This God of Gods, to him resigned;
And thou his saving power shalt know
Victorious o'er thy giant foe."

[This Canto does not appear in the Bengal recension. It comes in awkwardly and may I think be considered as an interpolation, but I paraphrase a portion of it as a relief after so much fighting and carnage, and as an interesting glimpse of the monotheistic ideas which underlie the Hindu religion. The hymn does not readily lend itself to metrical translation, and I have not attempted here to give a faithful rendering of the whole. A literal version of the text and the commentary given in the Calcutta edition will be found in the Additional Notes.

A canto is here omitted. It contains fighting of the ordinary kind between Ráma and Rávaṇ, and a description of sights and sounds of evil omen foreboding the destruction of the giant.]

Canto CVIII
The Battle

He spoke, and vanished: Ráma raised
His eyes with reverence meet, and praised
The glorious Day-God full in view:
Then armed him for the fight anew.
Urged onward by his charioteer
The giant's foaming steeds came near,
And furious was the battle's din
Where each resolved to die or win.
The Rákshas host and Vánar bands
Stood with their weapons in their hands,
And watched in terror and dismay
The fortune of the awful fray.
The giant chief with rage inflamed
His darts at Ráma's pennon aimed;
But when they touched the chariot made
By heavenly hands their force was stayed.
Then Ráma's breast with fury swelled;
He strained the mighty bow he held,
And straight at Rávaṇ's banner flew
An arrow as the string he drew—
A deadly arrow swift of flight,
Like some huge snake ablaze with light,
Whose fury none might e'er repel,—
And, split in twain, the standard fell.
At Ráma's steeds sharp arrows, hot
With flames of fire, the giant shot.
Unmoved the heavenly steeds sustained

The furious shower the warrior rained,
As though soft lotus tendrils smote
Each haughty crest and glossy coat.
Then volleyed swift by magic art,
Tree, mountain peak and spear and dart,
Trident and pike and club and mace
Flew hurtling straight at Ráma's face.
But Ráma with his steeds and car
Escaped the storm which fell afar
Where the strange missiles, as they rushed
To earth, a thousand Vánars crushed.

Canto CIX
The Battle

With wondrous power and might and skill
The giant fought with Ráma still.
Each at his foe his chariot drove,
And still for death or victory strove.
The warriors' steeds together dashed,
And pole with pole reëchoing clashed.
Then Ráma launching dart on dart
Made Rávaṇ's coursers swerve and start.
Nor was the lord of Lanká slow
To rain his arrows on the foe,
Who showed, by fiery points assailed,
No trace of pain, nor shook nor quailed.
Dense clouds of arrows Ráma shot
With that strong arm which rested not,
And spear and mace and club and brand
Fell in dire rain from Rávaṇ's hand.
The storm of missiles fiercely cast
Stirred up the oceans with its blast,
And Serpent-Gods and fiends who dwell
Below were troubled by the swell.
The earth with hill and plain and brook
And grove and garden reeled and shook:
The very sun grew cold and pale,
And horror stilled the rising gale.
God and Gandharva, sage and saint
Cried out, with grief and terror faint:
"O may the prince of Raghu's line

Give peace to Bráhmans and to kine,
And, rescuing the worlds, o'erthrow
The giant king our awful foe."
Then to his deadly string the pride
Of Raghu's race a shaft applied.
Sharp as a serpent's venomed fang
Straight to its mark the arrow sprang,
And from the giant's body shred
With trenchant steel the monstrous head.
There might the triple world behold
That severed head adorned with gold.
But when all eyes were bent to view,
Swift in its stead another grew.
Again the shaft was pointed well:
Again the head divided fell;
But still as each to earth was cast
Another head succeeded fast.
A hundred, bright with fiery flame,
Fell low before the victor's aim,
Yet Rávan by no sign betrayed
That death was near or strength decayed.
The doubtful fight he still maintained,
And on the foe his missiles rained.
In air, on earth, on plain, on hill,
With awful might he battled still;
And through the hours of night and day
The conflict knew no pause or stay.

Canto CX
Rávan's Death

Then Mátali to Ráma cried:
"Let other arms the day decide.
Why wilt thou strive with useless toil
And see his might thy efforts foil?
Launch at the foe thy dart whose fire
Was kindled by the Almighty Sire."
He ceased: and Raghu's son obeyed:
Upon his string the hero laid
An arrow, like a snake that hissed.
Whose fiery flight had never missed:
The arrow Saint Agastya gave
And blessed the chieftain's life to save
That dart the Eternal Father made
The Monarch of the Gods to aid;
By Brahmá's self on him bestowed
When forth to fight Lord Indra rode.
'Twas feathered with the rushing wind;
The glowing sun and fire combined
To the keen point their splendour lent;
The shaft, ethereal element,
By Meru's hill and Mandar, pride
Of mountains, had its weight supplied.
He laid it on the twisted cord,
He turned the point at Lanká's lord,
And swift the limb-dividing dart
Pierced the huge chest and cleft the heart,
And dead he fell upon the plain

Like Vritra by the Thunderer slain.
The Rákahas host when Rávaṇ fell
Sent forth a wild terrific yell,
Then turned and fled, all hope resigned,
Through Lanká's gates, nor looked behind.
His voice each joyous Vánar raised,
And Ráma, conquering Ráma, praised.
Soft from celestial minstrels came
The sound of music and acclaim.
Soft, fresh, and cool, a rising breeze
Brought odours from the heavenly trees,
And ravishing the sight and smell
A wondrous rain of blossoms fell:
And voices breathed round Raghu's son:
"Champion of Gods, well done, well done."

Canto CXI
Vibhishan's Lament

Vibhishaṇ saw his brother slain,
Nor could his heart its woe contain.
O'er the dead king he sadly bent
And mourned him with a loud lament:
"O hero, bold and brave," he cried,
"Skilled in all arms, in battle tried.
Spoiled of thy crown, with limbs outspread,
Why wilt thou press thy gory bed?
Why slumber on the earth's cold breast,
When sumptuous couches woo to rest?
Ah me, my brother over bold,
Thine is the fate my heart foretold:
But love and pride forbade to hear
The friend who blamed thy wild career.
Fallen is the sun who gave us light,
Our lordly moon is veiled in night.
Our beacon fire is dead and cold
A hundred waves have o'er it rolled.
What could his light and fire avail
Against Lord Ráma's arrowy hail?
Woe for the giants' royal tree,
Whose stately height was fair to see.
His buds were deeds of kingly grace,
His bloom the sons who decked his race.
With rifled bloom and mangled bough
The royal tree lies prostrate now."
"Nay, idly mourn not," Ráma cried,

"The warrior king has nobly died,
Intrepid hero, firm through all,
So fell he as the brave should fall;
And ill beseems it chiefs like us
To weep for those who perish thus.
Be firm: thy causeless grief restrain,
And pay the dues that yet remain."
Again Vibhishan sadly spoke:
"His was the hero arm that broke
Embattled Gods' and Indra's might,
Unconquered ere to-day in fight.
He rushed against thee, fought and fell,
As Ocean, when his waters swell,
Hurling his might against a rock,
Falls spent and shattered by the shock.
Woe for our king's untimely end,
The generous lord the trusty friend:
Our sure defence when fear arose,
A dreaded scourge to stubborn foes.
O, let the king thy hand has slain
The honours of the dead obtain."
Then Ráma answered. "Hatred dies
When low in dust the foeman lies.
Now triumph bids the conflict cease,
And knits us in the bonds of peace.
Let funeral rites be duly paid.
And be it mine thy toil to aid."

Canto CXII
The Rákshas Dames

High rose the universal wail
That mourned the monarch's death, and, pale
With crushing woe, her hair unbound,
Her eyes in floods of sorrow drowned,
Forth from the inner chambers came
With trembling feet each royal dame,
Heedless of those who bade them stay
They reached the field where Rávaṇ lay;
There falling by their husband's side,
"Ah, King! ah dearest lord!" they cried.
Like creepers shattered by the storm
They threw them on his mangled form.
One to his bleeding bosom crept
And lifted up her voice and wept.
About his feet one mourner clung,
Around his neck another hung,
One on the giant's severed head,
Her pearly tears in torrents shed
Fast as the drops the summer shower
Pours down upon the lotus flower.
"Ah, he whose arm in anger reared
The King of Gods and Yáma feared,
While panic struck their heavenly train,
Lies prostrate in the battle slain.
Thy haughty heart thou wouldst not bend,
Nor listen to each wiser friend.
Ah, had the dame, as they implored,

Been yielded to her injured lord,
We had not mourned this day thy fall,
And happy had it been for all.
Then Ráma and thy friends content
In blissful peace their days had spent.
Thine injured brother had not fled,
Nor giant chiefs and Vánars bled.
Yet for these woes we will not blame.
Thy fancy for the Maithil dame,
Fate, ruthless Fate, whom none may bend
Has urged thee to thy hapless end."

Canto CXIII
Mandodarí's Lament

While thus they wept, supreme in place,
The loveliest for form and face,
Mandodarí drew near alone,
Looked on her lord and made her moan:
"Ah Monarch, Indra feared to stand
In fight before thy conquering hand.
From thy dread spear the Immortals ran;
And art thou murdered by a man?
Ah, 'twas no child of earth, I know,
That smote thee with that mortal blow.
'Twas Death himself in Ráma's shape,
That slew thee: Death whom none escape.
Or was it he who rules the skies
Who met thee, clothed in man's disguise?
Ah no, my lord, not Indra: he
In battle ne'er could look on thee.
One only God thy match I deem:
'Twas Vishṇu's self, the Lord Supreme,
Whose days through ceaseless time extend
And ne'er began and ne'er shall end:
He with the discus, shell, and mace,
Brought ruin on the giant race.
Girt by the Gods of heaven arrayed
Like Vánar hosts his strength to aid,
He Ráma's shape and arms assumed
And slew the king whom Fate had doomed.
In Janasthán when Khara died

With giant legions by his side,
No mortal was the unconquered foe
In Ráma's form who struck the blow.
When Hanumán the Vanár came
And burnt thy town with hostile flame,
I counselled peace in anxious fear:
I counselled, but thou wouldst not hear.
Thy fancy for the foreign dame
Has brought thee death and endless shame.
Why should thy foolish fancy roam?
Hadst thou not wives as fair at home?
In beauty, form and grace could she,
Dear lord, surpass or rival me?
Now will the days of Sítá glide
In tranquil joy by Ráma's side:
And I—ah me, around me raves
A sea of woe with whelming waves.
With thee in days of old I trod
Each spot beloved by nymph and God;
I stood with thee in proud delight
On Mandar's side and Meru's height;
With thee, my lord, enchanted strayed
In Chaitraratha's 1013 lovely shade,
And viewed each fairest scene afar
Transported in thy radiant car.
But source of every joy wast thou,
And all my bliss is ended now."
Then Ráma to Vibhishaṇ cried:
"Whate'er the ritual bids, provide.
Obsequial honours duly pay,
And these sad mourners' grief allay."
Vibhishaṇ answered, wise and true,
For duty's changeless law he knew:
"Nay one who scorned all sacred vows

And dared to touch another's spouse,
Fell tyrant of the human race,
With funeral rites I may not grace."
Him Raghu's royal son, the best
Of those who love the law, addressed:
"False was the rover of the night,
He loved the wrong and scorned the right.
Yet for the fallen warrior plead
The dauntless heart, the valorous deed.
Let him who ne'er had brooked defeat,
The chief whom Indra feared to meet,
The ever-conquering lord, obtain
The honours that should grace the slain."
Vibhishan bade his friends prepare
The funeral rites with thoughtful care.
Himself the royal palace sought
Whence sacred fire was quickly brought,
With sandal wood and precious scents
And pearl and coral ornaments.
Wise Bráhmans, while the tears that flowed
Down their wan cheeks their sorrow sowed,
Upon a golden litter laid
The corpse in finest ropes arrayed.
Thereon were flowers and pennons hung,
And loud the monarch's praise was sung.
Then was the golden litter raised,
While holy fire in order blazed.
And first in place Vibhishan led
The slow procession of the dead,
Behind, their cheeks with tears bedewed,
Came sad the widowed multitude.
Where, raised as Bráhmans ordered, stood
Piled sandal logs, and scented wood,
The body of the king was set

High on a deerskin coverlet.
Then duly to the monarch's shade
The offerings for the dead they paid,
And southward on the eastern side
An altar formed and fire supplied.
Then on the shoulder of the dead
The oil and clotted milk were shed.
All rites were done as rules ordain:
The sacrificial goat was slain.
Next on the corpse were perfumes thrown
And many a flowery wreath was strown;
And with Vibhishan's ready aid
Rich vesture o'er the king was laid.
Then while the tears their cheeks bedewed
Parched grain upon the dead they strewed;
Last, to the wood, as rules require,
Vibhishan set the kindling fire.
Then having bathed, as texts ordain,
To Lanká went the mourning train.
Vibhishan, when his task was done,
Stood by the side of Raghu's son.
And Ráma, freed from every foe,
Unstrung at last his deadly bow,
And laid the glittering shafts aside,
And mail by Indra's love supplied.

Canto CXIV
Vibhishan Consecrated

Joy reigned in heaven where every eye
Had seen the Lord of Lanká die.
In cars whose sheen surpassed the sun's
Triumphant rode the radiant ones:
And Rávan's death, by every tongue,
And Ráma's glorious deeds were sung.
They praised the Vánars true and brave,
The counsel wise Sugríva gave.
The deeds of Hanúmán they told,
The valiant chief supremely bold,
The strong ally, the faithful friend,
And Sítá's truth which naught could bend.
To Mátali, whom Indra sent,
His head the son of Raghu bent:
And he with fiery steeds who clove
The clouds again to Swarga drove.
Round King Sugríva brave and true
His arms in rapture Ráma threw,
Looked on the host with joy and pride,
And thus to noble Lakshman cried:
"Now let king-making drops be shed,
Dear brother, on Vibhishan's head
For truth and friendship nobly shown,
And make him lord of Rávan's throne."
This longing of his heart he told:
And Lakshman took an urn of gold
And bade the wind-fleet Vánars bring

Sea water for the giants' king.
The brimming urn was swiftly brought:
Then on a throne superbly wrought
Vibhishan sat, the giants' lord,
And o'er his brows the drops were poured.
As Raghu's son the rite beheld
His loving heart with rapture swelled:
But tenderer thoughts within him woke,
And thus to Hanúmán he spoke:
"Go to my queen: this message give:
Say Lakshman and Sugríva live.
The death of Lanká's monarch tell,
And bid her joy, for all is well."

Canto CXV
Sítá's Joy

The Vánar chieftain bowed his head,
Within the walls of Lanká sped,
Leave from the new-made king obtained,
And Sítá's lovely garden gained.
Beneath a tree the queen he found,
Where Rákshas warders watched around.
Her pallid cheek, her tangled hair,
Her raiment showed her deep despair,
Near and more near the envoy came
And gently hailed the weeping dame.
She started up in sweet surprise,
And sudden joy illumed her eyes.
For well the Vánar's voice she knew,
And hope reviving sprang and grew.
"Fair Queen," he said, "our task is done:
The foe is slain and Lanká won.
Triumphant mid triumphant friends
Kind words of greeting Ráma sends.
"Blest for thy sake, O spouse most true,
My deadly foe I met and slew.
Mine eyes are strangers yet to sleep:
I built a bridge athwart the deep
And crossed the sea to Lanká's shore
To keep the mighty oath I swore.
Now, gentle love, thy cares dispel,
And weep no more, for all is well.
Fear not in Rávaṇ's house to stay

For good Vibhishaṇ now bears sway,
For constant truth and friendship known
Regard his palace as thine own."
He greets thee thus thy heart to cheer,
And urged by love will soon be here."
Then flushed with joy the lady's cheek.
Her eyes o'erflowed, her voice was weak;
But struggling with her sobs she broke
Her silence thus, and faintly spoke:
"So fast the flood of rapture came,
My trembling tongue no words could frame.
Ne'er have I heard in days of bliss
A tale that gave such joy as this.
More precious far than gems and gold
The message which thy lips have told."
His reverent hands the Vánar raised
And thus the lady's answer praised:
"Sweet are the words, O Queen, which thou
True to thy lord, hast spoken now,
Better than gems and pearls of price,
Yea, or the throne of Paradise.
But, lady, ere I leave this place,
Grant me, I pray, a single grace.
Permit me, and this vengeful hand
Shall slay thy guards, this Rákshas band,
Whose cruel insult threat and scorn
Thy gentle soul too long has borne."
Thus, stern of mood, Hanúmán cried:
The Maithil lady thus replied:
"Nay, be not wroth with servants: they,
When monarchs bid must needs obey.
And, vassals of their lords, fulfil
Each fancy of their sovereign will.
To mine own sins the blame impute,

For as we sow we reap the fruit.
The tyrant's will these dames obeyed
When their fierce threats my soul dismayed."
She ceased: with admiration moved
The Vánar chief her words approved:
"Thy speech," he cried, "is worthy one
Whom love has linked to Raghu's son.
Now speak, O Queen, that I may know
Thy pleasure, for to him I go."
The Vánar ceased: then Janak's child
Made answer as she sweetly smiled:
"'My first, my only wish can be,
O chief, my loving lord to see."
Again the Vánar envoy spoke,
And with his words new rapture woke:
"Queen, ere this sun shall cease to shine
Thy Ráma's eyes shall look in thine.
Again the lord of Raghu's race
Shall turn to thee his moon-bright face.
His faithful brother shall thou see
And every friend who fought for thee,
And greet once more thy king restored
Like Śachí 1014 to her heavenly lord."
To Raghu's son his steps he bent
And told the message that she sent.

Canto CXVI
The Meeting

He looked upon that archer chief
Whose full eye mocked the lotus leaf,
And thus the noble Vánar spake:
"Now meet the queen for whose dear sake
Thy mighty task was first begun,
And now the glorious fruit is won.
O'erwhelmed with woe thy lady lies,
The hot tears streaming from her eyes.
And still the queen must long and pine
Until those eyes be turned to thine."
But Ráma stood in pensive mood,
And gathering tears his eyes bedewed.
His sad looks sought the ground: he sighed
And thus to King Vibhishaṇ cried:
"Let Sítá bathe and tire her head
And hither to my sight be led
In raiment sweet with precious scent,
And gay with golden ornament."
The Rákshas king his palace sought,
And Sítá from her bower was brought.
Then Rákshas bearers tall and strong,
Selected from the menial throng,
Through Lanká's gate the queen, arrayed
In glorious robes and gems, conveyed.
Concealed behind the silken screen,
Swift to the plain they bore the queen,
While Vánars, close on every side,

With eager looks the litter eyed.
The warders at Vibhishaṇ's hest
The onward rushing throng repressed,
While like the roar of ocean loud
Rose the wild murmur of the crowd.
The son of Raghu saw and moved
With anger thus the king reproved:
"Why vex with hasty blow and threat
The Vánars, and my rights forget?
Repress this zeal, untimely shown:
I count this people as mine own.
A woman's guard is not her bower,
The lofty wall, the fenced tower:
Her conduct is her best defence,
And not a king's magnificence.
At holy rites, in war and woe,
Her face unveiled a dame may show;
When at the Maiden's Choice 1015 they meet,
When marriage troops parade the street.
And she, my queen, who long has lain
In prison racked with care and pain,
May cease a while her face to hide,
For is not Ráma by her side?
Lay down the litter: on her feet
Let Sítá come her lord to meet.
And let the hosts of woodland race
Look near upon the lady's face."
Then Lakshmaṇ and each Vánar chief
Who heard his words were filled with grief.
The lady's gentle spirit sank,
And from each eye in fear she shrank,
As, her sweet eyelids veiled for shame,
Slowly before her lord she came.
While rapture battled with surprise

She raised to his her wistful eyes.
Then with her doubt and fear she strove,
And from her breast all sorrow drove.
Regardless of the gathering crowd,
Bright as the moon without a cloud,
She bent her eyes, no longer dim,
In joy and trusting love on him.

Canto CXVII
Sítá's Disgrace

He saw her trembling by his side,
And looked upon her face and cried:
"Lady, at length my task is done,
And thou, the prize of war, art won,
This arm my glory has retrieved,
And all that man might do achieved;
The insulting foe in battle slain
And cleared mine honour from its stain.
This day has made my name renowned
And with success my labour crowned.
Lord of myself, the oath I swore
Is binding on my soul no more.
If from my home my queen was reft,
This arm has well avenged the theft,
And in the field has wiped away
The blot that on mine honour lay.
The bridge that spans the foaming flood,
The city red with giants' blood;
The hosts by King Sugríva led
Who wisely counselled, fought and bled;
Vibhishaṇ's love, our guide and stay—
All these are crowned with fruit to-day.
But, lady, 'twas not love for thee
That led mine army o'er the sea.
'Twas not for thee our blood was shed,
Or Lanká filled with giant dead.
No fond affection for my wife

Inspired me in the hour of strife.
I battled to avenge the cause
Of honour and insulted laws.
My love is fled, for on thy fame
Lies the dark blot of sin and shame;
And thou art hateful as the light
That flashes on the injured sight.
The world is all before thee: flee:
Go where thou wilt, but not with me.
How should my home receive again
A mistress soiled with deathless stain?
How should I brook the foul disgrace,
Scorned by my friends and all my race?
For Rávan bore thee through the sky,
And fixed on thine his evil eye.
About thy waist his arms he threw,
Close to his breast his captive drew,
And kept thee, vassal of his power,
An inmate of his ladies' bower."

Canto CXVIII
Sítá's Reply

Struck down with overwhelming shame
She shrank within her trembling frame.
Each word of Ráma's like a dart
Had pierced the lady to the heart;
And from her sweet eyes unrestrained
The torrent of her sorrows, rained.
Her weeping eyes at length she dried,
And thus mid choking sobs replied:
"Canst thou, a high-born prince, dismiss
A high-born dame with speech like this?
Such words befit the meanest hind,
Not princely birth and generous mind,
By all my virtuous life I swear
I am not what thy words declare.
If some are faithless, wilt thou find
No love and truth in womankind?
Doubt others if thou wilt, but own
The truth which all my life has shown.
If, when the giant seized his prey,
Within his hated arms I lay,
And felt the grasp I dreaded, blame
Fate and the robber, not thy dame.
What could a helpless woman do?
My heart was mine and still was true,
Why when Hanúmán sent by thee
Sought Lanká's town across the sea,
Couldst thou not give, O lord of men,

Thy sentence of rejection then?
Then in the presence of the chief
Death, ready death, had brought relief,
Nor had I nursed in woe and pain
This lingering life, alas in vain.
Then hadst thou shunned the fruitless strife
Nor jeopardied thy noble life,
But spared thy friends and bold allies
Their vain and weary enterprise.
Is all forgotten, all? my birth,
Named Janak's child, from fostering earth?
That day of triumph when a maid
My trembling hand in thine I laid?
My meek obedience to thy will,
My faithful love through joy and ill,
That never failed at duty's call—
O King, is all forgotten, all?"
To Lakshmaṇ then she turned and spoke
While sobs and sighs her utterance broke:
"Sumitrá's son, a pile prepare,
My refuge in my dark despair.
I will not live to bear this weight
Of shame, forlorn and desolate.
The kindled fire my woes shall end
And be my best and surest friend."
His mournful eyes the hero raised
And wistfully on Ráma gazed,
In whose stern look no ruth was seen,
No mercy for the weeping queen.
No chieftain dared to meet those eyes,
To pray, to question or advise.
The word was passed, the wood was piled
And fain to die stood Janak's child.
She slowly paced around her lord,

The Gods with reverent act adored,
Then raising suppliant hands the dame
Prayed humbly to the Lord of Flame:
"As this fond heart by virtue swayed
From Raghu's son has never strayed,
So, universal witness, Fire
Protect my body on the pyre,
As Raghu's son has idly laid
This charge on Sítá, hear and aid."
She ceased: and fearless to the last
Within the flame's wild fury passed.
Then rose a piercing cry from all
Dames, children, men, who saw her fall
Adorned with gems and gay attire
Beneath the fury of the fire.

Canto CXIX
Glory To Vishnu

The shrill cry pierced through Ráma's ears
And his sad eyes o'erflowed with tears,
When lo, transported through the sky
A glorious band of Gods was nigh.
Ancestral shades, 1016 by men revered,
In venerable state appeared,
And he from whom all riches flow, 1017
And Yáma Lord who reigns below:
King Indra, thousand-eyed, and he
Who wields the sceptre of the sea. 1018
The God who shows the blazoned bull, 1019
And Brahmá Lord most bountiful
By whose command the worlds were made
All these on radiant cars conveyed,
Brighter than sun-beams, sought the place
Where stood the prince of Raghu's race,
And from their glittering seats the best
Of blessed Gods the chief addressed:
"Couldst thou, the Lord of all, couldst thou,
Creator of the worlds, allow
Thy queen, thy spouse to brave the fire
And give her body to the pyre?
Dost thou not yet, supremely wise,
Thy heavenly nature recognize?"
They ceased: and Ráma thus began:
"I deem myself a mortal man.
Of old Ikshváku's line, I spring

From Daśaratha Kośal's king."
He ceased: and Brahmá's self replied:
"O cast the idle thought aside.
Thou art the Lord Náráyaṇ, thou
The God to whom all creatures bow.
Thou art the saviour God who wore
Of old the semblance of a boar;
Thou he whose discus overthrows
All present, past and future foes;
Thou Brahmá, That whose days extend
Without beginning, growth or end;
The God, who, bears the bow of horn,
Whom four majestic arms adorn;
Thou art the God who rules the sense
And sways with gentle influence;
Thou all-pervading Vishṇu Lord
Who wears the ever-conquering sword;
Thou art the Guide who leads aright,
Thou Krishṇa of unequalled might.
Thy hand, O Lord, the hills and plains,
And earth with all her life sustains;
Thou wilt appear in serpent form
When sinks the earth in fire and storm.
Queen Sítá of the lovely brows
Is Lakshmí thy celestial spouse.
To free the worlds from Rávaṇ thou
Wouldst take the form thou wearest now.
Rejoice: the mighty task is done:
Rejoice, thou great and glorious one.
The tyrant, slain, thy labours end:
Triumphant now to heaven ascend.
High bliss awaits the devotee
Who clings in loving faith to thee,
Who celebrates with solemn praise

The Lord of ne'er beginning days.
On earth below, in heaven above
Great joy shall crown his faith and love.
And he who loves the tale divine
Which tells each glorious deed of thine
Through life's fair course shall never know
The fierce assault of pain and woe." 1020

Canto CXX
Sítá Restored

Thus spoke the Self-existent Sire:
Then swiftly from the blazing pyre
The circling flames were backward rolled,
And, raising in his gentle hold
Alive unharmed the Maithil dame,
The Lord of Fire embodied came.
Fair as the morning was her sheen,
And gold and gems adorned the queen.
Her form in crimson robes arrayed,
Her hair was bound in glossy braid.
Her wreath was fresh and sweet of scent,
Undimmed was every ornament.
Then, standing close to Ráma'a side,
The universal witness cried:
"From every blot and blemish free
Thy faithful queen returns to thee.
In word or deed, in look or mind
Her heart from thee has ne'er declined.
By force the giant bore away
From thy lone cot his helpless prey;
And in his bowers securely kept
She still has longed for thee and wept.
With soft temptation, bribe and threat,
He bade the dame her love forget:
But, nobly faithful to her lord,
Her soul the giant's suit abhorred.
Receive, O King, thy queen again,

Pure, ever pure from spot and stain."
Still stood the king in thoughtful mood
And tears of joy his eyes bedewed.
Then to the best of Gods the best
Of warrior chiefs his mind expressed:
"'Twas meet that mid the thousands here
The searching fire my queen should clear;
For long within the giant's bower
She dwelt the vassal of his power.
For else had many a slanderous tongue
Reproaches on mine honour flung,
And scorned the king who, love-impelled,
His consort from the proof withheld.
No doubt had I, but surely knew
That Janak's child was pure and true,
That, come what might, in good and ill
Her faithful heart was with me still.
I knew that Rávaṇ could not wrong
My queen whom virtue made so strong.
I knew his heart would sink and fail,
Nor dare her honour to assail,
As Ocean, when he raves and roars,
Fears to o'erleap his bounding shores.
Now to the worlds her truth is shown,
And Sítá is again mine own.
Thus proved before unnumbered eyes,
On her pure fame no shadow lies.
As heroes to their glory cleave,
Mine own dear spouse I ne'er will leave."
He ceased: and clasped in fond embrace
On his dear breast she hid her face.

Canto CXXI
Dasaratha

To him Maheśvar thus replied:
"O strong-armed hero, lotus-eyed,
Thou, best of those who love the right,
Hast nobly fought the wondrous fight.
Dispelled by thee the doom that spread
Through trembling earth and heaven is fled.
The worlds exult in light and bliss,
And praise thy name, O chief, for this.
Now peace to Bharat's heart restore,
And bid Kausalyá weep no more.
Thy face let Queen Kaikeyí see,
Let fond Sumitrá gaze on thee.
The longing of thy friends relieve,
The kingdom of thy sires receive.
Let sons of gentle Sítá born
Ikshváku's ancient line adorn.
Then from all care and foemen freed
Perform the offering of the steed.
In pious gifts thy wealth expend,
Then to the home of Gods ascend,
Thy sire, this glorious king, behold,
Among the blest in heaven enrolled.
He comes from where the Immortals dwell:
Salute him, for he loves thee well."
His mandate Raghu's sons obeyed,

And to their sire obeisance made,

Where high he stood above the car

In wondrous light that shone afar,

His limbs in radiant garments dressed

Whereon no spot of dust might rest.

When on the son he loved so well

The eyes of Daśaratha fell,

He strained the hero to his breast

And thus with gentle words addressed:

"No joy to me is heavenly bliss,

For there these eyes my Ráma miss.

Enrolled on high with saint and sage,

Thy woes, dear son, my thoughts engage.

Kaikeyí's guile I ne'er forget:

Her cruel words will haunt me yet,

Which sent thee forth, my son, to roam

The forest far from me and home.

Now when I look on each dear face,

And hold you both in fond embrace,

My heart is full of joy to see

The sons I love from danger free.

Now know I what the Gods designed,

And how in Ráma's form enshrined

The might of Purushottam lay,

The tyrant of the worlds to slay.

Ah, how Kausalyá will rejoice

To hear again her darling's voice,

And, all thy weary wanderings o'er,

To gaze upon thy face once more.

Ah blest, for ever blest are they

Whose eyes shall see the glorious day

Of thy return in joy at last,

Thy term of toil and exile past.
Ayodhyá's lord, begin thy reign,
And day by day new glory gain."
He ceased: and Ráma thus replied:
"Be not this grace, O sire, denied.
Those hasty words, that curse revoke
Which from thy lips in anger broke:
"Kaikeyí, be no longer mine:
I cast thee off, both thee and thine."
O father, let no sorrow fall
On her or hers: thy curse recall."
"Yea, she shall live, if so thou wilt,"
The sire replied, "absolved from guilt."
Round Lakshmaṇ then his arms he threw,
And moved by love began anew:
"Great store of merit shall be thine,
And brightly shall thy glory shine;
Secure on earth thy brother's grace.
And high in heaven shall be thy place.
Thy glorious king obey and fear:
To him the triple world is dear.
God, saint, and sage, by Indra led,
To Ráma bow the reverent head,
Nor from the Lord, the lofty-souled,
Their worship or their praise withhold.
Heart of the Gods, supreme is he,
The One who ne'er shall cease to be."
On Sítá then he looked and smiled;
"List to my words" he said, "dear child,
Let not thy gentle breast retain
One lingering trace of wrath or pain.
When by the fire thy truth be proved,

By love for thee his will was moved.
The furious flame thy faith confessed
Which shrank not from the awful test:
And thou, in every heart enshrined,
Shalt live the best of womankind."
He ceased: he bade the three adieu,
And home to heaven exulting flew.

Canto CXXII
Indra's Boon

Then Indra, he whose fiery stroke
Slew furious Páka, turned and spoke:
"A glorious day, O chief, is this,
Rich with the fruit of lasting bliss.
Well pleased are we: we love thee well
Now speak, thy secret wishes tell."
Thus spake the sovereign of the sky,
And this was Ráma's glad reply:
"If I have won your grace, incline
To grant this one request of mine.
Restore, O King: the Vánar dead
Whose blood for me was nobly shed.
To life and strength my friends recall,
And bring them back from Yáma's hall.
When, fresh in might the warriors rise,
Prepare a feast to glad their eyes.
Let fruits of every season glow,
And streams of purest water flow."
Thus Raghu's son, great-hearted, prayed,
And Indra thus his answer made:
"High is the boon thou seekest: none
Should win this grace but Raghu's son.
Yet, faithful to the word I spake,
I grant the prayer for thy dear sake.
The Vánars whom the giants slew
Their life and vigour shall renew.
Their strength repaired, their gashes healed

Whose torrents dyed the battle field,
The warrior hosts from death shall rise
Like sleepers when their slumber flies."
Restored from Yáma's dark domain
The Vánar legions filled the plain,
And, round the royal chief arrayed,
With wondering hearts obeisance paid.
Each God the son of Raghu praised,
And cried as loud his voice he raised:
"Turn, King, to fair Ayodhyá speed,
And leave thy friends of Vánar breed.
Thy true devoted consort cheer
After long days of woe and fear.
Bharat, thy loyal brother, see,
A hermit now for love of thee.
The tears of Queen Kauśalyá dry,
And light with joy each stepdame's eye;
Then consecrated king of men
Make glad each faithful citizen."
They ceased: and borne on radiant cars
Sought their bright home amid the stars.

Canto CXXIII
The Magic Car

Then slept the tamer of his foes
And spent the night in calm repose.
Vibhishan came when morning broke,
And hailed the royal chief, and spoke:
"Here wait thee precious oil and scents,
And rich attire and ornaments.
The brimming urns are newly filled,
And women in their duty skilled,
With lotus-eyes, thy call attend,
Assistance at thy bath to lend."
"Let others," Ráma cried, "desire
These precious scents, this rich attire,
I heed not such delights as these,
For faithful Bharat, ill at ease,
Watching for me is keeping now
Far far away his rigorous vow.
By Bharat's side I long to stand,
I long to see my fatherland.
Far is Ayodhyá: long, alas,
The dreary road and hard to pass."
"One day," Vibhishan cried, "one day
Shall bear thee o'er that length of way.
Is not the wondrous chariot mine,
Named Pushpak, wrought by hands divine.
The prize which Rávan seized of old
Victorious o'er the God of Gold?
This chariot, kept with utmost care,

Will waft thee through the fields of air,
And thou shalt light unwearied down
In fair Ayodhyá's royal town.
But yet if aught that I have done
Has pleased thee well, O Raghu's son;
If still thou carest for thy friend,
Some little time in Lanká spend;
There after toil of battle rest
Within my halls an honoured guest."
Again the son of Raghu spake:
"Thy life was perilled for my sake.
Thy counsel gave me priceless aid:
All honours have been richly paid.
Scarce can my love refuse, O best
Of giant kind, thy last request.
But still I yearn once more to see
My home and all most dear to me;
Nor can I brook one hour's delay:
Forgive me, speed me on my way."
He ceased: the magic car was brought.
Of yore by Viśvakarmá wrought.
In sunlike sheen it flashed and blazed;
And Raghu's sons in wonder gazed.

Canto CXXIV
The Departure

The giant lord the chariot viewed,
And humbly thus his speech renewed:
"Behold, O King, the car prepared:
Now be thy further will declared."
He ceased: and Ráma spake once more:
"These hosts who thronged to Lanká's shore
Their faith and might have nobly shown,
And set thee on the giants' throne.
Let pearls and gems and gold repay
The feats of many a desperate day,
That all may go triumphant hence
Proud of their noble recompense."
Vibhishaṇ, ready at his call,
With gold and gems enriched them all.
Then Ráma clomb the glorious car
That shone like day's resplendent star.
There in his lap he held his dame
Vailing her eyes in modest shame.
Beside him Lakshmaṇ took his stand,
Whose mighty bow still armed his hand,
"O King Vibhishaṇ," Ráma cried,
"O Vánar chiefs, so long allied,
My comrades till the foemen fell,
List, for I speak a long farewell.

The task, in doubt and fear begun,
With your good aid is nobly done.
Leave Lanká's shore, your steps retrace,
Brave warriors of the Vánar race.
Thou, King Sugríva, true, through all,
To friendship's bond and duty's call,
Seek far Kishkindhá with thy train
And o'er thy realm in glory reign.
Farewell, Vibhishan, Lanká's throne
Won by our arms is now thine own,
Thou, mighty lord, hast nought to dread
From heavenly Gods by Indra led.
My last farewell, 0 King, receive,
For Lanká's isle this hour I leave."
Loud rose their cry in answer: "We,
O Raghu's son, would go with thee.
With thee delighted would we stray
Where sweet Ayodhyá's groves are gay,
Then in the joyous synod view
King-making balm thy brows bedew;
Our homage to Kauśalyá pay,
And hasten on our homeward way."
Their prayer the son of Raghu heard,
And spoke, his heart with rapture stirred:
"Sugríva, O my faithful friend,
Vibhishan and ye chiefs, ascend.
A joy beyond all joys the best
Will fill my overflowing breast,
If girt by you, O noble band,
I seek again my native land."
With Vánar lords in danger tried

Sugríva sprang to Ráma's side,
And girt by chiefs of giant kind
Vibhíshan's step was close behind.
Swift through the air, as Ráma chose,
The wondrous car from earth arose.
And decked with swans and silver wings
Bore through the clouds its freight of kings.

Canto CXXV
The Return

Then Ráma, speeding through the skies,
Bent on the earth his eager eyes:
"Look, Sítá, see, divinely planned
And built by Viśvakarmá's hand,
Lanká the lovely city rest
Enthroned on Mount Trikúṭa's crest
Behold those fields, ensanguined yet,
Where Vánar hosts and giants met.
There, vainly screened by charm and spell,
The robber Rávan fought and fell.
There knelt Mandodarí 1021 and shed
Her tears in floods for Rávan dead.
And every dame who loved him sent
From her sad heart her wild lament.
There gleams the margin of the deep,
Where, worn with toil, we sank to sleep.
Look, love, the unconquered sea behold,
King Varuṇ's home ordained of old,
Whose boundless waters roar and swell
Rich with their store of pearl and shell.
O see, the morning sun is bright
On fair Hiraṇyanábha's 1022 height,
Who rose from Ocean's sheltering breast
That Hanumán might stay and rest.
There stretches, famed for evermore,
The wondrous bridge from shore to shore.
The worlds, to life's remotest day,·

Due reverence to the work shall pay,
Which holier for the lapse of time
Shall give release from sin and crime.
Now thither bend, dear love, thine eyes
Where green with groves Kishkindhá lies,
The seat of King Sugríva's reign,
Where Báli by this hand was slain. 1023
There Ríshyamúka's hill behold
Bright gleaming with embedded gold.
There too my wandering foot I set,
There King Sugríva first I met.
And, where yon trees their branches wave,
My promise of assistance gave.
There, flushed with lilies, Pampá shines
With banks which greenest foliage lines,
Where melancholy steps I bent
And mourned thee with a mad lament.
There fierce Kabandha, spreading wide
His giant arms, in battle died.
Turn, Sítá, turn thine eyes and see
In Janasthán that glorious tree:
There Rávan, lord of giants slew
Our friend Jaṭáyus brave and true,
Thy champion in the hopeless strife,
Who gave for thee his noble life.
Now mark that glade amid the trees
Where once we lived as devotees.
See, see our leafy cot between
Those waving boughs of densest green,
Where Rávan seized his prize and stole
My love the darling of my soul.
O, look again: beneath thee gleams
Godávarí the best of streams,
Whose lucid waters sweetly glide

By lilies that adorn her side.
There dwelt Agastya, holy sage,
In plantain-sheltered hermitage.
See Śarabhanga's humble shed
Which sovereign Indra visited.
See where the gentle hermits dwell
Neath Atri's rule who loved us well;
Where once thine eyes were blest to see
His sainted dame who talked with thee.
Now rest thine eyes with new delight
On Chitrakúṭa's woody height,
See Jumna flashing in the sun
Through groves of brilliant foliage run.
Screened by the shade of spreading boughs.
There Bharadvája keeps his vows,
There Gangá, river of the skies,
Rolls the sweet wave that purifies,
There Śringavera's towers ascend
Where Guha reigns, mine ancient friend.
I see, I see thy glittering spires,
Ayodhyá, city of my sires.
Bow down, bow down thy head, my sweet,
Our home, our long-lost home to greet."

Canto CXXVI
Bharat Consoled

But Ráma bade the chariot stay,
And halting in his airy way,
In Bharadvája's holy shade
His homage to the hermit paid.
"O saint," he cried, "I yearn to know
My dear Ayodhyá's weal and woe.
O tell me that the people thrive,
And that the queens are yet alive."
Joy gleamed in Bhardvája's eye,
Who gently smiled and made reply:
"Thy brother, studious of thy will,
Is faithful and obedient still.
In tangled twine he coils his hair:
Thy safe return is all his care.
Before thy shoes he humbly bends,
And to thy house and realm attends.
When first these dreary years began,
When first I saw the banished man,
With Sítá, in his hermit coat,
At this sad heart compassion smote.
My breast with tender pity swelled:
I saw thee from thy home expelled,
Reft of all princely state, forlorn,
A hapless wanderer travel-worn,
Firm in thy purpose to fulfil
Thy duty and thy father's will.
But boundless is my rapture now:

Triumphant, girt with friends, art thou.
Where'er thy wandering steps have been,
Thy joy and woe mine eyes have seen.
Thy glorious deeds to me art known,
The Bráhmans saved, the foes o'erthrown.
Such power have countless seasons spent
In penance and devotion lent.
Thy virtues, best of chiefs, I know,
And now a boon would fain bestow.
This hospitable gift 1024 receive:
Then with the dawn my dwelling leave."
The bended head of Ráma showed
His reverence for the grace bestowed;
Then for each brave companion's sake
He sought a further boon and spake:
"O let that mighty power of thine
The road to fair Ayodhyá line
With trees where fruit of every hue
The Vánars' eye and taste may woo,
And flowers of every season, sweet
With stores of honeyed juice, may meet."
The hero ceased: the hermit bent
His reverend head in glad assent;
And swift, as Bharadvája willed,
The prayer of Ráma was fulfilled.
For many a league the lengthening road
Trees thick with fruit and blossom showed
With luscious beauty to entice
The taste like trees of Paradise.
The Vánars passed beneath the shade
Of that delightful colonnade,
Still tasting with unbounded glee
The treasures of each wondrous tree.

Canto CXXVII
Ráma's Message

But Ráma, when he first looked down
And saw afar Ayodhyá's town,
Had called Hanumán to his side,
The chief on whom his heart relied,
And said: "Brave Vánar, good at need,
Haste onward, to Ayodhyá speed,
And learn, I pray, if all be well
With those who in the palace dwell.
But as thou speedest on thy way
Awhile at Śringavera stay.
Tell Guha the Nishádas' lord,
That victor, with my queen restored,
In health and strength with many a friend
Homeward again my steps I bend.
Thence by the road that he will show
On to Ayodhyá swiftly go.
There with my love my brother greet,
And all our wondrous tale repeat.
Say that victorious in the strife
I come with Lakshman and my wife,
Then mark with keenest eye each trace
Of joy or grief on Bharat's face.
Be all his gestures closely viewed,
Each change of look and attitude.
Where breathes the man who will not cling
To all that glorifies a king?
Where beats the heart that can resign

An ancient kingdom, nor repine
To lose a land renowned for breeds
Of elephants and warrior steeds?
If, won by custom day by day,
My brother Bharat thirsts for sway,
Still let him rule the nations, still
The throne of old Ikshváku fill.
Go, mark him well: his feelings learn,
And, ere we yet be near return."
He ceased: and, garbed in human form,
Forth sped Hanúmán swift as storm.
Sublime in air he rose, and through
The region of his father flew.
He saw far far beneath his feet
Where Gangá's flood and Jumna meet.
Descending from the upper air
He entered Śringavera, where
King Guha's heart was well content
To hear the message Ráma sent.
Then, with his mighty strength renewed,
The Vánar chief his way pursued,
Válúkiní was far behind,
And Gomatí with forests lined,
And golden fields and pastures gay
With flocks and herds beneath him lay.
Then Nandigráma charmed his eye
Where flowers were bright with every dye,
And trees of lovely foliage made
With meeting boughs delightful shade,
Where women watched in trim array
Their little sons' and grandsons' play.
His eager eye on Bharat fell
Who sat before his lonely cell.
In hermit weed, with tangled hair,

Pale, weak, and worn with ceaseless care.
His royal pomp and state resigned
For Ráma still he watched and pined,
Still to his dreary vows adhered,
And royal Ráma's shoes revered.
Yet still the terror of his arm
Preserved the land from fear and harm.
The Wind-God's son, in form a man,
Raised reverent hands and thus began:
"Fond greeting, Prince, I bring to thee,
And Ráma's self has sent it: he
For whom thy spirit sorrows yet
As for a hapless anchoret
In Daṇḍak wood, in dire distress,
With matted hair and hermit dress.
This sorrow from thy bosom fling,
And hear the tale of joy I bring.
This day thy brother shalt thou meet
Exulting in his foe's defeat,
Freed from his toil and lengthened vow,
The light of victory on his brow,
With Sítá, Lakshmaṇ and his friends
Homeward at last his steps he bends."
Then joy, too mighty for control,
Rushed in full flood o'er Bharat's soul;
His reeling sense and strength gave way,
And fainting on the earth he lay,
At length upspringing from the ground,
His arms about Hanúmán wound,
With tender tears of rapture sprung,
He dewed the neck to which he clung:
"Art thou a God or man," he cried,
"Whom love and pity hither guide?
For this a hundred thousand kine,

A hundred villages be thine.
A score of maids of spotless lives
To thee I give to be thy wives,
Of golden hue and bright of face,
Each lovely for her tender grace."
He ceased a while by joy subdued,
And then his eager speech renewed.

Canto CXXVIII
Hanumán's Story

"In doubt and fear long years have passed
And glorious tidings come at last.
True, true is now the ancient verse
Which men in time of bliss rehearse:
"Once only in a hundred years
Great joy to mortal men appears."
But now his woes and triumph tell,
And loss and gain as each befell."
He ceased: Hanúmán mighty-souled
The tale of Ráma's wanderings told
From that first day on which he stood
In the drear shade of Daṇḍak wood.
He told how fierce Virádha fell;
He told of Śarabhanga's cell
Where Ráma saw with wondering eyes
Indra descended from the skies.
He told how Śúrpaṇakhí came,
Her soul aglow with amorous flame,
And fled repulsed, with rage and tears,
Reft of her nose and severed ears.
He told how Ráma's might subdued
The giants' furious multitude;
How Khara with the troops he led
And Triśirás and Dúshaṇ bled:
How Ráma, tempted from his cot,
The golden deer pursued and shot,
And Rávaṇ came and stole away

The Maithil queen his hapless prey,
When, as he fought, the dame to save,
His noble life Jatáyus gave:
How Ráma still the the search renewed,
The robber to his hold pursued,
Bridging the sea from shore to shore,
And found his queen to part no more. 1025

Canto CXXIX
The Meeting With Bharat

O'erwhelmed with rapture Bharat heard
The tale that all his being stirred,
And, heralding the glad event,
This order to Śatrughna sent:
"Let every shrine with flowers be gay
Let incense burn and music play.
Go forth, go forth to meet your king,
Let tabours sound and minstrels sing,
Let bards swell high the note of praise
Skilled in the lore of ancient days,
Call forth the royal matrons: call
Each noble from the council hall.
Send all we love and honour most,
Send Bráhmans and the warrior host,
A glorious company to bring
In triumph home our lord the king."
Great rapture filled Śatrughna's breast,
Obedient to his brother's hest.
"Send forth ten thousand men" he cried,
"Let brawny arms be stoutly plied,
And, smoothing all with skilful care,
The road for Kośal's king prepare.
Then o'er the earth let thousands throw
Fresh showers of water cool as snow,
And others strew with garlands gay
With loveliest blooms our monarch's way.
On tower and temple porch and gate

Let banners wave in royal state,
And be each roof and terrace lined
With blossoms loose and chaplets twined."
The nobles hasting forth fulfilled
His order as Śatrughna willed.
Sublime on elephants they rode
Whose gilded girths with jewels glowed.
Attended close by thousands more
Gay with the gear and flags they bore.
A thousand chiefs their steeds bestrode,
Their glittering cars a thousand showed.
And countless hosts in rich array
Pursued on foot their eager way.
Veiled from the air with silken screens
In litters rode the widowed queens.
Kausalyá first, acknowledged head
And sovereign of the household, led:
Sumitrá next, and after, dames
Of lower rank and humbler names.
Then compassed by a white-robed throng
Of Bráhmans, heralded with song,
With shouts of joy from countless throats,
And shells' and tambours' mingled notes,
And drums resounding long and loud,
Exulting Bharat joined the crowd.
Still on his head, well-trained in lore
Of duty, Ráma's shoes he bore.
The moon-white canopy was spread
With flowery twine engarlanded,
And jewelled cheuries, meet to hold
O'er Ráma's brow, shone bright with gold,
Though Nandigráma's town they neared,
Of Ráma yet no sign appeared.
Then Bharat called the Vánar chief

And questioned thus in doubt and grief:
"Hast thou uncertain, like thy kind,
A sweet delusive guile designed?
Where, where is royal Ráma? show
The hero, victor of the foe.
I gaze, but see no Vánars still
Who wear each varied shape at will."
In eager love thus Bharat cried,
And thus the Wind-God's son replied:
"Look, Bharat, on those laden trees
That murmur with the song of bees;
For Ráma's sake the saint has made
Untimely fruits, unwonted shade.
Such power in ages long ago
Could Indra's gracious boon bestow.
O, hear the Vánars' voices, hear
The shouting which proclaims them near.
E'en now about to cross they seem
Sweet Gomatí's delightful stream.
I see, I see the car designed
By Brahmá's own creative mind,
The car which, radiant as the moon,
Moves at the will by Brahmá's boon;
The car which once was Rávan's pride,
The victor's spoil when Rávan died.
Look, there are Raghu's sons: between
The brothers stands the rescued queen.
There is Vibhishaṇ full in view,
Sugríva and his retinue."
He ceased: then rapture loosed each tongue:
From men and dames, from old and young,
One long, one universal cry,
'Tis he, 'tis Ráma, smote the sky.
All lighted down with eager speed

From elephant and car and steed,
And every joyful eye intent
On Ráma's moonbright face was bent.
Entranced a moment Bharat gazed:
Then reverential hands he raised,
And on his brother humbly pressed
The honours due to welcome guest.
Then Bharat clomb the car to greet
His king and bowed him at his feet,
Till Ráma raised him face to face
And held him in a close embrace.
Then Lakshman and the Maithil dame
He greeted as he spoke his name 1026
He greeted next, supreme in place,
The sovereign of the Vánar race,
And Jámbaván and Báli's son,
And lords and chiefs, omitting none. 1027
Sugríva to his heart he pressed
And thus with grateful words addressed:
"Four brothers, Vánar king, were we,
And now we boast a fifth in thee.
By kindly acts a friend we know:
Offence and wrong proclaim the foe."
To King Vibhishan then he spake:
"Well hast thou fought for Ráma's sake."
Nor was the brave Śatrughna slow
His reverential love to show
To both his brothers, as was meet,
And venerate the lady's feet.
Then Ráma to his mother came,
Saw her pale cheek and wasted frame,
With gentle words her heart consoled,
And clasped her feet with loving hold.
Then at Sumitrá's feet he bent,

And fair Kaikeyí's, reverent,
Greeted each dame from chief to least,
And bowed him to the household priest.
Up rose a shout from all the throng:
"O welcome, Ráma, mourned so long.
Welcome, Kausalyá's joy and pride,"
Ten hundred thousand voices cried.
Then Bharat placed, in duty taught,
On Ráma's feet the shoes he brought:
"My King," he cried, "receive again
The pledge preserved through years of pain,
The rule and lordship of the land
Entrusted to my weaker hand.
No more I sigh o'er sorrows past,
My birth and life are blest at last
In the glad sight this day has shown,
When Ráma comes to rule his own."
He ceased: the faithful love that moved
The prince's soul each heart approved;
Nor could the Vánar chiefs refrain
From tender tears that fell like rain.
Then Ráma, stirred with joy anew,
His arms about his brother threw,
And to the grove his course he bent
Where Bharat's hermit days were spent.
Alighting in that pure retreat
He pressed the earth with eager feet.
Then, at his hest, the car rose high
And sailing through the northern sky
Sped homeward to the Lord of Gold
Who owned the wondrous prize of old. 1028

Canto CXXX
The Consecration

Then, reverent hand to hand applied,
Thus Bharat to his brother cried:
"Thy realm, O King, is now restored,
Uninjured to the rightful lord.
This feeble arm with toil and pain,
The weighty charge could scarce sustain.
And the great burthen wellnigh broke
The neck untrained to bear the yoke.
The royal swan outspeeds the crow:
The steed is swift, the mule is slow,
Nor can my feeble feet be led
O'er the rough ways where thine should tread.
Now grant what all thy subjects ask:
Begin, O King, thy royal task.
Now let our longing eyes behold
The glorious rite ordained of old,
And on the new-found monarch's head
Let consecrating drops be shed."
He ceased; victorious Ráma bent
His head in token of assent.
He sat, and tonsors trimmed with care
His tangles of neglected hair
Then, duly bathed, the hero shone
With all his splendid raiment on.
And Sítá with the matrons' aid
Her limbs in shining robes arrayed,
Sumantra then, the charioteer,

Drew, ordered by Śatrughna near,
And stayed within the hermit grove
The chariot and the steeds he drove.
Therein Sugríva's consorts, graced
With gems, and Ráma's queen were placed,
All fain Ayodhyá to behold:
And swift away the chariot rolled.
Like Indra Lord of Thousand Eyes,
Drawn by fleet lions through the skies.
Thus radiant in his glory showed
King Ráma as he homeward rode,
In power and might unparalleled.
The reins the hand of Bharat held.
Above the peerless victor's head
The snow-white shade Śatrughna spread,
And Lakshmaṇ's ever-ready hand
His forehead with a chourie fanned.
Vibhishaṇ close to Lakshmaṇ's side
Sharing his task a chourie plied.
Sugríva on Śatrunjay came,
An elephant of hugest frame:
Nine thousand others bore, behind,
The chieftains of the Vánar kind
All gay, in forms of human mould,
With rich attire and gems and gold.
Thus borne along in royal state
King Ráma reached Ayodbyá's gate
With merry noise of shells and drums
And joyful shouts, He comes, he comes,
A Bráhman host with solemn tread,
And kine the long procession led,
And happy maids in ordered bands
Threw grain and gold with liberal hands.
Neath gorgeous flags that waved in rows

On towers and roofs and porticoes.
Mid merry crowds who sang and cheered
The palace of the king they neared.
Then Raghu's son to Bharat, best
Of duty's slaves, these words addressed:
"Pass onward to the monarch's hall.
The high-souled Vánars with thee call,
And let the chieftains, as is meet,
The widows of our father greet.
And to the Vánar king assign
Those chambers, best of all, which shine
With lazulite and pearl inlaid,
And pleasant grounds with flowers and shade."
He ceased: and Bharat bent his head;
Sugríva by the hand he led
And passed within the palace where
Stood couches which Śatrughna's care,
With robes and hangings richly dyed,
And burning lamps, had seen supplied.
Then Bharat spake: "I pray thee, friend,
Thy speedy messengers to send,
Each sacred requisite to bring
That we may consecrate our king."
Sugríva raised four urns of gold,
The water for the rite to hold,
And bade four swiftest Vánars flee
And fill them from each distant sea.
Then east and west and south and north
The Vánar envoys hastened forth.
Each in swift flight an ocean sought
And back through air his treasure brought,
And full five hundred floods beside
Pure water for the king supplied.
Then girt by many a Bráhman sage,

Vaśishṭha, chief for reverend age,
High on a throne with jewels graced
King Ráma and his Sítá placed.
There by Jábáli, far revered,
Vijay and Kaśyap's son appeared;
By Gautam's side Kátváyan stood,
And Vámadeva wise and good,
Whose holy hands in order shed
The pure sweet drops on Ráma's head.
Then priests and maids and warriors, all
Approaching at Vaśishṭha's call,
With sacred drops bedewed their king,
The centre of a joyous ring,
The guardians of the worlds, on high,
And all the children of the sky
From herbs wherewith their hands were filled
Rare juices on his brow distilled.
His brows were bound with glistering gold
Which Manu's self had worn of old,
Bright with the flash of many a gem
His sire's ancestral diadem.
Śatrughna lent his willing aid
And o'er him held the regal shade:
The monarchs whom his arm had saved
The chouries round his forehead waved.
A golden chain, that flashed and glowed
With gems the God of Wind bestowed:
Mahendra gave a glorious string
Of fairest pearls to deck the king,
The skies with acclamation rang,
The gay nymphs danced, the minstrels sang.
On that blest day the joyful plain
Was clothed anew with golden grain.
The trees the witching influence knew,

And bent with fruits of loveliest hue,
And Ráma's consecration lent
New sweetness to each flowret's scent.
The monarch, joy of Raghu's line,
Gave largess to the Bráhmans, kine
And steeds unnumbered, wealth untold
Of robes and pearls and gems and gold.
A jewelled chain, whose lustre passed
The glory of the sun, he cast
About his friend Sugríva's neck;
And, Angad Báli's son to deck,
He gave a pair of armlets bright
With diamond and lazulite.
A string of pearls of matchless hue
Which gleams like tender moonlight threw
Adorned with gems of brightest sheen,
He gave to grace his darling queen.
The offering from his hand received
A moment on her bosom heaved;
Then from her neck the chain she drew,
A glance on all the Vánars threw,
And wistful eyes on Ráma bent
As still she held the ornament.
Her wish he knew, and made reply
To that mute question of her eye:
"Yea, love; the chain on him bestow
Whose wisdom truth and might we know,
The firm ally, the faithful friend
Through toil and peril to the end."
Then on Hanúmán's bosom hung
The chain which Sítá's hand had flung:
So may a cloud, when winds are still
With moon-lit silver gird a hill.
To every Vánar Ráma gave

Rich treasures from the mine and wave.
And with their honours well content
Homeward their steps the chieftains bent.
Ten thousand years Ayodhyá, blest
With Ráma's rule, had peace and rest,
No widow mourned her murdered mate,
No house was ever desolate.
The happy land no murrain knew,
The flocks and herds increased and grew.
The earth her kindly fruits supplied,
No harvest failed, no children died.
Unknown were want, disease, and crime:
So calm, so happy was the time. 1029

APPENDIX

Section XIII. Rávan Doomed.

Afterwards Rishyaśring said again to the King "I will perform another sacrificial act to secure thee a son." Then the son of Vibhándak, of subdued passions, seeking the happiness of the king, proceeded to perform the sacrifice for the accomplishment of his wishes. Hither were previously collected the gods, with the Gandharvas, the Siddhas and the sages, for the sake of receiving their respective shares, Brahmá too, the sovereign of the gods, with Sthánu, and Náráyana, chief of beings and the four supporters of the universe, and the divine mothers of all the celestials, met together there. To the Aśvamedha, the great sacrifice of the magnanimous monarch, came also Indra the glorious one, surrounded by the Maruts. Rishyaśring then supplicated the gods assembled for their share of the sacrifice (saying), "This devout king Daśaratha, who, through the desire of offspring, confiding in you, has performed sacred austerities, and who has offered to you the sacrifice called Aśvamedha, is about to perform another sacrifice for the sake of obtaining sons: To him thus desirous of offspring be pleased to grant the blessing: I supplicate you all with joined hands. May he have four sons, renowned through the universe." The gods replied to the sage's son supplicating with joined hands, "Be it so: thou, O Bráhman, art ever to be regarded by us, as the king is in a peculiar manner. The lord of men by this sacrifice shall obtain the great object of his desires." Having thus said, the gods preceded by Indra, disappeared.

They all then having seen that (sacrifice) performed by the great sage according to the ordinance went to Prajápati the lord of mankind, and with joined hands addressed Brahmá the giver of blessings, "O Brahmá, the Ráksha Rávana by name, to whom a blessing was awarded by thee, through pride troubleth all of us the gods, and even the great sages, who perpetually practise sacred austerities. We, O glorious one, regarding the promise formerly granted by thy kindness that he should be invulnerable to the gods, the Dánavas and the Yakshas have born (sic) all, (his oppression); this lord of Rákshas therefore distresses the universe; and, inflated by this promise unjustly vexes the divine sages, the Yakshas, and Gandharvas, the Asuras, and men: where Rávana remains there the sun loses his force, the winds through fear of him do not blow; the fire ceases to burn; the rolling ocean, seeing him, ceases to move its waves. Viśravas, distressed by his power, has abandoned Lanká and fled. O divine one save us from Rávana, who fills the world with noise and tumult. O giver of desired things, be pleased to contrive a way for his destruction."

Brahmá thus informed by the devas, reflecting, replied, "Oh! I have devised the method for slaying this outrageous tyrant. Upon his requesting, 'May I be invulnerable to the divine sages, the Gaundharvas, the Yakshas, the Rákshasas and the serpents,' I replied 'Be it so.' This Ráksha, through contempt, said nothing respecting man; therefore this wicked one shall be destroyed by man." The gods, preceded by Śakra, hearing these words spoken by Brahmá, were filled with joy.

At this time Vishnu the glorious, the lord of the world, arrayed in yellow, with hand ornaments of glowing gold, riding on Vinateya, as the sun on a cloud, arrived with his conch, his discus, and his club in his hand. Being adored by the excellent celestials, and welcomed by Brahmá, he drew near and stood before him. All the gods then addressed Vishnu, "O Madhusudana, thou art able to abolish the distress of the distressed. We intreat thee, be our sanctuary, O Vishnu." Vishnu replied, "Say, what shall I do?" The celestials hearing these his words added further. "The virtuous, the encourager of excellence, eminent for truth, the firm observer of his vows, being childless, is performing an Aśvamedha for the purpose of obtaining offspring. For the sake of the good of the universe, we intreat thee, O Vishnu, to become his son. Dividing thyself into four parts, in the wombs of his three consorts equal to Hari, Śrí, and Kirti, assume the sonship of king Daśaratha, the lord of Ayodhyá, eminent in the knowledge of duty, generous and illustrious, as the great sages. Thus becoming man, O Vishnu, conquer in battle Rávana, the terror of the universe, who is invulnerable to the gods. This ignorant Rákshasa Rávana, by the exertion of his power, afflicts the gods, the Gandharvaa, the Siddhas, and the most excellent sages; these sages, the Gandharvas, and the Apsaras, sporting in the forest Nandana have been destroyed by that furious one. We, with the sages, are come to thee seeking his destruction. The Siddhas, the Gandharvas, and the Yakshas betake themselves to thee, thou art our only refuge; O Deva, afflicter of enemies, regard the world of men, and destroy the enemy of the gods."

Vishnu, the sovereign of the gods, the chief of the celestials, adored by all beings, being thus supplicated, replied to all the assembled gods (standing) before Brahmá, "Abandon fear; peace be with you; for your benefit having killed Rávana the cruel, destructively active, the cause of fear to the divine sages, together with all his posterity, his courtiers and counsellors, and his relations, and friends, protecting the earth, I will remain incarnate among men for the space of eleven thousand years."

Having given this promise to the gods, the divine Vishṇu, ardent in the work, sought a birth-place among men. Dividing himself into four parts, he whose eyes resemble the lotus and the pulasa, the lotus petal-eyed, chose for his father Daśaratha the sovereign of men. The divine sages then with the Gandharvas, the Rudras, and the (different sorts of) Apsaras, in the most excellent strains, praised the destroyer of Madhu, (saying) "Root up Rávaṇa, of fervid energy, the devastator, the enemy of Indra swollen with pride. Destroy him, who causes universal lamentation, the annoyer of the holy ascetics, terrible, the terror of the devout Tapaswis. Having destroyed Rávaṇa, tremendously powerful, who causes universal weeping, together with his army and friends, dismissing all sorrow, return to heaven, the place free from stain and sin, and protected by the sovereign of the celestial powers."

Thus far the Section, containing the plan for the death of Rávaṇ.

Carey and Marshman.

Caput XIV. RATIO NECANDI RAVANAE EXCOGITATA.

Prudens ille, voluminum sacrorum gnarus, responsum quod dederat aliquamdiu meditatus, mente ad se revocata regem deuno est effatus: Parabo tibi aliud sacrum, genitale, prolis masculae adipiscendae gratia, cum carminibus in Atharvanis exordio expressis rite peragendum. Tum coepit modestus Vibhândaci filius, regis commodis intentus, parare sacrum, quo eius desiderium expleret. Iam'antea eo convenerant, ut suam quisque portionem acciperent, Dî cum fidicinum coelestium choris, Beatique cum Sapientibus; Brachman Superûm regnator, Sthânus nec non augustus Nârâyanus, Indrasque almus, coram visendus Ventorum cohorte circumdatus, in magno isto sacrificio equino regis magnanimi. Ibidem vates ille deos, qui portiones suas accipiendi gratia advenerant, apprecatus, En inquit, hicce ex Dasarathus filiorum desiderio castimoniis adstrictus, fidei plenus, vestrum numen adoravit sacrificio equino. Nunc iterum accingit se ad aliud sacrum peragendum: quamobrem aequum est, ut filios cupienti vos faveatis. Ille ego, qui manus supplices tendo, vos universos pro eo apprecor: nascantur ei filii quatuor, faina per triplicem mundum clari. Divi supplicem vatis filium invicem affari: Fiat quod petis! Tu nobis, virsancte, imprimis es venerandus, nee minus rex ille; compos fiet voti sui egregii hominum princeps. Ita locuti Dî Indra duce, ex oculis evanuerunt.

Superi vero, legitime in concilio congregati. Brachmanem mundi creatorem his verbis compellarunt: Tuo munere auctus, O Brachman! gigas nomine Râvanas, prae superbia nos omnes vexat, pariterque Sapientes castimoniis gaudentes. A te propitio olim ex voto ei hoc munus concessum fuit, ut ne a diis, Danuidis, Geniisve necari posset. Nos, oraculum tuum reveriti, facinora eius qualiacunque toleramus. At ille gigantum tyrannus ternos mundos gravibus iniuriis vexat Deos, Sapientes, Genios, Fidicines coelestes, Titanes, mortales denique, exsuperat ille aegre cohibendus, tuoque munere demens. Non ibi calet sol, neque Ventus prae timore spirat, nee flagrat ignis, ubi Râvanas versatur. Ipse oceanus, vagis fluctibus redimitus, isto viso stat immotus; eiectus fuit e sede sua Cuvêrus, huius robore vexatus. Ergo ingens nobis periculum imminet ab hoc gigante visu horribili; tuum est, alme Parens! auxilium parare, quo hic deleatur. Ita admonitus ille a diis universis, paulisper meditatus, Ehem! inquit, hancce inveni rationem nefarium istum necandi. Petierat is a me, ut a Gandharvis, a Geniis, a Divis, Danuibus Gigantibusque necari non posset et me annuente voto suo potitus est. Prae contemptu vero monstrum illud homines non commemoravit: ideo ab homine est necandus: nullum aliud exstat leti genus, quod ei sit fatale. Postquam audiverant gratum hunc sermonem Brachmanis ore prolatum, Dî cum duce suo Indra summopere gaudio erecti sunt. Eodem temporis momento Vishnus, istuc accessit, splendore insignis, concham, discum et clavum manibus gestans, croceo vestitu, mundi dominus, vulturis Vinateii dorso, sicuti sol nimbo, vectus, armillas ex auro candente gerens, salutatus a Superûm primoribus. Quem laudibus celebratum reverenter Dî universi compellarunt. Tu animantium afflictorum es vindex, Madhûs interfector! quamobrem nos afflicti te apprecamur. Sis praesidio nobis numine tuo inconcusso. Dicite, inquit Vishnus, quid pro vobis facere me oporteat. Audito eius sermone, Dî hunc in modum respondent: Rex quidam, nomine Dasarathus, austeris castimoniis sese castigavit, litavit sacrificio equino, prolis cupidus et prole carens. Nostro hortatu tu, Vishnus, conditionem natorum eius subeas: ex tribus eius uxoribus, Pudicitiae, Venustatis et Famae similibus, nasci, velis, temetipsum quadrifariam dividens. Ibi tu in humanam naturam conversus Râvanam, gravissimam mundi pestem, diis insuperabilem, O Vishnus! proelio caede. Gigas ille vecors Râvanas Deos cum Fidicinum choris, Beatos et Sapientes praestantissimos vexat, audacia superbiens. Etenim ab hoc furioso Sapientes Fidicines et nymphae, ludentes in Nandano viridario, sunt proculcati. Tu es nostrum omnium summa salus, divine bellator! Ut deoram hostes extinguas, ad sortem humanam animum converte. Augustus ille Nârâyanus, diis hunc in modum coram hortantibus, eosdem apto hoc sermone compellavit: Quare, quaeso, hac in re negotium vestrum a me potissimum, corporea specie palam facto, est peragendum aut unde tantus vobis terror fuit iniectus? His verbis a Vishnû interrogati Dî talia proferre: Terror nobis instat, O Vishnus! a Râvana mundi direptore; a quo nos vindicare, corpore humano assumpto, tuum est. Nemo alius coelicoiarum praeter te hunc scelestum enecare potis est. Nimirum ille,

O hostium domitor! per diuturnum tempus sese excruciaverat severissima abstinentia, qua magnus hicce rerum Parens propitius ipsi redditus est. Itaque almus votorum sponsor olim ei concessit securitatem ab ommibus animantibus, hominibus tamen exceptis. Hinc ilium, voti compotem, non aliunde quam ab homine necis periculum urget: tu ergo, humanitate assumpta eum intertice. Sic monitus Vishnus, Superûm princeps, quem mundus universus adorat, magnum Parentem oeterosque deos, in concilio congregatos, recti auctores, affatur: Mittite timorem; bene bobis eveniat! Vestrae salutis gratia, postquam praelio necavero Râvanam cum filiis nepotibusque, cum amicis, ministris, cognatis sociisque, crudelem istum aegre cohibendum, qui divinis Sapientibus terrorem meutit, per decem millia annorum decies centenis additis, commorabor in mortalium sedibus, orbem terrarum imperio regens. Tum divini sapientes et Fidicines conjuncti cum Rudris nympharumque choris celebravere Madhûs interfectorem hymnis, quales sedem aetheriam decent.

"Râvanam ilium insolentem, acri impetu actum, superbia elatum, Superûm hostem, tumultus cientem, bonorum piorumque pestem, humanitate assumpta pessamdare tuum est."

Schlegel.

Caput XIV. IL MEZZO STABILITO PER UCCIDERE RÁVANO.

Ma Riseyasringo soggiunse poscia al re: Tappresterò io un altro rito santissimo, genitale, onde tu conseguisca la prole che tu bramí. E in quel punto stesso il saggio figliuolo di Vibhândaco, intento alla prosperità del re, pose mano al sacro rito per condurre ad effetto il suo desiderio. Già erano prima, per ricevere ciascuno la sua parte, qui convenuti al gran sacrifizio del re magnanimo l'Asvamedha, i Devi coi Gandharvi, i Siddhi e i Muni, Brahma Signor dei Sari, Sthânu e l' Augusto Nârâyana, i quattio custodi dell' universo e le Madri degli Iddu, i Yacsi insieme cogli Dei, e il sovrano, venerando Indra, visibile, circondato dalla schiera dei Maruti. Quivi così parlò Riscyasringo agli Dei venuti a partecipare del sacrifizio: Questo è il re Dasaratha, che per desiderio di progenie già s' astrinse ad osservanze austeré, e testè pieno di fede ha a voi, O eccelsi, sacrificato con un Asvamedha. Ora egli, sollecito d' aver figli, si dispone ad adempiere un nuovo rito; vogliate essere favorevole a lui che sospira progenie. Io alzo a voi supplici le mani, e voi tutti per lui imploro: nascano a lui quattro figli degni d'essere celebrati pei tre mondi. Risposero gli Dei al supplichevole figliuolo del Risci: Sia fatto ciò che chiedi; a te ed al re parimente si debbe da noi, O Brahmano, sommo pregio; canseguirà il re per questo sacro rito il suo suppremo desiderio. Ciò detto disparvero i Numi preceduti da Indra.

Poichè videro gli Dei compiersi debitamente dal gran Risci l'oblazione, venuti al cospetto di Brahma facitor del mondo, signor delle creature, così parlarono reverenti a lui dator di grazie: O Brahma, un Racsaso per nome Râvano, cui tu fosti largo del tuo favore, è per superbia infesto a noi tutti e ai grandi Saggi penitenti. Un di, O Nume, augusto, tu propizio a lui gli accordasti il favore, ch' egli bramava, di non poter essere ucciso dagli Dei, dai Dânavi nè dai Yacsi: noi venerando i tuoi oracoli, ogni cosa sopportiamo da costui. Quindi il signor dei Racsasi infesta con perpetue offese i tre mondi, i Devi, i Risci, i Yacsi ed i Gandharvi, gli Asuri e gli uomini: tutti egli opprime indegnamente inorgoglito pel tuo dono. Colà dove si trova Râvano, più non isfavilla per timore il sole, più non spira il vento, più non fiammeggia il fuoco: l' oceano stesso cui fan corona i vasti flutti, veggendo costui, tutto si turba e si commuove. Stretto dalla forza di costui e ridotto allo stremo dovette Vaisravano abbandonare Lancâ. Da questo Râvano, terror del mondo, tu ne proteggi, O almo Nume: degna, O dator d'ogni bene, trovar modo ad estirpar costui. Fatto di queste cose conscio dai Devi, stette alquanto meditando, poi rispose Brahma: Orsù! è stabilito il modo onde distruggere questo iniquo. Egli a me chiese, ed io gliel concessi, di non poter essere ucciso dai Devi, dai Risci, dai Gandharvi, dai Yacsi, dai Racsasi nè dai Serpenti; ma per disprezzo non fece menzione degli uomini quel Racso: or bene, sarà quell' empio ucciso da un uomo. Udite le fauste parole profferte da Brahma, furono per ogni parte liete gli Iddii col loro duce Indra. In questo mezzo quì sopravvenne raggiante d'immensa luce il venerando Visnu, pensato da Brahma nell' immortal sua mente, siccome atto ad estirpar colui; Allora Brahma colla schiera de' Celesti così parlò a Visnu: Tu sei il conforto delle gente oppresse, O distruttor di Madhu: noi quindi a te supplichiamo afflitti: sia tu nostro sostegno, O Aciuto. Dite, loro rispose Visnu, quale cosa io debba far per voi; e gli Dei, udite queste parole, cosi soggiunsero: Un re per nome Dasaratha, giusto, virtuoso, veridico e pio, non ha progenie e la desidera: ei già s' impose durissime penitenze, ed ora ha sacrificato con un Asvamedha: tu, per nostro consiglio, O Visnu, consenti a divenir suo figlio: fatte di te quattro parti, ti manifesta, O invocato dalle genti, nel seno delle quattro sue consorti, simili alla venusta Dea. Così esortato dagli Dei quivi presenti, l'augusto Nârâyana loro rispose queste opportune parole: Quale opra s'ha da me, fatto visibile nel mondo, a compiere per voi, O Devi? e d'onde in voi cotal terrore? Intese le parole di Visnu, così risposero gli Dei: Il nostro terrore. O Visnu, nasce da un Racsaso per nome Râvano, spavento dell' universo. Vestendo umano corpo, tu debbi esterminar costui. Nessuno fra i Celesti, fuorchè tu solo, è valevole ad uccidere quell' iniquo. Egli, O domator de' tuoi nemici, sostenne per lungo tempo acerbissime macerazioni: per esse fu di lui contento l'augusto sommo Genitore: e un di gli accordò propizio la sicurezza da tutti gli esseri, eccettutine gli uomini. Per questo favore a lui concesso nou ha egli a temere offesa da alcuna parte, fuorchè dall' uomo, perciò, assumendo la natura umana, costui tu uccidi. Egli, il peggior di tutti i Racsasi, insano per la forza che gli infonde il dono avuto, da travaglio ai Devi ed ai Gaudharvi, ai Risci, ai Muni ed ai mortali. Egli, sicuro da morte pel favore ottenuto, è turbatore dei sacrifizj, nemico ed uccisor dei Brahmi, divoratore degli uomini, peste del mondo. Da lui furono assaliti re coi loro carri ed elefanti; altri percessi e fugati si dispersero per ogni dove. Da lui furono divorati Risci ed Apsarase: egli insomma oltracotato continuamente e quasi per ischerzo tutti travaglia i sette mondi. Perciò, O terribile ai nemici è stabilita la morte di costui per opra d'un uomo; poich' un di per superbia del dono tutti sprezzò gli uomini. Tu, O supremo fra i Numi, dei, umanandoti, estirpare questo tremendo, superbo Ràvano, oltracotato, a noi nemico, terrore e flagello dei penitenti.

Gorresio.

XIV.

De nouveau Rishyaçringa tint ce langage au Monarque: "Je vais célébrer un autre sacrifice, afin que le ciel accorde à tes vœux les enfants que tu souhaites." Cela dit, cherchant le bonheur du roi et pour l'accomplissement de son désir, le fils puissant de Vibhándaka se mit à célébrer ce nouveau sacrifice.

Là auparavant, étaient venus déjà recevoir une part de l' offrande les Dieux, accompagnés des Gaudharvas, et les Siddhas avec les Mounis divins, Brahma, le monarque des Souras, l' immuable Śiva, et l' auguste Náráyana, et les quatre gardiens vigilants du monde, et les mères des Immortels, et tous les Dieux, escortés des Yakshas, et le maître éminent du ciel, Indra, qui se manifestait aux yeux, environné par l' essaim des Maroutes. Alors ce jeune anachorète avait supplié tous les Dieux, que le désir d'une part dans l' offrande avait conduits á l' açwamédha, cette grande cérémonie de ce roi magnanime; *et, dans ce moment, l' époux de Śántá les conjurait ainsi pour la seconde fois:* "Cet homme *en prières,* c'est le roi Daçaratha, qui est privé de fils. Il est rempli d' une foi vive; il s'est infligé de pénibles austérités; il vous a déjà servi, divinités augustes, le sacrifice d'un açwa-médha, et maintenant il s'étudie encore à vous plaire avec ce nouveau sacrifice dans l'espérance que vous lui donnerez les fils, où tendent ses désirs. Versez donc sur lui votre bienveillance et daignez sourire à son vœu pour des fils. C'est pour lui que moi ici, les mains jointes, je vous adresse à tous mes supplications: envoyez-lui quatre fils, qui soient vantés dans les trois mondes!"

"Ouí! répondirent les Dieux au fils suppliant du rishi; tu mérites que nous t'écoutions avec faveur, toi, brahme saint, et même, en premier lieu, ce roi. Comme récompense de ces différents sacrifices, le monarque obtendra cet objet le plus cher de ses désirs."

Ayant aussi parlé et vu que le grand saint avait mis fin suivant les rites à son *pieux* sacrifice, les Dieux, Indra à leur tête, s'évanouissent dans le vide des airs et se rendent vers l' architecte des mondes, le souverain des créatures, le donateur des biens, vers Brahma enfin, auquel tous, les mains jointes, ils adressent les paroles suivantes: "O Brahma, un rakshasa, nommé Râvana, tourne su mal les grâces, qu'il a reçues de toi. Dans son orgueil, il nous opprime tous; il opprime avec nous les grands anchorètes, qui se font un bonheur des macérations: car jadis, ayant su te plaire, O Bhagavat, il a reçu de toi ce don incomparable. 'Oui, as-tu dit, exauçant le vœu du mauvais Génie; Dieu. Yaksha ou Démon ne pourra jamais causer ta mort!' Et nous, par qui ta parole est respectée, nous avons tout supporté de ce roi des rakshasas, qui écrase de sa tyrannie les trois mondes, ou il promène l' injure impunément. Enorgueilli de ce don victorieux, il opprime indignement les Dieux, les rishis, les Yakshas, les Gandharvas, les Asouras et les enfants de Manou. Là ou se tient Râvana, la peur empêche le soleil d'échauffer, le vent craint de souffler, et le feu n'ose flamboyer. A son aspect, la guirlande même des grands flots tremble au sein de la mer. Accablé par sa vigueur indomptable, Kouvéra défait lui a cédé Lanká. Suave-nous donc, ô toi, qui reposes daus le bonheur absolu; sauve-nous de Râvana, le fléau des mondes. Daigne, ô toi, qui souris aux vœux du suppliant, daigne imaginer un expedient pour ôter la vie à ce cruel Démon." Les Dieux ayant ainsi dénoncé leurs maux à Brahma, il réfléchit un instant et leur tint ce langage: "Bien, voici que j'ai découvert un moyen pour tuer ce Génie scélérat. Que ni les Dieux, a-t-il dit, ni les rishis, ni les Gandharvas ni les Yakshas, ni les rakshasas, ni les Nágas même ne puissent me donner la mort! Soit lui ai-je répondu. Mais, par dédain pour la force humaine, les hommes n'ont pas été compris daus sa demande. C'est donc par la main d' un homme, qu'il faut immoler ce méchant." Ainsi tombée de la bouche du créateur, cette parole salutaire satisfit pleinement le roi des habitants du ciel et tous les Dieux avec lui. Lá, dans ce même instant, survint le fortuné Visnou, revêtu d' une splendeur infinie; car c'était a lui, que Brahma avait pensé dans son âme pour la mort du tyran. Celui-ci donc avec l'essaim des Immortels adresse à Vishnou ces paroles: "Meurtrier de Madhou, comme tu aimes á tirer de l'affliction les êtres malheureux, nous te supplions, nous qui sommes plongés dans la tristesse, Divinité auguste, sois notre asyle!" "Dites! reprit Vishnou; que dois-je faire?" "Ayant oui les paroles de l'ineffable, tous les Dieux repondirent: Il est un roi nommé Daçaratha; il a embrassé une très-duré pénitence; il a célébré même le sacrifice d'un açwa-medha, parce qu'il n'a point de fils et qu'il veut en obtenir du ciel. Il est inébranlable dars sa piété, il est vanté pour ses vertus; la justice est son caractère, la verite est sa parole. Acquiesce donc à notre demande, ô toi, Vishnou, et consens à naître comme son fils. Divisé en quatre portions de toi-même, daigne, ô toi, qui foules aux pieds tes ennemis, daigne t' incarner dans le sein de ses trois épouses, belles comme la déesse de la beauté." Nárâyana, le maître, *non perceptible aux sens, mais qui alors s' était rendu* visible, Nárâyana répondit cette parole salutaire aux Dieux, qui i invitaient à cet *heroique avatâra*. Quelle chose, une fois revêtu de cette incarnation, faudra-t-il encore que je fasse pour vous, et de quelle part vient la terreur, qui vous trouble ainsi? A ces mots du grand Vishnou: "C'est le démon Rávana, reprirent les Dieux; c'est lui, Vishnou, cette désolation des mondes, qui nous inspire un tel effroi. Enveloppe-toi d'un corps, humain, et qu'il te plaise arrâcher du monde cette blessante epine; car nul autre que toi parmi les habitants du ciel n'est capable d'immoler ce pécheur. *Sache que* longtemps il s'est imposé la plus austére pénitence, et *que* par elle il s'est rendu agreable au suprême ayeul de toutes les créatures. Aussi le distributeur ineffable des gràces lui a-t-il accordé ce don insigne d'être invulnérable à tous les êtres, l' homme seul excepté. Puisque, doué ainsi de cette faveur, la mort terrible et sûre ne peut venir à lui de nulle autre part que de l'homme, va, dompteur *puissant* de tes ennemis, va dans la condition humaine, et tue-le. Car ce don, auquel on ne peut résister, élevant au plus haut point l'ivresse de sa force, le vil rakshasa tourmente les Dieux, les rishis, les Gandharvas, les hommes sanctifiés par la pénitence; et, quoique, destructeur des sacrifices, lacérateur des Saintes Ecritures, ennemi des brahmes, dévorateur des hommes, cette faveur incomparable sauve de la mort Rávana le triste fléau des mondes. Il ose attaquer les rois, que défendant les chars de guerre, que remparent les éléphants: d'autres blessés et mis en fuite, sont dissipés ça et là devant lui. Il a dévoré des saints, il a dévoré même une foule d'apsaras. Sans cesse, dans son délire, il s'amuse à tourmenter les sept mondes. Comme *on vient de nous apprendre qu'* il n'a point daigné parler d'eux ce jour, que lui fut donnée cette faveur, *dont il abuse*, entre dans un corps humain, ô toi, qui peux briser tes ennemis, et jette sans vie à tes pieds, roi puissant des treize Dieux, ce Rávana superbe, d'une force épouvantable, d'un orgueil immense, l'ennemi de tous les ascètes, ce ver, *qui les ronge*, cette cause de leurs gémissements."

Ici, dans le premier tome du saint Râmâyana, Finit le quatorzième chapitre, nommé: Un Expédient pour tuer Rávana.

Hippolyte Fauche.

Uttarakánda.

The Rámáyan ends, epically complete, with the triumphant return of Ráma and his rescued queen to Ayodhyá and his consecration and coronation in the capital of his forefathers. Even if the story were not complete, the conclusion of the last Canto of the sixth Book, evidently the work of a later hand than Válmíki's, which speaks of Ráma's glorious and happy reign and promises blessings to those who read and hear the Rámáyan, would be sufficient to show that, when these verses were added, the poem was considered to be finished. The Uttarakáṇḍa or Last Book is merely an appendix or a supplement and relates only events antecedent and subsequent to those described in the original poem. Indian scholars however, led by reverential love of tradition, unanimously ascribe this Last Book to Válmíki, and regard it as part of the Rámáyan.

Signor Gorresio has published an excellent translation of the Uttarakáṇḍa, in Italian prose, from the recension current in Bengal; 1030 and Mr. Muir has epitomized a portion of the book in the Appendix to the Fourth Part of his Sanskrit Texts (1862). From these scholars I borrow freely in the following pages, and give them my hearty thanks for saving me much wearisome labour.

"After Ráma had returned to Ayodhyá and taken possession of the throne, the rishis [saints] assembled to greet him, and Agastya, in answer to his questions recounted many particulars regarding his old enemies. In the Krita Yuga (or Golden Age) the austere and pious Brahman rishi Pulastya, a son of Brahmá, being teased with the visits of different damsels, proclaimed that any one of them whom he again saw near his hermitage should become pregnant. This had not been heard by the daughter of the royal rishi Triṇavindu, who one day came into Pulastya's neighbourhood, and her pregnancy was the result (Sect. 2, vv. 14 ff.). After her return home, her father, seeing her condition, took her to Pulastya, who accepted her as his wife, and she bore a son who received the name of Viśravas. This son was, like his father, an austere and religious sage. He married the daughter of the muni Bharadvája, who bore him a son to whom Brahmá gave the name of Vaiśravaṇ-Kuvera (Sect. 3, vv. 1 ff.). He performed austerities for thousands of years, when he obtained from Brahmá as a boon that he should be one of the guardians of the world (along with Indra, Varuṇa, and Yáma) and the god of riches. He afterwards consulted his father Viśravas about an abode, and at his suggestion took possession of the city of Lanká, which had formerly been built by Viśvakarmán for the Rákshasas, but had been abandoned by them through fear of Vishṇu, and was at that time unoccupied. Ráma then (Sect. 4) says he is surprised to hear that Lanká had formerly belonged to the Rákshasas, as he had always understood that they were the descendants of Pulastya, and now he learns that they had also another origin. He therefore asks who was their ancestor, and what fault they had committed that they were chased away by Vishṇu. Agastya replies that when Brahmá created the waters, he formed certain beings,—some of whom received the name of Rákshasas,—to guard them. The first Rákshasas kings were Heti and Praheti. Heti married a sister of Kála (Time). She bore him a son Vidyutkeśa, who in his turn took for his wife Lankatanka[t.]á, the daughter of Sandhyá (V. 21). She bore him a son Sukeśa, whom she abandoned, but he was seen by Śiva as he was passing by with his wife Párvatí, who made the child as old as his mother, and immortal, and gave him a celestial city. Sukeśa married a Gandharví called Devavatí who bore three sons, Mályavat, Sumáli and Máli. These sons practised intense austerities, when Brahmá appeared and conferred on them invincibility and long life. They then harassed the gods. Viśvakarmá gave them a city, Lanká, on the mountain Trikúṭa, on the shore of the southern ocean, which he had built at the command of Indra…. The three Rákshasa, Mályavat and his two brothers, then began to oppress the gods, rishis, etc.; who (Sect. 6, v. 1 ff.) in consequence resort for aid to Mahádeva, who having regard to his protégé Sukeśa the father of Mályavat, says that he cannot kill the Rákshasas, but advises the suppliants to go to Vishṇu, which they do, and receive from him a promise that he will destroy their enemies. The three Rákshasa kings, hearing of this, consult together, and proceed to heaven to attack the gods. Vishṇu prepares to meet them. The battle is described in the seventh section. The Rákshasas are defeated by Vishṇu with great slaughter, and driven back to Lanká, one of their leaders, Máli, being slain. Mályavat remonstrates with Vishṇu, who was assaulting the rear of the fugitives, for his unwarrior-like conduct, and wishes to renew the combat (Sect. 8, v. 3 ff.). Vishṇu replies that he must fulfil his promise to the gods by slaying the Rákshasas, and that he would destroy them even if they fled to Pátála. These Rákshasas, Agastya says, were more powerful than Rávaṇa, and, could only be destroyed by Náráyaṇa, i.e. by Ráma himself, the eternal, indestructible god. Sumáli with his family lived for along time in Pátála, while Kuvera dwelt in Lanká. In section 9 it is related that Sumáli once happened to visit the earth, when he observed Kuvera going in his chariot to see his father Viśravas. This leads him to consider how he might restore his own fortunes. He consequently desires his daughter Kaikasí to go and woo Viśravas, who receives her graciously. She becomes the mother of the dreadful Rávaṇa, of the huge Kumbhakarṇa, of Śúrpaṇakhá, and of the righteous Vibhishaṇa, who was the last son. These children grow up in the forest. Kumbhakarṇa goes about eating rishis. Kuvera comes to visit his father, when Kaikasí takes occasion to urge her son Rávaṇa to strive to become like his brother (Kuvera) in splendour. This Rávaṇa promises to do. He then goes to the hermitage of Gokarna with his brothers to perform austerity. In section 10 their austere observances are described: after a thousand years' penance Rávaṇa throws his head into the fire. He repeats this oblation nine times

after equal intervals, and is about to do it the tenth time, when Brahmá appears, and offers a boon. Rávaṇa asks immortality, but is refused. He then asks that he may be indestructible by all creatures more powerful than men; which boon is accorded by Brahmá together with the recovery of all the heads he had sacrificed and the power of assuming any shape he pleased. Vibhishaṇa asks as his boon that even amid the greatest calamities he may think only of righteousness, and that the weapon of Brahmá may appear to him unlearnt, etc. The god grants his request, and adds the gift of immortality. When Brahmá is about to offer a boon to Kumbhakarṇa, the gods interpose, as, they say, he had eaten seven Apsarases and ten followers of Indra, besides rishis and men; and beg that under the guise of a boon stupefaction may be inflicted on him. Brahmá thinks on Sarasvatí, who arrives and, by Brahmá's command, enters into Kumbhakarṇa's mouth that she may speak for him. Under this influence he asks that he may receive the boon of sleeping for many years, which is granted. When however Sarasvatí has left him, and he recovers his own consciousness, he perceives that he has been deluded. Kuvera by his father's advice, gives up the city of Lanká to Rávaṇ."
1031 Rávaṇa marries (Sect. 12) Mandodarí the beautiful daughter of the Asur Maya whose name has several times occurred in the Rámáyan as that of an artist of wonderful skill. She bears a son Meghanáda or the Roaring Cloud who was afterwards named Indrajít from his victory over the sovereign of the skies. The conquest of Kuvera, and the acquisition of the magic self-moving chariot which has done much service in the Rámáyan, form the subject of sections XIII., XIV. and XV. "The rather pretty story of Vedavatí is related in the seventeenth section, as follows: Rávaṇa in the course of his progress through the world, comes to the forest on the Himálaya, where he sees a damsel of brilliant beauty, but in ascetic garb, of whom he straightway becomes enamoured. He tells her that such an austere life is unsuited to her youth and attractions, and asks who she is and why she is leading an ascetic existence. She answers that she is called Vedavatí, and is the vocal daughter of Vṛihaspati's son, the rishi Kuśadhwaja, sprung from him during his constant study of the Veda. The gods, gandharvas, etc., she says, wished that she should choose a husband, but her father would give her to no one else than to Vishṇu, the lord of the world, whom he desired for his son-in-law. Vedavatí then proceeds: 'In order that I may fulfil this desire of my father in respect of Náráyaṇa, I wed him with my heart. Having entered into this engagement I practise great austerity. Náráyaṇa and no other than he, Purushottama, is my husband. From the desire of obtaining him, I resort to this severe observance.' Rávaṇa's passion is not in the least diminished by this explanation and he urges that it is the old alone who should seek to become distinguished by accumulating merit through austerity, prays that she who is so young and beautiful shall become

his bride; and boasts that he is superior to Vishṇu. She rejoins that no one but he would thus contemn that deity. On receiving this reply he touches the hair of her head with the tip of his finger. She is greatly incensed, and forthwith cuts off her hair and tells him that as he has so insulted her, she cannot continue to live, but will enter into the fire before his eyes. She goes on 'Since I have been insulted in the forest by thee who art wicked-hearted, I shall be born again for thy destruction. For a man of evil desire cannot be slain by a woman; and the merit of my austerity would be lost if I were to launch a curse against thee. But if I have performed or bestowed or sacrificed aught may I be born the virtuous daughter, not produced from the womb, of a righteous man.' Having thus spoken she entered the blazing fire. Then a shower of celestial flowers fell (from every part of the sky). It is she, lord, who, having been Vedavatí in the Krita age, has been born (in the Treta age) as the daughter of the king of the Janakas, and (has become) thy [Ráma's] bride; for thou art the eternal Vishṇu. The mountain-like enemy who was [virtually] destroyed before by her wrath, has now been slain by her having recourse to thy superhuman energy." On this the commentator remarks: "By this it is signified that Sítá was the principal cause of Rávaṇa's death; but the function of destroying him is ascribed to Ráma." On the words, "thou art Vishṇu," in the preceding verse the same commentator remarks: "By this it is clearly affirmed that Sítá was Lakshmí." This is what Parásara says: "In the god's life as Ráma, she became Sítá, and in his birth as Krishṇa [she became] Rukminí." 1032

In the following section (XVIII.) "Rávaṇa is described as violently interrupting a sacrifice which is being performed by king Marutta, and the assembled gods in terror assume different shapes to escape; Indra becomes a peacock, Yáma a crow, Kuvera a lizard, and Varuṇa a swan; and each deity bestows a boon on the animal he had chosen. The peacock's tail recalls Indra's thousand eyes; the swan's colour becomes white, like the foam of the ocean (Varuṇa being its lord); the lizard obtains a golden colour; and the crow is never to die except when killed by a violent death, and the dead are to enjoy the funeral oblations when they have been devoured by the crows." 1033

Rávaṇ then attacks Arjuna or Kárttavírya the mighty king of Máhishmati on the banks of the Narmadá, and is defeated, captured and imprisoned by Arjuna. At the intercession of Pulastya (Sect. XXII.) he is released from his bonds. He then visits Kishkindhá where he enters into alliance with Báli the King of the Vánars: "We will have all things in common," says Rávaṇ, "dames, sons, cities and kingdoms, food, vesture, and all delights." His next exploit is the invasion of the kingdom of departed spirits and his terrific battle with the sovereign Yáma. The poet in his description of these regions with the detested river with waves of blood, the dire lamentations, the cries for a drop of water, the devouring worm, all the tortures of the guilty and the somewhat insipid pleasures of the just, reminds one of the scenes in the under world so vividly described by Homer, Virgil, and Dante. Yáma is defeated (Sect. XXVI.) by the giant, not so much by his superior power as because at the request of Brahmá Yáma refrains from smiting with his deadly weapon the Rákshas enemy to whom that God had once given the promise that preserved him. In the twenty-seventh section Rávaṇ goes "under the earth into Pátála the treasure-house of the waters inhabited by swarms of serpents and Daityas, and well defended by Varuṇ." He subdues Bhogavatí the city ruled by Vásuki and reduces the Nágas or serpents to subjection. He penetrates even to the imperial seat of Varuṇ. The God himself is absent, but his sons come forth and do battle with the invader. The giant is victorious and departs triumphant. The twenty-eighth section gives the details of a terrific battle between Rávaṇ and Mándhátá King of Ayodhyá, a distinguished ancestor of Ráma. Supernatural weapons are employed on both sides and the issue of the conflict is long doubtful. But at last Mándhátá prepares to use the mighty weapon "acquired by severe austerities through the grace and favour of Rudra." The giant would inevitably have been slain. But two pre-eminent Munis Pulastya and Gálava beheld the fight through the power given by contemplation, and with words of exhortation they parted King Mándhátá and the sovereign of the Rákshases. Rávaṇ at last (Sect. XXXII.) returns homeward carrying with him in his car Pushpak the virgin daughters of kings, of Rishis, of Daityas, and Gandharvas whom he has seized upon his way. The thirty-sixth section describes a battle with Indra, in which the victorious Meghanáda son of the giant, makes the King of the Gods his prisoner, binds him with his magic art, and carries him away (Sect. XXVII.) in triumph to Lanká. Brahmá intercedes (Sect. XXXVIII.) and Indrajít releases his prisoner on obtaining in return the boon that sacrifice to the Lord of Fire shall always make him invincible in the coming battle. In sections XXXIX., XL, "we have a legend related to Ráma by the sage Agastya to account for the stupendous strength of the monkey Hanumán, as it had been described in the *Rámáyaṇa*. Rama naturally wonders (as perhaps many readers of the *Rámáyaṇa* have done since) why a monkey of such marvellous power and prowess had not easily overcome Báli and secured the throne for his friend Sugríva. Agastya replies that Hanumán was at that time under a curse from a Rishi, and consequently was not conscious of his own might." 1034 The whole story of the marvellous Vánar is here given at length, but nothing else of importance is added to the tale already given in the Rámáyaṇa. The Rishis or saints then (Sect. XL.) return to their celestial seats, and the Vánars, Rákshases and bears also (Sect. XLIII.) take their departure.

The chariot Pushpak is restored to its original owner Kuvera, as has already been related in the Rámáyaṇ.

The story of Ráma and Sítá is then continued, and we meet with matter of more human interest. The winter is past and the pleasant spring-time is come, and Ráma and Sítá sit together in the shade of the Aśoka trees happy as Indra and Śachí when they drink in Paradise the nectar of the Gods. "Tell me, my beloved," says Ráma, "for thou wilt soon be a mother, hast thou a wish in thy heart for me to gratify?" And Sítá smiles and answers: "I long, O son of Raghu, to visit the pure and holy hermitages on the banks of the Ganges and to venerate the feet of the saints who there perform their rigid austerities and live on roots and berries. This is my chief desire, to stand within the hermits' grove were it but for a single day." And Ráma said: "Let not the thought trouble thee: thou shalt go to the grove of the ascetics." But slanderous tongues have been busy in Ayodhyá, and Sítá has not been spared. Ráma hears that the people are lamenting his blind folly in taking back to his bosom the wife who was so long a captive in the palace of Rávaṇ. Ráma well knows her spotless purity in thought, word, and deed, and her perfect love of him; but he cannot endure the mockery and the shame and resolves to abandon his unsuspecting wife. He orders the sad but still obedient Lakshmaṇ to convey her to the hermitage which she wishes to visit and to leave her there, for he will see her face again no more. They arrive at the hermitage, and Lakshmaṇ tells her all. She falls fainting on the ground, and when she recovers her consciousness sheds some natural tears and bewails her cruel and undeserved lot. But she resolves to live for the sake of Ráma and her unborn son, and she sends by Lakshmaṇ a dignified message to the husband who has forsaken her: "I grieve not for myself," she says "because I have been abandoned on account of what the people say, and not for any evil that I have done. The husband is the God of the wife, the husband is her lord and guide; and what seems good unto him she should do even at the cost of her life."

Sítá is honourably received by the saint Válmíki himself, and the holy women of the hermitage are charged to entertain and serve her. In this calm retreat she gives birth to two boys who receive the names of Kuśa and Lava. They are carefully brought up and are taught by Válmíki himself to recite the Rámáyaṇ. The years pass by: and Ráma at length determines to celebrate the Aśvamedha or Sacrifice of the Steed. Válmíki, with his two young pupils, attends the ceremony, and the unknown princes recite before the delighted father the poem which recounts his deeds. Ráma inquires into their history and recognizes them as his sons. Sítá is invited to return and solemnly affirm her innocence before the great assembly.

"But Sítá's heart was too full; this second ordeal was beyond even her power to submit to, and the poet rose above the ordinary Hindu level of women when he ventured to paint her conscious purity as rebelling: 'Beholding all the spectators, and clothed in red garments, Sítá clasping her hands and bending low her face, spoke thus in a voice choked with tears: "as I, even in mind, have never thought of any other than Ráma, so may Mádhaví the goddess of Earth, grant me a hiding-place." As Sítá made this oath, lo! a marvel appeared. Suddenly cleaving the earth, a divine throne of marvellous beauty rose up, borne by resplendent dragons on their heads: and seated on it, the goddess of Earth, raising Sítá with her arm, said to her, "Welcome to thee!" and placed her by her side. And as the queen, seated on the throne, slowly descended to Hades, a continuous shower of flowers fell down from heaven on her head.' 1035 "

"Both the great Hindu epics thus end in disappointment and sorrow. In the *Mahábhárata* the five victorious brothers abandon the hardly won throne to die one by one in a forlorn pilgrimage to the Himálaya; and in the same way Ráma only regains his wife, after all his toils, to lose her. It is the same in the later Homeric cycle—the heroes of the *Iliad* perish by ill-fated deaths. And even Ulysses, after his return to Ithaca, sets sail again to Thesprotia, and finally falls by the hand of his own son. But in India and Greece alike this is an afterthought of a self-conscious time, which has been subsequently added to cast a gloom on the strong cheerfulness of the heroic age." 1036

"The termination of Ráma's terrestrial career is thus told in Sections 116 ff. of the Uttarakáṇḍa. Time, in the form of an ascetic, comes to his palace gate, and asks, as the messenger of the great rishi (Brahmá) to see Ráma. He is admitted and received with honour, but says, when he is asked what he has to communicate, that his message must be delivered in private, and that any one who witnesses the interview is to lose his life. Ráma informs Lakshmaṇ of all this, and desires him to stand outside. Time then tells Ráma that he has been sent by Brahmá, to say that when he (Ráma, *i.e.* Vishṇu) after destroying the worlds was sleeping on the ocean, he had formed him (Brahmá) from the lotus springing from his navel, and committed to him the work of creation; that he (Brahmá) had then entreated Ráma to assume the function of Preserver, and that the latter had in consequence become Vishṇu, being born as the son of Aditi, and had determined to deliver mankind by destroying Rávaṇa, and to live on earth ten thousand and ten hundred years; that period, adds Time, was now on the eve of expiration, and Ráma could either at his pleasure prolong his stay on earth, or ascend to heaven and rule over the gods. Ráma replies, that he had been born for the good of the three worlds, and would now return to the place whence he had come, as it was his function to fulfil the purposes of the gods. While they are speaking the irritable rishi Durvásas comes, and insists on seeing Ráma immediately, under a threat, if refused, of cursing Ráma and all his family."

Lakshmaṇ, preferring to save his kinsman, though knowing that his own death must be the consequence of interrupting the interview of Ráma with Time, enters the palace and reports the rishi's message to Ráma. Ráma comes out, and when Durvásas has got the food he wished, and departed, Ráma reflects with great distress on the words of Time, which require that Lakshmaṇ should die. Lakshmaṇ however exhorts Ráma not to grieve, but to abandon him and not break his own promise. The counsellors concurring in this advice, Ráma abandons Lakshmaṇ, who goes to the river Sarayú, suppresses all his senses, and is conveyed bodily by Indra to heaven. The gods are delighted by the arrival of the fourth part of Vishṇu. Ráma then resolves to install Bharata as his successor and retire to the forest and follow Lakshmaṇ. Bharata however refuses the succession, and determines to accompany his brother. Ráma's subjects are filled with grief, and say they also will follow him wherever he goes. Messengers are sent to Śatrughna, the other brother, and he also resolves to accompany Ráma; who at length sets out in procession from his capital with all the ceremonial appropriate to the "great departure," silent, indifferent to external objects, joyless, with Śrí on his right, the goddess Earth on his left, Energy in front, attended by all his weapons in human shapes, by the Vedas in the forms of Bráhmans, by the Gáyatrí, the Omkára, the Vashaṭkára, by rishis, by his women, female slaves, eunuchs, and servants. Bharata with his family, and Śatrughna, follow together with Bráhmans bearing the sacred fire, and the whole of the people of the country, and even with animals, etc., etc. Ráma, with all these attendants, comes to the banks of the Sarayú. Brahmá, with all the gods and innumerable celestial cars, now appears, and all the sky is refulgent with the divine splendour. Pure and fragrant breezes blow, a shower of flowers falls. Ráma enters the waters of the Sarayú; and Brahmá utters a voice from the sky, saying: "Approach, Vishṇu; Rághava, thou hast happily arrived, with thy godlike brothers. Enter thine own body as Vishṇu or the eternal ether. For thou art the abode of the worlds: no one comprehends thee, the inconceivable and imperishable, except the large-eyed Máyá thy primeval spouse." Hearing these words, Ráma enters the glory of Vishṇu with his body and his followers. He then asks Brahmá to find an abode for the people who had accompanied him from devotion to his person, and Brahmá appoints them a celestial residence accordingly. 1037

ADDITIONAL NOTES

Queen Fortune.

"A curious festival is celebrated in honour of this divinity (Lakshmî) on the fifth lunar day of the light half of the month Mâgha (February), when she is identified with Saraswatí the consort of Brahmá, and the goddess of learning. In his treatise on festivals, a great modern authority, Raghunandana, mentions, on the faith of a work called *Samvatsara-sandîpa*, that Lakshmî is to be worshipped in the forenoon of that day with flowers, perfumes, rice, and water; that due honour is to be paid to inkstand and writing-reed, and no writing to be done. Wilson, in his essay on the *Religious Festivals of the Hindus* (works, vol. ii, p. 188. ff.) adds that on the morning of the 2nd February, the whole of the pens and inkstands, and the books, if not too numerous and bulky, are collected, the pens or reeds cleaned, the inkstands scoured, and the books wrapped up in new cloth, are arranged upon a platform, or a sheet, and strewn over with flowers and blades of young barley, and that no flowers except white are to be offered. After performing the necessary rites, ... all the members of the family assemble and make their prostrations; the books, the pens, and ink having an entire holiday; and should any emergency require a written communication on the day dedicated to the divinity of scholarship, it is done with chalk or charcoal upon a black or white board."

Chambers's Encyclopædia. *Lakshmî.*

Indra.

"The Hindu Jove or Jupiter Tonans, chief of the secondary deities. He presides over swarga or paradise, and is more particularly the god of the atmosphere and winds. He is also regent of the east quarter of the sky. As chief of the deities he is called Devapati, Devadeva, Surapati, etc.; as lord of the atmosphere Divaspati; as lord of the eight Vasus or demigods, Fire, etc., Vásava; as breaking cities into fragments, Purandara, Puranda; as lord of a hundred sacrifices (the performance of a hundred Aśvamechas elevating the sacrificer to the rank of Indra) Śatakratu, Śatamakha; as having a thousand eyes, Sahasráksha; as husband of Śachí, Śachípati. His wife is called Śachí, Indráṇí, Sakráṇí, Maghoni, Indraśakti, Pulomajá, and Paulomí. His son is Jayanta. His pleasure garden or elysium is Nandana; his city,

Amarávatí; his palace, Vaijayanta; his horse, Uchchaihśravas, his elephant, Airávata; his charioteer, Mátali."

Professor M. Williams's English-Sanskrit Dictionary. *Indra.*

Vishnu.

"The second person of the Hindu triad, and the most celebrated and popular of all the Indian deities. He is the personification of the preserving power, and became incarnate in nine different forms, for the preservation of mankind in various emergencies. Before the creation of the universe, and after its temporary annihilation, he is supposed to sleep on the waters, floating on the serpent Śesha, and is then identified with Náráyaṇa. Brahmá, the creator, is fabled to spring at that time from a lotus which grows from his navel, whilst thus asleep.... His ten avatárs or incarnations are:

"1. The Matsya, or fish. In this avatár Vishṇu descended in the form of a fish to save the pious king Satyavrata, who with the seven Rishis and their wives had taken refuge in the ark to escape the deluge which then destroyed the earth. 2, The Kúrma, or Tortoise. In this he descended in the form of a tortoise, for the purpose of restoring to man some of the comforts lost during the flood. To this end he stationed himself at the bottom of the ocean, and allowed the point of the great mountain Mandara to be placed upon his back, which served as a hard axis, whereon the gods and demons, with the serpent Vásuki twisted round the mountain for a rope, churned the waters for the recovery of the amrita or nectar, and fourteen other sacred things. 3. The Varáha, or Boar. In this he descended in the form of a boar to rescue the earth from the power of a demon called 'golden-eyed,' Hiraṇyáksha. This demon had seized on the earth and carried it with him into the depths of the ocean. Vishṇu dived into the abyss, and after a contest of a thousand years slew the monster. 4. The Narasinha, or Man-lion. In this monstrous shape of a creature half-man, half-lion, Vishṇu delivered the earth from the tyranny of an insolent demon called Hiraṇyakaśipu. 5. Vámana, or Dwarf. This avatár happened in the second age of the Hindús or Tretáyug, the four preceding are said to have occurred in the first or Satyayug; the object of this avatár was to trick Bali out of the dominion of the three worlds. Assuming the form of a wretched dwarf he appeared before the king and asked, as a boon, as much land as he could pace in three steps. This was granted; and Vishṇu immediately expanding himself till he filled the world, deprived Bali at two steps of heaven and earth, but in consideration of some merit, left Pátála still in his dominion. 6. Paraśuráma. 7. Rámchandra. 8. Krishṇa, or according to some Balaráma. 9. Buddha. In this avatár Vishṇu descended in the form of a sage for the purpose of making some reform in the religion of the Brahmins, and especially to reclaim them from their proneness to animal sacrifice. Many of the Hindús will not allow this to have been an incarnation of their favourite god. 10. Kalki, or White Horse. This is yet to come. Vishṇu mounted on a white horse, with a drawn scimitar, blazing like a comet, will, according to prophecy, end this present age, viz. the fourth or Kaliyug, by destroying the world, and then renovating creation by an age of purity."

William's Dictionary. *Vishṇu.*

Siva.

"A celebrated Hindú God, the Destroyer of creation, and therefore the most formidable of the Hindú Triad. He also personifies reproduction, since the Hindú philosophy excludes the idea of total annihilation without subsequent regeneration. Hence he is sometimes confounded with Brahmá, the creator or first person of the Triad. He is the particular God of the Tántrikas, or followers of the books called Tantras. His worshippers are termed Śaivas, and although not so numerous as the Vaishṇavas, exalt their god to the highest place in the heavens, and combine in him many of the attributes which properly belong to the other deities. According to them Śiva is Time, Justice, Fire, Water, the Sun, the Destroyer and Creator. As presiding over generation, his type is the Linga, or Phallus, the origin probably of the Phallic emblem of Egypt and Greece. As the God of generation and justice, which latter character he shares with the god Yama, he is represented riding a white bull. His own colour, as well as that of the bull, is generally white, referring probably to the unsullied purity of Justice. His throat is dark-blue; his hair of a light reddish colour, and thickly matted together, and gathered above his head like the hair of an ascetic. He is sometimes seen with two hands, sometimes with four, eight, or ten, and with five faces. He has three eyes, one being in the centre of his forehead, pointing up and down. These are said to denote his view of the three divisions of time, past, present, and future. He holds a trident in his hand to denote, as some say, his relationship to water, or according to others, to show that the three great attributes of Creator, Destroyer, and Regenerator are combined in him. His loins are enveloped in a tiger's skin. In his character of Time, he not only presides over its extinction, but also its astronomical regulation. A crescent or half-moon on his forehead indicates the measure of time by the phases of the moon; a serpent forms one of his necklaces to denote the measure of time by years, and a second necklace of human skulls marks the lapse and revolution of ages, and the extinction and succession of the generations of mankind. He is often represented as entirely covered with serpents, which are the emblems of immortality. They are bound in his hair, round his neck, wrists, waist, arms and legs; they serve as rings for his fingers, and earrings for his ears, and are his constant companions. Śiva has more than a thousand names which are detailed at length in the sixty-ninth chapter of the Śiva Puráṇa." —Williams's Dictionary, *Śiva*.

Apsarases.

"Originally these deities seem to have been personifications of the vapours which are attracted by the sun, and form into mist or clouds: their character may be thus interpreted in the few hymns of the Rigveda where mention is made of them. At a subsequent period when the Gandharva of the Rigveda who personifies there especially the Fire of the Sun, expanded into the Fire of Lightning, the rays of the moon and other attributes of the elementary life of heaven as well as into pious acts referring to it, the Apsarasas become divinities which represent phenomena or objects both of a physical and ethical kind closely associated with that life; thus in the *Yajurveda* Sunbeams are called the Apsarasas associated with the Gandharva who is the Sun; Plants are termed the Apsarasas connected with the Gandharva Fire: Constellations are the Apsarasas of the Gandharva Moon: Waters the Apsarasas of the Gandharva Wind, etc. etc.… In the last Mythological epoch when the Gandharvas have saved from their elementary nature merely so much as to be musicians in the paradise of Indra, the Apsarasas appear among other subordinate deities which share in the merry life of Indra's heaven, as the wives of the Gandharvas, but more especially as wives of a licentious sort, and they are promised therefore, too, as a reward to heroes fallen in battle when they are received in the paradise of Indra; and while, in the Rigveda, they assist Soma to pour down his floods, they descend in the epic literature on earth merely to shake the virtue of penitent Sages and to deprive them of the power they would otherwise have acquired through unbroken austerities." —Goldstücker's *Sanskrit Dictionary*.

Vishnu's Incarnation As Ráma.

"Here is described one of the *avatárs*, descents or manifestations of Vishṇu in a visible form. The word *avatár* signifies literally *descent*. The *avatár* which is here spoken of, that in which, according to Indian traditions, Vishṇu descended and appeared upon earth in the corporeal form of Ráma, the hero of the Rámáyana, is the seventh in the series of Indian *avatárs*. Much has been said before now of these avatárs, and through deficient knowledge of the ideas and doctrines of India, they have been compared to the sublime dogma of the Christian Incarnation. This is one of the grossest errors that ignorance of the ideas and beliefs of a people has produced. Between the *avatárs* of India and the Christian Incarnation there is such an immensity of difference that it is impossible to find any reasonable analogy that can approximate them. The idea of the *avatárs* is intimately united with that of the Trimúrti; the bond of connection between these two ideas is an essential notion common to both, the notion of Vishṇu. What is the Trimúrti? I have already said that it is composed of three Gods, Brahmá (masculine), Vishṇu the God of *avatárs*, and Śiva. These three Gods, who when reduced to their primitive and most simple expression are but three cosmogonical personifications, three powers or forces of nature, these Gods, I say, are here found, according to Indian doctrines, entirely external to the true God of India, or Brahma in the neuter gender. Brahma is alone, unchangeable in the midst of creation: all emanates from him, he comprehends all, but he remains extraneous to all: he is Being and the negation of beings. Brahma is never worshipped; the indeterminate Being is never invoked; he is inaccessible to the prayers as the actions of man; humanity, as well as nature, is extraneous to him. External to Brahma rises the Trimúrti, that is to say, Brahmá (masculine) the power which creates, Vishṇu the power which preserves, and Śiva the power which destroys: theogony here commences at the same time with cosmogony. The three divinities of the Trimúrti govern the phenomena of the universe and influence all nature. The real God of India is by himself without power; real efficacious power is attributed only to three divinities who exist externally to him. Brahmá, Vishṇu, and Śiva, possessed of qualities in part contradictory and attributes that are mutually exclusive, have no other accord or harmony than that which results from the power of things itself, and which is found external to their own thoughts. Such is the Indian Trimúrti. What an immense difference between this Triad and the wonderful Trinity of Christianity! Here there is only one God, who created all, provides for all, governs all. He exists in three Persons equal to one another, and intimately united in one only infinite and eternal substance. The Father represents the eternal thought and the power which created, the Son infinite love, the Holy Spirit universal sanctification. This one and triune God completes by omnipotent power the great work of creation which, when it has come forth from His hands, proceeds in obedience to the laws which He has given it, governed with certain order by His infinite providence.

"The immense difference between the Trimúrti of India and the Christian Trinity is found again between the *avatárs* of Vishṇu and the Incarnation of Christ. The *avatár* was effected altogether externally to the Being who is in India regarded as the true God. The manifestation of one essentially cosmogonical divinity wrought for the most part only material and cosmogonical prodigies. At one time it takes the form of the gigantic tortoise which sustains Mount Mandar from sinking in the ocean; at another of the fish which raises the lost Veda from the bottom of the sea, and saves mankind from the waters. When these *avatárs* are not cosmogonical they consist in some protection accorded to men or Gods, a protection which is neither universal nor permanent. The very manner in which the *avatár* is effected corresponds to its material nature, for instance the mysterious vase and the magic liquor by means of which the *avatár* here spoken of takes place. What are the forms which Vishṇu takes in his descents? They are the simple forms of life; he becomes a tortoise, a boar, a fish, but he is not obliged to take the form of intelligence and liberty, that is to say, the form of man. In the *avatár* of Vishṇu is discovered the inpress of pantheistic ideas which have always more or less prevailed in India. Does the *avatár* produce a permanent and definitive result in the world? By no means. It is renewed at every catastrophe either of nature or man, and its effects are only transitory.... To sum up then, the Indian *avatár* is effected externally to the true God of India, to Brahma; it has only a cosmogonical or historical mission which is neither lasting nor decisive; it is accomplished by means of strange prodigies and magic transformations; it may assume promiscuously all the forms of life; it may be repeated indefinitely. Now let the whole of this Indian idea taken from primitive tradition be compared with the Incarnation of Christ and it will be seen that there is between the two an irreconcilable difference. According to the doctrines of Christianity the Everlasting Word, Infinite Love, the Son of God, and equal to Him, assumed a human body, and being born as a man accomplished by his divine act the great miracle of the spiritual redemption of man. His coming had for its sole object to bring erring and lost humanity back to Him; this work being accomplished, and the divine union of men with God being re-established, redemption is complete and remains eternal.

"The superficial study of India produced in the last century many erroneous ideas, many imaginary and false parallels between Christianity and the Brahmanical religion. A profounder knowledge of Indian civilization and religion, and philological studies enlarged and guided by more certain principles have dissipated one by one all those errors. The attributes of the Christian God, which by one of those intellectual errors, which Vico attributes to the vanity of the learned, had been transferred to Vishṇu, have by a better inspired philosophy been reclaimed for Christianity, and the result of the two religions, one immovable and powerless, the other diffusing itself with all its inherent force and energy, has shown further that there is a difference, a real opposition, between the two principles." — Gorresio.

Kusa and Lava.

As the story of the banishment of Sítá and the subsequent birth in Válmíki's hermitage of Kuśa and Lava the rhapsodists of the Rámáyan, is intimately connected with the account in the introductory cantos of Válmíki's composition of the poem, I shall, I trust, be pardoned for extracting it from my rough translation of Kálidása's Raghuvaṇśa, parts only of which have been offered to the public.

"Then, day by day, the husband's hope grew high,
Gazing with love on Sítá's melting eye:
With anxious care he saw her pallid cheek,
And fondly bade her all her wishes speak.
"Once more I fain would see," the lady cried,
"The sacred groves that rise on Gangá's side,
Where holy grass is ever fresh and green,
And cattle feeding on the rice are seen:
There would I rest awhile, where once I strayed
Linked in sweet friendship to each hermit maid."
And Ráma smiled upon his wife, and sware,
With many a tender oath, to grant her prayer.
It chanced, one evening, from a lofty seat
He viewed Ayodhyá stretched before his feet:
He looked with pride upon the royal road
Lined with gay shops their glittering stores that showed,
He looked on Sarjú's silver waves, that bore
The light barks flying with the sail and oar;
He saw the gardens near the town that lay,
Filled with glad citizens and boys at play.
Then swelled the monarch's bosom with delight,
And his heart triumphed at the happy sight.
He turned to Bhadra, standing by his side,—
Upon whose secret news the king relied.—
And bade him say what people said and thought
Of all the exploits that his arm had wrought.
The spy was silent, but, when questioned still,
Thus spake, obedient to his master's will:
"For all thy deeds in peace and battle done
The people praise thee, King, except for one:
This only act of all thy life they blame,—

Thy welcome home of her, thy ravished dame."
Like iron yielding to the iron's blow,
Sank Ráma, smitten by those words of woe.
His breast, where love and fear for empire vied,
Swayed, like a rapid swing, from side to side.
Shall he this rumour scorn, which blots his life,
Or banish her, his dear and spotless wife?
But rigid Duty left no choice between
His perilled honour and his darling queen.
Called to his side, his brothers wept to trace
The marks of anguish in his altered face.
No longer bright and glorious as of old,
He thus addressed them when the tale was told:
"Alas! my brothers, that my life should blot
The fame of those the Sun himself begot:
As from the labouring cloud the driven rain
Leaves on the mirror's polished face a stain.
E'en as an elephant who loathes the stake
And the strong chain he has no power to break,
I cannot brook this cry on every side,
That spreads like oil upon the moving tide.
I leave the daughter of Videha's King,
And the fair blossom soon from her to spring,
As erst, obedient to my sire's command,
I left the empire of the sea-girt land.
Good is my queen, and spotless; but the blame
Is hard to bear, the mockery and the shame.
Men blame the pure Moon for the darkened ray,
When the black shadow takes the light away.
And, O my brothers, if ye wish to see
Ráma live long from this reproach set free,
Let not your pity labour to control
The firm sad purpose of his changeless soul."
Thus Ráma spake. The sorrowing brothers heard

His stern resolve, without an answering word;
For none among them dared his voice to raise,
That will to question:—and they could not praise.
"Beloved brother," thus the monarch cried
To his dear Lakshmaṇ, whom he called aside.—
Lakshmaṇ, who knew no will save his alone
Whose hero deeds through all the world were known:—
"My queen has told me that she longs to rove
Beneath the shade of Saint Válmíki's grove:
Now mount thy car, away my lady bear;
Tell all, and leave her in the forest there."
The car was brought, the gentle lady smiled,
As the glad news her trusting heart beguiled.
She mounted up: Sumantra held the reins;
And forth the coursers bounded o'er the plains.
She saw green fields in all their beauty dressed,
And thanked her husband in her loving breast.
Alas! deluded queen! she little knew
How changed was he whom she believed so true;
How one she worshipped like the Heavenly Tree
Could, in a moment's time, so deadly be.
Her right eye throbbed,—ill-omened sign, to tell
The endless loss of him she loved so well,
And to the lady's saddening heart revealed
The woe that Lakshmaṇ, in his love, concealed.
Pale grew the bloom of her sweet face,—as fade
The lotus blossoms,—by that sign dismayed.
"Oh, may this omen,"—was her silent prayer,—
"No grief to Ráma or his brothers bear!"
When Lakshmaṇ, faithful to his brother, stood
Prepared to leave her in the distant wood,
The holy Gangá, flowing by the way,
Raised all her hands of waves to bid him stay.
At length with sobs and burning tears that rolled

Down his sad face, the king's command he told;
As when a monstrous cloud, in evil hour,
Rains from its labouring womb a stony shower.
She heard, she swooned, she fell upon the earth,
Fell on that bosom whence she sprang to birth.
As, when the tempest in its fury flies,
Low in the dust the prostrate creeper lies,
So, struck with terror sank she on the ground,
And all her gems, like flowers, lay scattered round.
But Earth, her mother, closed her stony breast,
And, filled with doubt, denied her daughter rest.
She would not think the Chief of Raghu's race
Would thus his own dear guiltless wife disgrace.
Stunned and unconscious, long the lady lay,
And felt no grief, her senses all astray.
But gentle Lakshman, with a brother's care,
Brought back her sense, and with her sense, despair.
But not her wrongs, her shame, her grief, could wring
One angry word against her lord the King:
Upon herself alone the blame she laid,
For tears and sighs that would not yet be stayed.
To soothe her anguish Lakshman gently strove;
He showed the path to Saint Válmíki's grove;
And craved her pardon for the share of ill
He wrought, obedient to his brother's will.
"O, long and happy, dearest brother, live!
I have to praise," she cried, "and not forgive:
To do his will should be thy noblest praise;
As Vishnu ever Indra's will obeys.
Return, dear brother: on each royal dame
Bestow a blessing in poor Sítá's name,
And bid them, in their love, kind pity take
Upon her offspring, for the father's sake.
And speak my message in the monarch's ear,

The last last words of mine that he shall hear:
"Say, was it worthy of thy noble race
Thy guiltless queen thus lightly to disgrace?
For idle tales to spurn thy faithful bride,
Whose constant truth the searching fire had tried?
Or may I hope thy soul refused consent,
And but thy voice decreed my banishment?
Hope that no care could turn, no love could stay
The lightning stroke that falls on me to-day?
That sins committed in the life that's fled
Have brought this evil on my guilty head?
Think not I value now my widowed life,
Worthless to her who once was Ráma's wife.
I only live because I hope to see
The dear dear babe that will resemble thee.
And then my task of penance shall be done,
With eyes uplifted to the scorching sun;
So shall the life that is to come restore
Mine own dear husband, to be lost no more."
And Lakshmaṇ swore her every word to tell,
Then turned to go, and bade the queen farewell.
Alone with all her woes, her piteous cries
Rose like a butchered lamb's that struggling dies.
The reverend sage who from his dwelling came
For sacred grass and wood to feed the flame,
Heard her loud shrieks that rent the echoing wood,
And, quickly following, by the mourner stood.
Before the sage the lady bent her low,
Dried her poor eyes, and strove to calm her woe.
With blessings on her hopes the blameless man
In silver tones his soothing speech began:
"First of all faithful wives, O Queen, art thou;
And can I fail to mourn thy sorrows now?
Rest in this holy grove, nor harbour fear

Where dwell in safety e'en the timid deer.
Here shall thine offspring safely see the light,
And be partaker of each holy rite.
Here, near the hermits' dwellings, shall thou lave
Thy limbs in Tonse's sin-destroying wave,
And on her isles, by prayer and worship, gain
Sweet peace of mind, and rest from care and pain.
Each hermit maiden with her sweet soft voice,
Shall soothe thy woe, and bid thy heart rejoice:
With fruit and early flowers thy lap shall fill,
And offer grain that springs for us at will.
And here, with labour light, thy task shall be
To water carefully each tender tree,
And learn how sweet a nursing mother's joy
Ere on thy bosom rest thy darling boy...."
That very night the banished Sítá bare
Two royal children, most divinely fair....
The saint Válmíki, with a friend's delight,
Graced Sítá's offspring with each holy rite.
Kuśa and Lava—such the names they bore—
Learnt, e'en in childhood, all the Vedas' lore;
And then the bard, their minstrel souls to train,
Taught them to sing his own immortal strain.
And Ráma's deeds her boys so sweetly sang,
That Sítá's breast forgot her bitterest pang....
Then Sítá's children, by the saint's command,
Sang the Rámáyan, wandering through the land.
How could the glorious poem fail to gain
Each heart, each ear that listened to the strain!
So sweet each minstrel's voice who sang the praise
Of Ráma deathless in Válmíki's lays.
Ráma himself amid the wondering throng
Marked their fair forms, and loved the noble song,
While, still and weeping, round the nobles stood,

As, on a windless morn, a dewy wood.

On the two minstrels all the people gazed,

Praised their fair looks and marvelled as they praised;

For every eye amid the throng could trace

Ráma's own image in each youthful face.

Then spoke the king himself and bade them say

Who was their teacher, whose the wondrous lay.

Soon as Válmíki, mighty saint, he saw,

He bowed his head in reverential awe.

"These are thy children" cried the saint, "recall

Thine own dear Sítá, pure and true through all."

"O holy father," thus the king replied,

"The faithful lady by the fire was tried;

But the foul demon's too successful arts

Raised light suspicions in my people's hearts.

Grant that their breasts may doubt her faith no more,

And thus my Sítá and her sons restore."

Raghuvaṇśa Cantos XIV, XV.

Parasuráma, Page 87.

"He cleared the earth thrice seven times of the Kshatriya caste, and filled with their blood the five large lakes of Samanta, from which he offered libations to the race of Bhrigu. Offering a solemn sacrifice to the King of the Gods Paraśuráma presented the earth to the ministering priests. Having given the earth to Kaśyapa, the hero of immeasurable prowess retired to the Mahendra mountain, where he still resides; and in this manner was there enmity between him and the race of the Kshatriyas, and thus was the whole earth conquered by Paraśuráma." The destruction of the Kshatriyas by Paraśuráma had been provoked by the cruelty of the Kshatriyas. *Chips from a German Workshop, Vol.* II. p. 334.

The scene in which he appears is probably interpolated for the sake of making him declare Ráma to be Vishṇu. "Herr von Schlegel has often remarked to me," says Lassen, "that without injuring the connexion of the story all the chapters [of the Rámáyan] might be omitted in which Ráma is regarded as an incarnation of Vishṇu. In fact, where the incarnation of Vishṇu as the four sons of Daśaratha is described, the great sacrifice is already ended, and all the priests remunerated at the termination, when the new sacrifice begins at which the Gods appear, then withdraw, and then first propose the incarnation to Vishṇu. If it had been an original circumstance of the story, the Gods would certainly have deliberated on the matter earlier, and the celebration of the sacrifice would have continued without interruption." Lassen, *Indische Alterthumskunde, Vol. I.* p. 489.

Yáma, Page 68.

Son of Vivasvat=Jima son of Vivanghvat, the Jamshíd of the later Persians.

Fate, Page 68.

"The idea of fate was different in India from that which prevailed in Greece. In Greece fate was a mysterious, inexorable power which governed men and human events, and from which it was impossible to escape. In India Fate was rather an inevitable consequence of actions done in births antecedent to one's present state of existence, and was therefore connected with the doctrine of metempsychosis. A misfortune was for the most part a punishment, an expiation of ancient faults not yet entirely cancelled." Gorresio.

Visvámitra, Page 76.

"Though of royal extraction, Viśvámitra conquered for himself and his family the privileges of a Brahman. He became a Brahman, and thus broke through all the rules of caste. The Brahmans cannot deny the fact, because it forms one of the principal subjects of their legendary poems. But they have spared no pains to represent the exertions of Viśvámitra, in his struggle for Brahmanhood, as so superhuman that no one would easily be tempted to follow his example. No mention is made of these monstrous penances in the Veda, where the struggle between Viśvámitra, the leader of the Kuśikas or Bharatas, and the Brahman Vaśishtha, the leader of the white-robed Tritsus, is represented as the struggle of two rivals for the place of Purohita or chief priest and minister at the court of King Sudás, the son of Pijavana." *Chips from a German Workshop, Vol. II.* p. 336.

Household Gods, Page 102.

"No house is supposed to be without its tutelary divinity, but the notion attached to this character is now very far from precise. The deity who is the object of hereditary and family worship, the *Kuladevatá,* is always one of the leading personages of the Hindu mythology, as Śiva, Vishṇu or Durgá, but the *Grihadevatá* rarely bears any distinct appellation. In Bengal, the domestic god is sometimes the *Sálagrám* stone, sometimes the *tulasi* plant, sometimes a basket with a little rice in it, and sometimes a water-jar—to either of which a brief adoration is daily addressed, most usually by the females of the family. Occasionally small images of Lakshmi or Chaṇḍi fulfil the office, or should a snake appear, he is venerated as the guardian of the dwelling. In general, however, in former times, the household deities were regarded as the unseen spirits of ill, the ghosts and goblins who hovered about every spot, and claimed some particular sites as their own. Offerings were made to them in the open air, by scattering a little rice with a short formula at the close of all ceremonies to keep them in good humour.

"The household gods correspond better with the genii locorum than with the lares or penates of autiquity."

H. H. Wilson.

Page 107.

Śaivya, a king whom earth obeyed,
Once to a hawk a promise made.

The following is a free version of this very ancient story which occurs more than once in the *Mahábhárat*:

The Suppliant Dove.

Chased by a hawk there came a dove
With worn and weary wing,
And took her stand upon the hand
Of Káśí's mighty king.
The monarch smoothed her ruffled plumes
And laid her on his breast,
And cried, "No fear shall vex thee here,
Rest, pretty egg-born, rest!
Fair Káśí's realm is rich and wide,
With golden harvests gay,
But all that's mine will I resign
Ere I my guest betray."
But panting for his half won spoil
The hawk was close behind.
And with wild cry and eager eye
Came swooping down the wind:
"This bird," he cried, "my destined prize,

'Tis not for thee to shield:
'Tis mine by right and toilsome flight
O'er hill and dale and field.
Hunger and thirst oppress me sore,
And I am faint with toil:
Thou shouldst not stay a bird of prey
Who claims his rightful spoil.
They say thou art a glorious king,
And justice is thy care:
Then justly reign in thy domain,
Nor rob the birds of air."
Then cried the king: "A cow or deer
For thee shall straightway bleed,
Or let a ram or tender lamb
Be slain, for thee to feed.
Mine oath forbids me to betray
My little twice-born guest:
See how she clings with trembling wings
To her protector's breast."
"No flesh of lambs," the hawk replied,
"No blood of deer for me;
The falcon loves to feed on doves
And such is Heaven's decree.
But if affection for the dove
Thy pitying heart has stirred,
Let thine own flesh my maw refresh,
Weighed down against the bird."
He carved the flesh from off his side,
And threw it in the scale,
While women's cries smote on the skies
With loud lament and wail.
He hacked the flesh from side and arm,
From chest and back and thigh,
But still above the little dove

The monarch's scale stood high.
He heaped the scale with piles of flesh,
With sinews, blood and skin,
And when alone was left him bone
He threw himself therein.
Then thundered voices through the air;
The sky grew black as night;
And fever took the earth that shook
To see that wondrous sight.
The blessed Gods, from every sphere,
By Indra led, came nigh:
While drum and flute and shell and lute
Made music in the sky.
They rained immortal chaplets down,
Which hands celestial twine,
And softly shed upon his head
Pure Amrit, drink divine.
Then God and Seraph, Bard and Nymph
Their heavenly voices raised,
And a glad throng with dance and song
The glorious monarch praised.
They set him on a golden car
That blazed with many a gem;
Then swiftly through the air they flew,
And bore him home with them.
Thus Káśí's lord, by noble deed,
Won heaven and deathless fame:
And when the weak protection seek
From thee, do thou the same.
Scenes from the Rámáyan, &c.

Page 108.

The ceremonies that attended the consecration of a king (*Abhikshepa lit. Sprinkling over*) are fully described in Goldstücker's Dictionary, from which the following extract is made: "The type of the inauguration ceremony as practised at the Epic period may probably be recognized in the history of the inauguration of *Ráma*, as told in the *Rámáyana*, and in that of the inauguration of *Yudhishthira*, as told in the *Mahábháratha*. Neither ceremony is described in these poems with the full detail which is given of the vaidik rite in the *Aitareya-Bráhmaṇam*; but the allusion that Ráma was inaugurated by *Vaśishṭha* and the other Bráhmanas in the same manner as Indra by the Vasus ... and the observation which is made in some passages that a certain rite of the inauguration was performed 'according to the sacred rule' ... admit of the conclusion that the ceremony was supposed to have taken place in conformity with the vaidik injunction.... As the inauguration of *Ráma* was intended and the necessary preparations for it were made when his father Daśaratha was still alive, but as the ceremony itself, through the intrigues of his step-mother *Kaikeyí*, did not take place then, but fourteen years later, after the death of *Daśaratha*, an account of the preparatory ceremonies is given in the *Ayodhyákáṇḍa* (Book II) as well as in the *Yuddha-Káṇḍa* (Book VI.) of the Rámáyaṇa, but an account of the complete ceremony in the latter book alone. According to the *Ayodhyákáṇḍa*, on the day preceding the intended inauguration *Ráma* and his wife *Sítá* held a fast, and in the night they performed this preliminary rite: *Ráma* having made his ablutions, approached the idol of *Náráyaṇa*, took a cup of clarified butter, as the religious law prescribes, made a libation of it into the kindled fire, and drank the remainder while wishing what was agreeable to his heart. Then, with his mind fixed on the divinity he lay, silent and composed, together with *Sítá*, on a bed of Kuśa-grass, which was spread before the altar of Vishṇu, until the last watch of the night, when he awoke and ordered the palace to be prepared for the solemnity. At day-break reminded of the time by the voices of the bards, he performed the usual morning devotion and praised the divinity. In the meantime the town Ayodhyá had assumed a festive appearance and the inauguration implements had been arranged ... golden water-jars, an ornamented throne-seat, a chariot covered with a splendid tiger-skin, water taken from the confluence of the Ganges and Jumna, as well as from other sacred rivers, tanks, wells, lakes, and from all oceans, honey, curd, clarified butter, fried grain, Kuśa-grass, flowers, milk; besides, eight beautiful damsels, and a splendid furious elephant, golden and silver jars, filled with water, covered with *Udumbara* branches and various lotus flowers, besides a white jewelled *chourie*, a white splendid parasol, a white bull, a white horse, all manner of musical instruments and bards.... In the preceding chapter ... there are mentioned *two* white *chouries* instead of one, and all kinds of seeds, perfumes and jewels, a scimitar, a bow, a litter, a golden vase, and a blazing fire, and amongst the living implements of the pageant, instead of the bards, gaudy courtesans, and besides the eight damsels, professors of divinity, Bráhmaṇas, cows and pure kinds of wild beasts and birds, the chiefs of town and country-people and the citizens with their train."

Page 109.

Then with the royal chaplains they
Took each his place in long array.
The twice born chiefs, with zealous heed,
Made ready what the rite would need.

"Now about the office of a Purohita (house priest). The gods do not eat the food offered by a king, who has no house-priest (Purohita). Thence the king even when (not) intending to bring a sacrifice, should appoint a Bráhman to the office of house-priest." Haug's *Autareya Bráhmanam. Voi. II. p. 528.*

Page 110.

There by the gate the Sáras screamed.

The Sáras or Indian Crane is a magnificent bird easily domesticated and speedily constituting himself the watchman of his master's house and garden. Unfortunately he soon becomes a troublesome and even dangerous dependent, attacking strangers with his long bill and powerful wings, and warring especially upon "small infantry" with unrelenting ferocity.

Page 120.

My mothers or my sire the king.

All the wives of the king his father are regarded and spoken of by Ráma as his mothers.

Page 125.

Such blessings as the Gods o'erjoyed
Poured forth when Vritra was destroyed.

"Mythology regards Vritra as a demon or Asur, the implacable enemy of Indra, but this is not the primitive idea contained in the name of Vritra. In the hymns of the Veda Vritra appears to be the thick dark cloud which Indra the God of the firmament attacks and disperses with his thunderbolt." Gorresio.

"In that class of Rig-veda hymns which there is reason to look upon as the oldest portion of Vedic poetry, the character of Indra is that of a mighty ruler of the firmament, and his principal feat is that of conquering the demon *Vritra*, a symbolical personification of the cloud which obstructs the clearness of the sky, and withholds the fructifying rain from the earth. In his battles with Vritra he is therefore described as 'opening the receptacles of the waters,' as 'cleaving the cloud' with his 'far-whirling thunderbolt,' as 'casting the waters down to earth,' and 'restoring the sun to the sky.' He is in consequence 'the upholder of heaven, earth, and firmament,' and the god 'who has engendered the sun and the dawn.' " Chambers's Cyclopædia, *Indra*.

"Throughout these hymns two images stand out before us with overpowering distinctness. On one side is the bright god of the heaven, as beneficent as he is irresistible: on the other the demon of night and of darkness, as false and treachorous as he is malignant.... The latter (as his name Vritra, from var, to veil, indicates) is pre-eminently the thief who hides away the rain-clouds.... But the myth is yet in too early a state to allow of the definite designations which are brought before us in the conflicts of Zeus with Typhôn and his monstrous progeny, of Apollôn with the Pythôn, of Bellerophôn with Chimaira of Oidipous with the Sphinx, of Hercules with Cacus, of Sigurd with the dragon Fafnir; and thus not only is Vritra known by many names, but he is opposed sometimes by Indra, sometimes by Agni the fire-god, sometimes by Trita, Brihaspati, or other deities; or rather these are all names of one and the same god." Cox's *Mythology of the Aryan Nations. Vol. II. p. 326.*

Page 125.

And that prized herb whose sovereign power
Preserves from dark misfortune's hour.

"And yet more medicinal is it than that Moly,

That Hermes once to wise Ulysses gave;

He called it Hæmony, and gave it me,

And bade me keep it as of sovereign use

'Gainst all enchantment, mildew, blast, or damp,

Or ghastly furies' apparition." *Comus.*

The *Moly* of Homer, which Dierbach considers to have been the *Mandrake*, is probably a corruption of the Sanskrit *Múla* a root.

Page 136.

True is the ancient saw: the Neem
Can ne'er distil a honeyed stream.

The Neem tree, especially in the Rains, emits a strong unpleasant smell like that of onions. Its leaves however make an excellent cooling poultice, and the Extract of Neem is an admirable remedy for cutaneous disorders.

Page 152.

Who of Nisháda lineage came.

The following account of the origin of the Nishádas is taken from Wilson's *Vishṇu Puráṇa*, Book I. Chap. 15. "Afterwards the Munis beheld a great dust arise, and they said to the people who were nigh: 'What is this?' And the people answered and said: 'Now that the kingdom is without a king, the dishonest men have begun to seize the property of their neighbours. The great dust that you behold, excellent Munis, is raised by troops of clustering robbers, hastening to fall upon their prey.' The sages, hearing this, consulted, and together rubbed the thigh of the king (Vena), who had left no offspring, to produce a son. From the thigh, thus rubbed, came forth a being of the complexion of a charred stake, with flattened features like a negro, and of dwarfish stature. 'What am I to do,' cried he eagerly to the Munis. 'Sit down (nishída),' said they. And thence his name was Nisháda. His descendants, the inhabitants of the Vindhyá mountain, great Muni, are still called Nishádas and are characterized by the exterior tokens of depravity." Professor Wilson adds, in his note on the passage: "The Matsya says that there were born outcast or barbarous races, Mlechchhas, as black as collyrium. The Bhágavata describes an individual of dwarfish stature, with short arms and legs, of a complexion as black as a crow, with projecting chin, broad flat nose, red eyes, and tawny hair, whose descendants were mountaineers and foresters. The Padma (Bhúmi Khaṇḍa) has a similar deccription; adding to the dwarfish stature and black complexion, a wide mouth, large ears, and a protuberant belly. It also particularizes his posterity as Nishádas, Kirátas, Bhillas, and other barbarians and Mlechchhas, living in woods and on mountains. These passages intend, and do not much exaggerate, the uncouth appearance of the Gonds, Koles, Bhils, and other uncivilized tribes, scattered along the forests and mountains of Central India from Behar to Khandesh, and who are, not improbably, the predecessors of the present occupants of the cultivated portions of the country. They are always very black, ill-shapen, and dwarfish, and have countenances of a very African character."

Manu gives a different origin of the Nishádas as the offspring of a Bráhman father and a Súdra mother. See Muir's *Sanskrit Texts*, Vol. I. p. 481.

Page 157.

Beneath a fig-tree's mighty shade,

With countless pendent shoots displayed.
"So counselled he, and both together went
Into the thickest wood; there soon they chose
The fig-tree: not that kind for fruit renowned,
But such as at this day, to Indians known,
In Malabar or Deccan spreads her arms
Branching so broad and long, that in the ground
The bended twigs take root, and daughters grow
About the mother tree, a pillared shade
High overarched, and echoing walks between."
Paradise Lost, Book IX.

Page 161.

Now, Lakshman, as our cot is made,
Must sacrifice be duly paid.

The rites performed in India on the completion of a house are represented in modern Europe by the familiar "house-warming."

Page 169.

I longed with all my lawless will
Some elephant by night to kill.

One of the regal or military caste was forbidden to kill an elephant except in battle.

Thy hand has made no Bráhman bleed.

"The punishment which the Code of Manu awards to the slayer of a Brahman was to be branded in the forehead with the mark of a headless corpse, and entirely banished from society; this being apparently commutable for a fine. The poem is therefore in accordance with the Code regarding the peculiar guilt of killing Brahmans; but in allowing a hermit who was not a *Divija* (twice-born) to go to heaven, the poem is far in advance of the Code. The youth in the poem is allowed to read the Veda, and to accumulate merit by his own as well as his father's pious acts; whereas the exclusive Code reserves all such privileges to *Divijas* invested with the sacred cord." Mrs. Speir's *Life in Ancient India*, p. 107.

Page 174. The Praise Of Kings

"Compare this magnificent eulogium of kings and kingly government with what Samuel says of the king and his authority: And Samuel told all the words of the Lord unto the people that asked of him a king.

And he said, This will be the manner of the king that shall reign over you: He will take your sons, and appoint them for himself, for his chariots, and to be his horsemen: and some shall run before his chariots.

And he will appoint him captains over thousands, and captains over fifties, and will set them to work his ground, and to reap his harvest, and to make his instrument of war, and instruments of his chariots.

And he will take your daughters to be confectionaries, and to be cooks, and to be bakers.

And he will take your fields, and your vineyards and your oliveyards, even the best of them, and give them to his servants.

And he will take the tenth of your seed, and of your vineyards, and give to his officers, and to his servants.

And he will take your men-servants, and your maid-servants, and your goodliest young men, and your asses, and put them to his work.

He will take the tenth of your sheep: and ye shall be his servants.

And ye shall cry out in that day because of your king which ye shall have chosen you. I. *Samuel*, VIII.

In India kingly government was ancient and consecrated by tradition: whence to change it seemed disorderly and revolutionary: in Judæa theocracy was ancient and consecrated by tradition, and therefore the innovation which would substitute a king was represented as full of dangers." Gorresio.

Page 176. Sálmalí.

According to the Bengal recension Sálmalí appears to have been another name of the Vipáśá. Sálmalí may be an epithet signifying rich in Bombax heptaphyllon. The commentator makes another river out of the word.

Page 178. Bharat's Return.

"Two routes from Ayodhyá to Rájagriha or Girivraja are described. That taken by the envoys appears to have been the shorter one, and we are not told why Bharat returned by a different road. The capital of the Kekayas lay to the west of the Vipáśá. Between it and the Śatadru stretched the country of the Báhíkas. Upon the remaining portion of the road the two recensions differ. According to that of Bengal there follow towards the east the river Indamatí, then the town Ajakála belonging to the Bodhi, then Bhulingá, then the river Śaradaṇḍá. According to the other instead of the first river comes the Ikshumatí ... instead of the first town Abhikála, instead of the second Kulingá, then the second river. According to the direction of the route both the above-mentioned rivers must be tributaries of the Śatadrú.... The road then crossed the Yamuná (Jumna), led beyond that river through the country of the Panchálas, and reached the Ganges at Hástinapura, where the ferry was. Thence it led over the Rámagangá and its eastern tributaries, then over the Gomati, and then in a southern direction along the Málini, beyond which it reached Ayodhyá. In Bharat's journey the following rivers are passed from west to east: *Kutikoshṭiká, Uttániká, Kuṭiká, Kapívatí, Gomatí* according to Schlegel, and *Hiraṇyavatí, Uttáriká, Kuṭilá, Kapívatí, Gomatí* according to Gorresio. As these rivers are to be looked for on the east of the Ganges, the first must be the modern *Koh*, a small affluent of the Rámagangá, over which the highway cannot have gone as it bends too far to the north. The Uttániká or Uttáriká must be the Rámagangá, the Kuṭiká or Kuṭilá its eastern tributary, Kośilá, the Kapívatí the next tributary which on the maps has different names, *Gurra* or above Kailas, lower down *Bhaigu*. The Gomatí (Goomtee) retains its old name. The Málini, mentioned only in the envoys' journey, must have been the western tributary of the Sarayú now called Chuká." Lassen's *Indische Alterthumskunde*, Vol. II. P. 524.

Page 183.

What worlds await thee, Queen, for this?

"Indian belief divided the universe into several worlds (*lokáh*). The three principal worlds were heaven, earth, and hell. But according to another division there were seven: Bhúrloka or the earth, Bhuvarloka or the space between the earth and the sun, the seat of the Munis, Siddhas, &c., Svarloka or the heaven of Indra between the sun and the polar star, and the seventh Brahmaloka or the world of Brahma. Spirits which reached the last were exempt from being born again." Gorresio.

Page 203.

When from a million herbs a blaze

Of their own luminous glory plays.

This mention of lambent flames emitted by herbs at night may be compared with Lucan's description of a similar phenomenon in the Druidical forest near Marseilles, (*Pharsalia*, III. 420.).

Non ardentis fulgere incendia silvae.

Seneca, speaking of Argolis, (Thyestes, Act IV), says:—

Tota solet

Micare flamma silva, et excelsae trabes

Ardent sine igni.

Thus also the bush at Horeb (Exod. II.) flamed, but was not consumed.

The Indian explanation of the phenomenon is, that the sun before he sets deposits his rays for the night with the deciduous plants. See *Journal of R. As. S. Bengal*, Vol. II. p. 339.

Page 219.

We rank the Buddhist with the thief.

Schlegel says in his Preface: "Lubrico vestigio insistit V. Cl. *Heerenius, prof. Gottingensis*, in libro suo de commerciis veterum populorum (Opp. Vol. Hist. XII, pag. 129,) dum putat, ex mentione sectatorum Buddhae secundo libro Rameidos iniecta de tempore, quo totum carmen sit conditum, quicquam legitime concludi posse.... Sunt versus spurii, reiecti a Bengalis in sola commentatorum recensione leguntur. Buddhas quidem mille fere annis ante Christum natun vixit: sed post multa demumsecula, odiointernecivo inter Brachmanos et Buddhae sectatores orto, his denique ex India pulsis, fingi potuit iniquissima criminatio, eos animi immortalitatem poenasque et praemia in vita futura negare. Praeterea metrum, quo concinnati sunt hi versus, de quo metro mox disseram, recentiorem aetatem arguit.... Poenitet me nunc mei consilii, quod non statim ab initio, ... eiecerim cuncta disticha diversis a sloco vulgari metris composita. Metra sunt duo: pariter ambo constant quatuor hemistichiis inter se aequalibus, alterum undenarum syllabarum, alterum duodenarum, hunc in modum:

[-)] [-] [)] [-] | [-] [)] [)] [-] | [)] [-] [-)]

[)] [-] [)] [-] | [-] [)] [)] [-] | [)] [-] [)] [-)]

Cuius generis versus in primo et secundo Rameidos libro nusquam nisi ad finem capitum apposita inveniuntur, et huic loco unice sunt accommodata, quasi peroratio, lyricis numeris assurgens, quo magis canorae cadant clausulae: sicut musici in concentibus extremis omnium vocum instrumentorumque ictu fortiore aures percellere amant. Igitur disticha illa non ante divisionem per capita illatam addi potuerunt: hanc autem grammaticis deberi argumento est ipse recensionum dissensus, manifesto inde ortus, quod singuli editores in ea constituenda suo quisque iudicio usi sunt; praeterquam quod non credibile est, poetam artis suae peritum narrationem continuam in membra tam minuta dissecuisse. Porro discolor est dictio: magniloquentia affectatur, sed nimis turgida illa atque effusa, nec sententiarum pondere satis suffulta. Denique nihil fere novi affertur: amplificantur prius dicta, rarius aliquid ex capite sequente anticipatur. Si quis appendices hosce legendo transiliat, sentiet slocum ultimum cum primo capitis proximi apte coagmentatum, nec sine vi quadam inde avulsum. Eiusmodi versus exhibet utraque recensio, sed modo haec modo illa plures paucioresve numero, et lectio interdum magnopere variat."

"The narrative of Ráma's exile in the jungle is one of the most obscure portions of the Rámáyana, inasmuch as it is difficult to discover any trace of the original tradition, or any illustration of actual life and manners, beyond the artificial life of self-mortification and selfdenial said to have been led by the Brahman sages of olden time. At the same time, however, the story throws some light upon the significance of the poem, and upon the character in which the Brahmanical author desired to represent Ráma; and consequently it deserves more serious consideration than the nature of the subject-matter would otherwise seem to imply.

"According to the Rámáyana, the hero Ráma spent more than thirteen years of his exile in wandering amongst the different Brahmanical settlements, which appear to have been scattered over the country between the Ganges and the Godáveri; his wanderings extending from the hill of Chitra-kúṭa in Bundelkund, to the modern town of Nasik on the western side of India, near the source of the Godáveri river, and about seventy-five miles to the north-west of Bombay. The appearance of these Brahmanical hermitages in the country far away to the south of the Raj of Kasala, seems to call for critical inquiry. Each hermitage is said to have belonged to some particular sage, who is famous in Brahmanical tradition. But whether the sages named were really contemporaries of Ráma, or whether they could possibly have flourished at one and the same period, is open to serious question. It is of course impossible to fix with any degree of certainty the relative chronology of the several sages, who are said to have been visited by Ráma; but still it seems tolerably clear that some belonged to an age far anterior to that in which the Rámáyana was composed, and probably to an age anterior to that in which Ráma existed as a real and living personage; whilst, at least, one sage is to be found who could only have existed in the age during which the Rámáyana was produced in its present form. The main proofs of these inferences are as follows. An interval of many centuries seems to have elapsed between the composition of the Rig-Veda and that of the Rámáyana: a conclusion which has long been proved by the evidence of language, and is generally accepted by Sanskrit scholars. But three of the sages, said to have been contemporary with Ráma, namely, Viśvámitra, Atri and Agastya, are frequently mentioned in the hymns of the Rig-Veda; whilst Válmíki, the sage dwelling at Chitra-kúta, is said to have been himself the composer of the Rámáyana. Again, the sage Atri, whom Ráma visited immediately after his departure from Chitra-kúṭa, appears in the genealogical list preserved in the Mahá Bhárata, as the progenitor of the Moon, and consequently as the first ancestor of the Lunar race: whilst his grandson Buddha [Budha] is said to have married Ilá, the daughter of Ikhsváku who was himself the remote ancestor of the Solar race of Ayodhyá, from whom Ráma was removed by many generations. These conclusions are not perhaps based upon absolute proof, because they are drawn from untrustworthy authorities; but still the chronological difficulties have been fully apprehended by the Pundits, and an attempt has been made to reconcile all contradictions by representing the sages to have lived thousands of years, and to have often re-appeared upon earth in different ages widely removed from each other. Modern science refuses to accept such explanations; and consequently it is impossible to escape the conclusion that if Válmíki composed the Rámáyana in the form of Sanskrit in which it has been preserved, he could not have flourished in the same age as the sages who are named in the Rig-Veda." Wheeler's *History of India, Vol.* II, 229.

Page 249.

And King Himálaya's Child.

Umá or Párvatí, was the daughter of Himálaya and Mená. She is the heroine of Kálidása's *Kumára-Sambhava* or *Birth of the War-God.*

Page 250.

Strong Kumbhakarṇa slumbering deep

In chains of never-ending sleep.

"Kumbhakarṇa, the gigantic brother of the titanic Rávaṇ,—named from the size of his ears which could contain a *Kumbha* or large water-jar— had such an appetite that he used to consume six months' provisions in a single day. Brahmá, to relieve the alarm of the world, which had begun to entertain serious apprehensions of being eaten up, decreed that the giant should sleep six months at a time and wake for only one day during which he might consume his six months' allowance without trespassing unduly on the reproductive capabilities of the " *Scenes front the Rámáyan,* p. 153, 2nd Edit.

Page 257.

Like Śiva when his angry might

Stayed Daksha's sacrificial rite.

The following spirited version of this old story is from the pen of Mr. W. Waterfield:

"This is a favorite subject of Hindú sculpture, especially on the temples of Shiva, such as the caves of Elephanta and Ellora. It, no doubt, is an allegory of the contest between the followers of Shiva and the worshippers of the Elements, who observed the old ritual of the Vedas; in which the name of Shiva is never mentioned.

Daksha for devotion
Made a mighty feast:
Milk and curds and butter,
Flesh of bird and beast,
Rice and spice and honey,
Sweetmeats ghí and gur, 1038
Gifts for all the Bráhmans,
Food for all the poor.
At the gates of Gangá 1039
Daksha held his feast;
Called the gods unto it,
Greatest as the least.
All the gods were gathered
Round with one accord;
All the gods but Umá,
All but Umá's lord.
Umá sat with Shiva
On Kailása hill:
Round them stood the Rudras
Watching for their will.
Who is this that cometh
Lilting to his lute?
All the birds of heaven
Heard his music, mute.
Round his head a garland
Rich of hue was wreathed:
Every sweetest odour
From its blossoms breathed.
'Tis the Muni Nárad;
'Mong the gods he fares,
Ever making mischief

By the tales he bears.
"Hail to lovely Umá!
Hail to Umá's lord!
Wherefore are they absent
For her father's board?
Multiplied his merits
Would be truly thrice,
Could he gain your favour
For his sacrifice."
Worth of heart was Umá;
To her lord she spake:—
"Why dost thou, the mighty,
Of no rite partake?
Straight I speed to Daksha
Such a sight to see:
If he be my father,
He must welcome thee."
Wondrous was in glory
Daksha's holy rite;
Never had creation
Viewed so brave a sight.
Gods, and nymphs, find fathers,
Sages, Bráhmans, sprites,—
Every diverge creature
Wrought that rite of rites.
Quickly then a quaking
Fell on all from far;
Umá stood among them
On her lion car.
"Greeting, gods and sages,
Greeting, father mine!
Work hath wondrous virtue,
Where such aids combine.
Guest-hall never gathered

Goodlier company:
Seemeth all are welcome.
All the gods but me."
Spake the Muni Daksha,
Stern and cold his tone:—
"Welcome thou, too, daughter,
Since thou com'st alone.
But thy frenzied husband
Suits another shrine;
He is no partaker
Of this feast of mine.
He who walks in darkness
Loves no deeds of light:
He who herds with demons
Shuns each kindly sprite.
Let him wander naked.—
Wizard weapons wield,—
Dance his frantic measure
Round the funeral field.
Art thou yet delighted
With the reeking hide,
Body smeared with ashes.
Skulls in necklace tied?
Thou to love this monster?
Thou to plead his part!
Know the moon and Gangá
Share that faithless heart
Vainly art thou vying
With thy rivals' charms.
Are not coils of serpents
Softer than thine arms?"
Words like these from Daksha
Daksha's daughter heard:
Then a sudden passion

All her bosom stirred.
Eyes with fury flashing.
Speechless in her ire,
Headlong did she hurl her
'Mid the holy fire.
Then a trembling terror
Overcame each one,
And their minds were troubled
Like a darkened sun;
And a cruel Vision,
Face of lurid flame,
Umá's Wrath incarnate,
From the altar came.
Fiendlike forms by thousands
Started from his side,
'Gainst the sacrificers
All their might they plied:
Till the saints availed not
Strength like theirs to stay,
And the gods distracted
Turned and fled away.
Hushed were hymns and chanting,
Priests were mocked and spurned;
Food defiled and scattered;
Altars overturned. —
Then, to save the object
Sought at such a price,
Like a deer in semblance
Sped the sacrifice.
Soaring toward the heavens,
Through the sky it fled?
But the Rudras chasing
Smote away its head.
Prostrate on the pavement

Daksha fell dismayed:—
"Mightiest, thou hast conquered
Thee we ask for aid.
Let not our oblations
All be rendered vain;
Let our toilsome labour
Full fruition gain."
Bright the broken altars
Shone with Shiva's form;
"Be it so!" His blessing
Soothed that frantic storm.
Soon his anger ceases,
Though it soon arise;—
But the Deer's Head ever
Blazes in the skies."

Indian Ballads and other Poems.

Page 286. Urvasí.

"The personification of Urvasî herself is as thin as that of Eôs or Selênê. Her name is often found in the Veda as a mere name for the morning, and in the plural number it is used to denote the dawns which passing over men bring them to old age and death. Urvasî is the bright flush of light overspreading the heaven before the sun rises, and is but another form of the many mythical beings of Greek mythology whose names take us back to the same idea or the same root. As the dawn in the Vedic hymns is called Urûkî, the far-going (Têlephassa, Têlephos), so is she also Uruasî, the wide-existing or wide-spreading; as are Eurôpê, Euryanassa, Euryphassa, and many more of the sisters of Athênê and Aphroditê. As such she is the mother of Vasishtha, the bright being, as Oidipous is the son of Iokastê; and although Vasishtha, like Oidipous, has become a mortal bard or sage, he is still the son of Mitra and Varuṇa, of night and day. Her lover Purûravas is the counterpart of the Hellenic Polydeukês; but the continuance of her union with him depends on the condition that she never sees him unclothed. But the Gandharvas, impatient of her long sojourn among mortal men resolved to bring her back to their bright home; and Purûravas is thus led unwitingly to disregard her warning. A ewe with two lambs was tied to her couch, and the Gandharvas stole one of them; Urvasî said, 'They take away my darling, as if I lived in a land where there is no hero and no man.' They stole the second, and she upbraided her husband again. Then Purûravas looked and said, 'How can that be a land without heroes or men where I am?' And naked he sprang up; he thought it was too long to put on his dress. Then the Gandharvas sent a flash of lighting, and Urvasî saw her husband naked as by daylight. Then she vanished. 'I come back,' she said, and went. 'Then he bewailed his vanished love in bitter grief.' Her promise to return was fulfilled, but for a moment only, at the Lotos-lake, and Purûravas in vain beseeches her to tarry longer. 'What shall I do with thy speech?' is the answer of Urvasî. 'I am gone like the first of the dawns. Purûravas, go home again. I am hard to be caught like the winds.' Her lover is in utter despair; but when he lies down to die, the heart of Urvasî was melted, and she bids him come to her on the last night of the year. On that night only he might be with her; but a son should be born to him. On that day he went up to the golden seats, and there Urvasî told him that the Gandharvas would grant him one wish, and that he must make his choice. 'Choose thou for me,' he said: and she answered, 'Say to them, Let me be one of you.' "

Cox's *Mythology of the Aryan Nations*. Vol. I. p. 397.

Page 324.

The sovereign of the Vánar race.

"Vánar is one of the most frequently occurring names by which the poem calls the monkeys of Ráma's army. Among the two or three derivations of which the word Vánar is susceptible, one is that which deduces it from vana which signifies a wood, and thus Vánar would mean a forester, an inhabitant of the wood. I have said elsewhere that the monkeys, the Vánars, whom Ráma led to the conquest of Ceylon were fierce woodland tribes who occupied the mountainous regions of the south of India, where their descendants may still be seen. I shall hence forth promiscuously employ the word *Vánar* to denote those monkeys, those fierce combatants of Ráma's army." Gorresio.

Page 326.

No change of hue, no pose of limb

Gave sign that aught was false in him.

Concise, unfaltering, sweet and clear,

Without a word to pain the ear,

From chest to throat, nor high nor low,

His accents came in measured flow.

Somewhat similarly in *The Squire's Tale*:

"He with a manly voice said his message,
After the form used in his language,
Withouten vice of syllable or of letter.
And for his talë shouldë seem the better
Accordant to his wordës was his chere,
As teacheth art of speech them that it lere."

Page 329. Ráma's Alliance With Sugríva.

"The literal interpretation of this portion of the Ramáyana is indeed deeply rooted in the mind of the Hindu. He implicitly believes that Ráma is Vishnu, who became incarnate for the purpose of destroying the demon Rávana: that he permitted his wife to be captured by Rávana for the sake of delivering the gods and Bráhmans from the oppressions of the Rákshasa; and that he ultimately assembled an army of monkeys, who were the progeny of the gods, and led them against the strong-hold of Rávana at Lanká, and delivered the world from the tyrant Rákshasa, whilst obtaining ample revenge for his own personal wrongs.

One other point seems to demand consideration, namely, the possibility of such an alliance as that which Ráma is said to have concluded with the monkeys. This possibility will of course be denied by modern critics, but still it is interesting to trace out the circumstances which seem to have led to the acceptance of such a wild belief by the dreamy and marvel loving Hindi. The south of India swarms with monkeys of curious intelligence and rare physical powers. Their wonderful instinct for organization, their attachment to particular localities, their occasional journeys in large numbers over mountains and across rivers, their obstinate assertion of supposed rights, and the ridiculous caricature which they exhibit of all that is animal and emotional in man, would naturally create a deep impression.... Indeed the habits of monkeys well deserve to be patiently studied; not as they appear in confinement, when much that is revolting in their nature is developed, but as they appear living in freedom amongst the trees of the forest, or in the streets of crowded cities, or precincts of temples. Such a study would not fail to awaken strange ideas; and although the European would not be prepared to regard monkeys as sacred animals he might be led to speculate as to their origin by the light of data, which are at present unknown to the naturalist whose observations have been derived from the menagerie alone.

Whatever, however, may have been the train of ideas which led the Hindú to regard the monkey as a being half human and half divine, there can be little doubt that in the Rámáyana the monkeys of southern India have been confounded with what may be called the aboriginal people of the country. The origin of this confusion may be easily conjectured. Perchance the aborigines of the country may have been regarded as a superior kind of monkeys; and to this day the features of the Marawars, who are supposed to be the aborigines of the southern part of the Carnatic, are not only different from those of their neighbours, but are of a character calculated to confirm the conjecture. Again, it is probable that the army of aborigines may have been accompanied by outlying bands of monkeys impelled by that magpie-like curiosity and love of plunder which are the peculiar characteristics of the monkey race; and this incident may have given rise to the story that the army was composed of Monkeys."

Wheeler's *History of India. Vol. II. pp. 316 ff.*

Page 342. The Fall Of Báli.

"As regards the narrative, it certainly seems to refer to some real event amongst the aboriginal tribes: namely, the quarrel between an elder and younger brother for the possession of a Ráj; and the subsequent alliance of Ráma with the younger brother. It is somewhat remarkable that Ráma appears to have formed an alliance with the wrong party, for the right of Báli was evidently superior to that of Sugríva; and it is especially worthy of note that Ráma compassed the death of Báli by an act contrary to all the laws of fair fighting. Again, Ráma seems to have tacitly sanctioned the transfer of Tárá from Báli to Sugríva, which was directly opposed to modern rule, although in conformity with the rude customs of a barbarous age; and it is remarkable that to this day the marriage of both widows and divorced women is practised by the Marawars, or aborigines of the southern Carnatic, contrary to the deeply-rooted prejudice which exists against such unions amongst the Hindús at large."

Wheeler's *History of India, Vol. II. 324.*

Page 370. The Vánar Host.

"The splendid Marutas form the army of Indras, the red-haired monkeys and bears that of Rámas; and the mythical and solar nature of the monkeys and bears of the Rámâyaṇam manifests itself several times. The king of the monkeys is a sun-god. The ancient king was named Bâlin, and was the son of Indras. His younger brother Sugrívas, he who changes his shape at pleasure (Kâmarúpas), who, helped by Rámas, usurped his throne, is said to be own child of the sun. Here it is evident that the Vedic antagonism between Indras and Vishṇus is reproduced in a zoological and entirely apish form. The old Zeus must give way to the new, the moon to the sun, the evening to the morning sun, the sun of winter to that of spring; the young son betrays and overthrows the old one.... Rámas, who treacherously kills the old king of the monkeys, Bâlin, is the equivalent of Vishṇus, who hurls his predecessor Indras from his throne; and Sugrívas, the new king of the monkeys resembles Indras when he promises to find the ravished Sítá, in the same way as Vishṇus in one of his incarnations finds again the lost vedás. And there are other indications in the Râmâyaṇam of opposition between Indras and the monkeys who assist Râmas. The great monkey Hanumant, of the reddish colour of gold, has his jaw broken, Indras having struck him with his thunderbolt and caused him to fall upon a mountain, because, while yet a child, he threw himself off a mountain into the air in order to arrest the course of the sun, whose rays had no effect upon him. (The cloud rises from the mountain and hides the sun, which is unable of itself to disperse it; the tempest comes, and brings flashes of lightning and thunder-bolts, which tear the cloud in pieces.)

The whole legend of the monkey Hanumant represents the sun entering into the cloud or darkness, and coming out of it. His father is said to be now the wind, now the elephant of the monkeys (Kapikunjaras), now Keśarin, the long-haired sun, the sun with a mane, the lion sun (whence his name of Keśariṇah putrah). From this point of view, Hanumant would seem to be the brother of Sugrívas, who is also the offspring of the sun....

All the epic monkeys of the Râmâyaṇam are described in the twentieth canto of the first book by expressions which very closely resemble those applied in the Vedic hymns to the Marutas, as swift as the tempestuous wind, changing their shape at pleasure, making a noise like clouds, sounding like thunder, battling, hurling mountain-peaks, shaking great uprooted trees, stirring up the deep waters, crushing the earth with their arms, making the clouds fall. Thus Bâlin comes out of the cavern as the sun out of the cloud....

But the legend of the monkey Hanumant presents another curious resemblance to that of Samson. Hanumant is bound with cords by Indrajit, son of Rávaṇas; he could easily free himself, but does not wish to do so. Rávaṇas to put him to shame, orders his tail to be burned, because the tail is the part most prized by monkeys....

The tail of Hanumant, which sets fire to the city of the monsters, is probably a personification of the rays of the morning or spring sun, which sets fire to the eastern heavens, and destroys the abode of the nocturnal or winter monsters."

De Gubernatis, *Zoological Mythology*, Vol. II. pp. 100 ff.

"The Jaitwas of Rajputana, a tribe politically reckoned as Rajputs, nevertheless trace their descent from the monkey-god Hanuman, and confirm it by alleging that their princes still bear its evidence in a tail-like prolongation of the spine; a tradition which has probably a real ethnological meaning, pointing out the Jaitwas as of non-Aryan race." 1040 Tylor's *Primitive Culture*, Vol. I. p. 341.

Page 372.

The names of peoples occurring in the following *ślokas* are omitted in the metrical translation:

"Go to the Brahmamálas, 1041 the Videhas, 1042 the Málavas, 1043 the Káśikośalas, 1044 the Mágadnas, 1045 the Puṇḍras, 1046 and the Angas, 1047 and the land of the weavers of silk, and the land of the mines of silver, and the hills that stretch into the sea, and the towns and the hamlets that are about the top of Mandar, and the Karṇaprávaraṇas, 1048 and the Oshṭhakarṇakas, 1049 and the Ghoralohamukhas, 1050 and the swift Ekapádakas, 1051 and the strong imperishable Eaters of Men, and the Kirátas 1052 with stiff hair-tufts, men like gold and fair to look upon: And the Eaters of Raw Fish, and the Kirátas who dwell in islands, and the fierce Tiger-men 1053 who live amid the waters."

Page 374.

"Go to the Vidarbhas 1054 and the Rishṭikas 1055 and the Mahishikas, 1056 and the Matsyas 1057 and Kalingas 1058 and the Kauśikas 1059 ... and the Andhras 1060 and the Puṇḍras 1061 and the Cholas 1062 and the Paṇḍyas 1063 and the Keralas, 1064 Mlechchhas 1065 and the Pulindas 1066 and the Śúrasenas, 1067 and the Prasthalas and the Bharatas and Madrakas 1068 and the Kámbojas 1069 and the Yavanas 1070 and the towns of the Śakas 1071 and the Varadas." 1072

Page 378. Northern Kurus.

Professor Lassen remarks in the Zeitschrift für die Kunde des Morgenlandes, ii. 62: "At the furthest accessible extremity of the earth appears Harivarsha with the northern Kurus. The region of Hari or Vishṇu belongs to the system of mythical geography; but the case is different with the Uttara Kurus. Here there is a real basis of geographical fact; of which fable has only taken advantage, without creating it. The Uttara Kurus were formerly quite independent of the mythical system of *dvípas*, though they were included in it at an early date." Again the same writer says at p. 65: "That the conception of the Uttara Kurus is based upon an actual country and not on mere invention, is proved (1) by the way in which they are mentioned in the Vedas; (2) by the existence of Uttara Kuru in historical times as a real country; and (3) by the way in which the legend makes mention of that region as the home of primitive customs. To begin with the last point the Mahábhárata speaks as follows of the freer mode of life which women led in the early world, Book I. verses 4719-22: 'Women were formerly unconfined and roved about at their pleasure, independent. Though in their youthful innocence they abandoned their husbands, they were guilty of no offence; for such was the rule in early times. This ancient custom is even now the law for creatures born as brutes, which are free from lust and anger. This custom is supported by authority and is observed by great rishis, and it is *still practiced among the northern Kurus.'*

"The idea which is here conveyed is that of the continuance in one part of the world of that original blessedness which prevailed in the golden age. To afford a conception of the happy condition of the southern Kurus it is said in another place (M.-Bh, i. 4346.) 'The southern Kurus vied in happiness with the northern Kurus and with the divine rishis and bards.'

Professor Lassen goes on to say: 'Ptolemy (vi. 16.) is also acquainted with *Uttara Kuru*. He speaks of a mountain, a people, and a city called *Ottorakorra*. Most of the other ancient authors who elsewhere mention this name, have it from him. It is a part of the country which he calls Serica; according to him the city lies twelve degrees west from the metropolis of Sera, and the mountain extends from thence far to the eastward. As Ptolemy has misplaced the whole of eastern Asia beyond the Ganges, the *relative* position which he assigns will guide us better that the absolute one, which removes *Ottorakorra* so far to the east that a correction is inevitable. According to my opinion the *Ottorakorra* of Ptolemy must be sought for to the east of Kashgar.' Lassen also thinks that Magasthenes had the Uttara Kurus in view when he referred to the Hyperboreans who were fabled by Indian writers to live a thousand years. In his Indian antiquities, (Ind. Alterthumskunde, i. 511, 512. and note,) the same writer concludes that though the passages above cited relative to the Uttara Kurus indicate a belief in the existence of a really existing country of that name in the far north, yet that the descriptions there given are to be taken as pictures of an ideal paradise, and not as founded on any recollections of the northern origin of the Kurus. It is probable, he thinks, that some such reminiscences originally existed, and still survived in the Vedic era, though there is no trace of their existence in latter times." Muir's *Sanskrit Texts*, Vol. II. pp. 336, 337.

Page 428.

Trust to these mighty Vánars.

The corresponding passage in the Bengal recension has "these silvans in the forms of monkeys, vánaráh kapirupinah." "Here it manifestly appears," says Gorresio, "that these hosts of combatants whom Ráma led to the conquest of Lanká (Ceylon) the kingdom and seat of the Hamitic race, and whom the poem calls monkeys, were in fact as I have elsewhere observed, inhabitants of the mountainous and southern regions of India, who were wild-looking and not altogether unlike monkeys. They were perhaps the remote ancestors of the Malay races."

Page 431.

"Art thou not he who slew of old
The Serpent-Gods, and stormed their hold."

All these exploits of Rávan are detailed in the *Uttarakánda*, and epitomized in the Appendix.

Page 434.

Within the consecrated hall.

The Bráhman householder ought to maintain three sacred fires, the *Gárhapatya*, the *Ahavaniya* and the *Dakshina*. These three fires were made use of in many Brahmanical solemnities, for example in funeral rites when the three fires were arranged in prescribed order.

Page 436.

Fair Punjikasthalá I met.

"I have not noticed in the Úttara Kánda any story about the daughter of Varuna, but the commentator on the text (VI 60, 11) explains the allusion to her thus:

"The daughter of Varuna was Punjikasthalí. On her account, a curse of Brahmá, involving the penalty of death, [was pronounced] on the rape of women." Muir, *Sanskrit Texts*, Part IV. Appendix.

Page 452.

"Shall no funereal honours grace
The parted lord of Raghu's race?"

"Here are indicated those admirable rites and those funeral prayers which Professor Müller has described in his excellent work, *Die Todtenbestattung bei den Brahmanen*, Sítá laments that the body of Ráma will not be honoured with those rites and prayers, nor will the Bráhman priest while laying the ashes from the pile in the bosom of the earth, pronounce over them those solemn and magnificent words: 'Go unto the earth, thy mother, the ample, wide, and blessed earth.... And do thou, O Earth, open and receive him as a friend with sweet greeting: enfold him in thy bosom as a mother wraps her child in her robes.' " Gorresio.

Page 462.

Each glorious sign

That stamps the future queen is mine.

We read in Josephus that Caesar was so well versed in chiromancy that when one day a *soi-disant* son of Herod had audience of him, he at once detected the impostor because his hand was destitute of all marks of royalty.

Page 466.

In battle's wild Gandharva dance.

"Here the commentator explains: 'the battle resembled the dance of the Gandharvas,' in accordance with the notion of the Gandharvas entertained in his day. They were regarded as celestial musicians enlivening with their melodies Indra's heaven and the banquets of the Gods. But the Gandharvas before becoming celestial musicians in popular tradition, were in the primitive and true signification of the name heroes, spirited and ardent warriors, followers of Indra, and combined the heroical character with their atmospherical deity. Under this aspect the dance of the Gandharvas may be a very different thing from what the commentator means, and may signify the horrid dance of war." Gorresio.

The Homeric expression is similar, "to dance a war-dance before Ares."

Page 470.

By Anaraṇya's lips of old.

"The story of Anaraṇya is told in the Uttara Kaṇḍa of the Rámáyaṇa.... Anaraṇya a descendant of Ixváku and King of Ayodhyá, when called upon to fight with Rávaṇa or acknowledge himself conquered, prefers the former alternative; but his army is overcome, and he himself is thrown from his chariot.

When Rávaṇa triumphs over his prostrate foe, the latter says that he has been vanquished not by him but by fate, and that Rávaṇa is only the instrument of his overthrow; and he predicts that Rávaṇa shall one day be slain by his descendant Ráma." *Sanskrit Texts*, IV., Appendix.

Page 497.

"With regard to the magic image of Sítá made by Indrajit, we may observe that this thoroughly oriental idea is also found in Greece in Homer's

Iliad, where Apollo forms an image of Æneas to save that hero beloved by the Gods: it occurs too in the Æneid of Virgil where Juno forms a fictitious Æneas to save Turnus:

Tum dea nube cava tenuem sine viribus umbram

In faciem Æneæ (visu mirabile monstrum)

Dardaniis ornat telis; clipeumque jubasque

Divini assimulat capitis; dat inania verba;

Dat sine mente sonum, gressusque effingit euntis.

(*Æneidos*, lib. X.)" Gorresio.

Page 489.

"To Raghu's son my chariot lend."

"Analogous to this passage of the Rámáyana, where Indra sends to Ráma his own chariot, his own charioteer, and his own arms, is the passage in the Æneid where Venus descending from heaven brings celestial arms to her son Æneas when he is about to enter the battle:

At Venus æthereos inter dea candida nimbos

Dona fereus aderat;...

...

Arma sub adversa posuit radiantia quercum.

Ille, deæ donis et tanto lætus honore,

Expleri nequit, atque oculus per singula volvit,

Miraturque, interque manus et brachia versat

Terribilem cristis galeam flammasque vomentem,

Fatiferumque ensem, loricam ex ære rigentem.

(*Æneidos*, lib. VIII)" Gorresio.

Page 489.

Agastya came and gently spake.

"The Muni or saint Agastya, author of several Vedic hymns, was celebrated in Indo-Sanskrit tradition for having directed the first brahmanical settlements in the southern regions of India; and the Mahábhárata gives him the credit of having subjected those countries, expelled the Rákshases. and given security to the solitary ascetics, who were settled there. Hence Agastya was regarded in ancient legend as the conqueror and ruler of the southern country. This tradition refers to the earliest migrations made by the Sanskrit Indians towards the south of India. To Agastya are attributed many marvellous mythic deeds which adumbrate and veil ancient events; some of which are alluded to here and there in the Rámáyana." Gorresio.

The following is the literal translation of the Canto, text and commentary, from the Calcutta edition:

Having found Ráma weary with fighting and buried in deep thought, and Rávaṇ standing before him ready to engage in battle, the holy Agastya, who had come to see the battle, approached Ráma and spoke to him thus: "O mighty Ráma, listen to the old mystery by which thou wilt conquer all thy foes in the battle. Having daily repeated the Ádityahridaya (the delighter of the mind of the Sun) the holy prayer which destroys all enemies (of him who repeats it) gives victory, removes all sins, sorrows and distress, increases life, and which is the blessing of all blessings, worship the rising and splendid sun who is respected by both the Gods and demons, who gives light to all bodies and who is the rich lord of all the worlds, (To the question why this prayer claims so great reverence; the sage answers) Since yonder 1073 sun is full of glory and all gods reside in him (he being their material cause) and bestows being and the active principle on all creatures by his rays; and since he protects all deities, demons and men with his rays.

He is Brahmá, 1074 Vishṇu, 1075 Śiva, 1076 Skanda, 1077 Prajápati, 1078 Mahendra, 1079 Dhanada, 1080 Kála, 1081 Yáma, 1082 Soma, 1083 Apàm Pati i.e. The lord of waters, Pitris, 1084 Vasus, 1085 Sádhyas, 1086 Aśvins, 1087 Maruts, 1088 Manu, 1089 Váyu, 1090 Vahni, 1091 Prajá, 1092 Práṇa, 1093 Ritukartá, 1094 Prabhákara, 1095 (Thou, 1096 art) Aditya, 1097 Savitá, 1098 Súrya, 1099 Khaga, 1100 Púshan, 1101 Gabhastimán, 1102 Śuvarṇasadriśa, 1103 Bhánu, 1104 Hiraṇyaretas, 1105 Divákara, 1106 Haridaśva, 1107 Sahasrárchish, 1108 Saptasapti, 1109 Marichimán, 1110 Timironmathana, 1111 Sambhu, 1112 Twashtá, 1113 Mártanda, 1114 Anśumán, 1115 Hiranyagarbha, 1116 Siśira, 1117 Tapana, 1118 Ahaskara, 1119 Ravi, 1120 Agnigarbha, 1121 Aditiputra, 1122 Sankha, 1123 Siśiranáśana, 1124 Vyomanátha, 1125 Tamobhedí, 1126 Rigyajussámapáraga, 1127 Ghanavríshti, 1128 Apám-Mitra, 1129 Vindhyavíthíplavangama, 1130 Átapí, 1131 Mandalí, 1132 Mrityu (death), Pingala, 1133 Sarvatápana, 1134 Kavi, 1135 Viśva, 1136 Mahátejas, 1137 Rakta, 1138 Sarvabhavodbhava. 1139 The Lord of stars, planets, and other luminous bodies, Viśvabhávana, 1140 Tejasvinám-Tejasvi, 1141 Dwádaśátman: 1142 I salute thee. I salute thee who art the eastern mountain. I salute thee who art the western mountain. I salute thee who art the Lord of all the luminous bodies. I salute thee who art the Lord of days.

I respectfully salute thee who art Jaya, 1143 Jayabhadra, 1144 Haryaśa, 1145 O Thou who hast a thousand rays, I repeatedly salute thee. I repeatedly and respectfully salute thee who art Áditya, I repeatedly salute thee who art

Ugra, 1146 Víra, 1147 and Sáranga. 1148 I salute thee who openest the lotuses (or the lotus of the heart). I salute thee who art furious. I salute thee who art the Lord of Brahmá, Śiva and Vishṇu. I salute thee who art the sun, Ádityavarchas, 1149 splendid, Sarvabhaksha, 1150 and Raudravapush. 1151

I salute thee who destroyest darkness, cold and enemies: whose form is boundless, who art the destroyer of the ungrateful; who art Deva; 1152 who art the Lord of the luminous bodies, and who appearest like the heated gold. I salute thee who art Hari, 1153 Viśvakarman, 1154 the destroyer of darkness, and who art splendid and Lokasákshin. 1155 Yonder sun destroys the whole of the material world and also creates it. Yonder sun dries (all earthly things), destroys them and causes rain with his rays. He wakes when our senses are asleep; and resides within all beings. Yonder sun is Agnihotra 1156 and also the fruit obtained by the performer of Agnihotra. He is identified with the gods, sacrifices, and the fruit of the sacrifices. He is the Lord of all the duties known to the world, if any man, O Rághava, in calamities, miseries, forests and dangers, prays to yonder sun, he is never overwhelmed by distress.

Worship, with close attention Him the God of gods and the Lord of the world; and recite these verses thrice, whereby thou wilt be victorious in the battle. O brave one, thou wilt kill Rávaṇa this very instant."

Thereupon Agastya having said this went away as he came. The glorious Ráma having heard this became free from sorrow. Rághava whose senses were under control, being pleased, committed the hymn to memory, recited it facing the sun, and obtained great delight. The brave Ráma having sipped water thrice and become pure took his bow, and seeing Rávaṇa, was delighted, and meditated on the sun.

Page 492. Rávan's Funeral.

"In the funeral ceremonies of India the fire was placed on three sides of the pyre; the *Dakshiṇa* on the south, the *Gárhapatya* on the west, and the *Áhavaníya* on the east. The funeral rites are not described in detail here, and it is therefore difficult to elucidate and explain them. The poem assigns the funeral ceremonies of Aryan Brahmans to the Rákshases, a race different from them in origin and religion, in the same way as Homer sometimes introduces into Troy the rites of the Grecian cult." Gorresio.

Mr. Muir translates the description of the funeral from the Calcutta edition, as follows: "They formed, with Vedic rites, a funeral pile of faggots of sandal-wood, with *padmaka* wood, *uśira* grass, and sandal, and covered with a quilt of deer's hair. They then performed an unrivalled obsequial ceremony for the Ráxasa prince, placing the sacrificial ground to the S.E.

and the fire in the proper situation. They cast the ladle filled with curds and ghee on the shoulder 1157 of the deceased; he (?) placed the car on the feet, and the mortar between the thighs. Having deposited all the wooden vessels, the [upper] and lower fire-wood, and the other pestle, in their proper places, they departed. The Ráxasas having then slain a victim to their prince in the manner prescribed in the Sástras, and enjoined by great rishis, cast [into the fire] the coverlet of the king saturated with ghee. They then, Vibhíshaṇa included, with afflicted hearts, adorned Rávaṇa with perfumes and garlands, and with various vestments, and besprinkled him with fried grain. Vibhíshaṇa having bathed, and having, with his clothes wet, scattered in proper form *tila* seeds mixed with *darbha* grass, and moistened with water, applied the fire [to the pile]."

Page 496.

The following is a literal translation of Brahmá's address to Ráma according to the Calcutta edition, text and commentary:

"O Ráma, how dost thou, being the creator of all the world, best of all those who have profound knowledge of the Upanishads and all-powerful as thou art, suffer Sítá to fall in the fire? How dost thou not know thyself as the best of the gods? Thou art one of the primeval Vasus, 1158 and also their lord and creator. Thou art thyself the lord and first creator of the three worlds. Thou art the eighth (that is Mahádeva) of the Rudras, 1159 and also the fifth 1160 of the Sádhyas. 1161 (The poet describes Ráma as made of the following gods) The Aśvinikumáras (the twin divine physicians of the gods) are thy ears; the sun and the moon are thy eyes; and thou hast been seen in the beginning and at the end of creation. How dost thou neglect the daughter of Videha (Janaka} like a man whose actions are directed by the dictates of nature?" Thus addressed by Indra, Brahmá and the other gods, Ráma the descendant of Raghu, lord of the world and the best of the virtuous, spoke to the chief of the gods. "As I take myself to be a man of the name of Ráma and son of Daśaratha, therefore, sir, please tell me who I am and whence have I come." "O thou whose might is never failing," said Brahmá to Kákutstha the foremost of those who thoroughly know Brahmá, "Thou art Náráyaṇa, 1162 almighty, possessed of fortune, and armed with the discus. Thou art the boar 1163 with one tusk; the conqueror of thy past and future foes. Thou art Brahmá true and eternal or undecaying. Thou art Viśvaksena, 1164 having four arms; Thou art Hrishíkeśa, 1165 whose bow is made of horn; Thou art Purusha, 1166 the best of all beings; Thou art one who is never defeated by any body; Thou art the holder of the sword (named Nandaka). Thou art Vishṇu (the pervader of all); blue in colour: of great might; the commander of armies; and lord of villages. Thou art truth. Thou art embodied intelligence, forgiveness, control over the senses, creation, and destruction. Thou art Upendra 1167 and Madhusúdana. 1168 Thou art the creator of Indra, the ruler over all the world, Padmanábha, 1169 and destroyer of enemies in the battle. The divine Rishis call thee shelter of refugees, as well as the giver of shelter. Thou hast a thousand horns, 1170 a hundred heads. 1171 Thou art respected of the respected; and the lord and first creator of the three worlds. Thou art the forefather and shelter of Siddhas, 1172 and Sádhyas. 1173 Thou art sacrifices; Vashatkára, 1174 Omkára. 1175 Thou art beyond those who are beyond our senses. There is none who knows who thou art and who knows thy beginning and end. Thou art seen in all material objects, in Bráhmans, in cows, and also in all the quarters, sky and streams. Thou hast a thousand feet, a hundred heads, and a thousand eyes. Thou hast borne the material objects and the earth with the mountains; and at the bottom of the ocean thou art seen the great serpent. O Ráma, Thou hast borne the three worlds, gods, Gandharvas, 1176 and demons. I am, O Ráma, thy heart; the goddess of learning is thy tongue; the gods are the hairs of thy body; the closing of thy eyelids is called the night: and their opening is called the day. The Vedas are thy Sanskáras. 1177 Nothing can exist without thee. The whole world is thy body; the surface of the earth is thy stability."

O Śrívatsalakshana, fire is thy anger, and the moon is thy favour. In the time of thy incarnation named Vámana, thou didst pervade the three worlds with thy three steps; and Mahendra was made the king of paradise by thee having confined the fearful Bali. 1178 Sítá (thy wife) is Lakshmí; and thou art the God Vishnu, 1179 Krishna, 1180 and Prajápati. To kill Rávan thou hast assumed the form of a man; therefore, O best of the virtuous, thou hast completed this task imposed by us (gods). O Ráma, Rávana has been killed by thee: now being joyful (i.e. having for some time reigned in the kingdom of Ayodhyá,) go to paradise. O glorious Ráma, thy power and thy valour are never failing. The visit to thee and the prayers made to thee are never fruitless. Thy devotees will never be unsuccessful. Thy devotees who obtain thee (thy favour) who art first and best of mankind, shall obtain their desires in this world as well as in the next. They who recite this prayer, founded on the Vedas (or first uttered by the sages), and the old and divine account of (Ráma) shall never suffer defeat."

Page 503. The Meeting.

The *Bharat-Miláp* or meeting with Bharat, is the closing scene of the dramatic representation of Ráma's great victory and triumphant return which takes place annually in October in many of the cities of Northern India.

The Rám-Lalá or Play of Ráma, as the great drama is called, is performed in the open air and lasts with one day's break through fifteen successive days. At Benares there are three nearly simultaneous performances, one provided by H. H. the Maharajah of Benares near his palace at Ramnaggur, one by H. H. the Maharajah of Vizianagram near the Missionary settlement at Sigra and at other places in the city, and one by the leading gentry of the city at Chowká Ghát near the College. The scene especially on the great day when the brothers meet is most interesting: the procession of elephants with their gorgeous howdahs of silver and gold and their magnificently dressed riders with priceless jewels sparkling in their turbans, the enthusiasm of the thousands of spectators who fill the streets and squares, the balconies and the housetops, the flowers that are rained down upon the advancing car, the wild music, the shouting and the joy, make an impression that is not easily forgotten.

Still on his head, well trained in lore

Of duty, Ráma's shoes he bore.

Ráma's shoes are here regarded as the emblems of royalty or possession. We may compare the Hebrew "Over Edom will I cast forth my shoe." A curiously similar passage occurs in Lyschander's *Chronicon Greenlandiæ Rhythmicon*:

"Han sendte til Irland sin skiden skoe,

Og böd den Konge. Som der monne boe,

Han skulde dem hæderlig bære

Pan Juuledag i sin kongelig Pragt,

Og kjende han havde sit Rige og Magt

Af Norges og Quernes Herre."

He sent to Ireland his dirty shoes,

And commanded the king who lived there

To wear them with honour

On Christmas Day in his royal state,

And to own that he had his kingdom and power

From the Lord of Norway and the Isles.

Notes & Queries, March 30, 1872.

Final Notes.

I end these notes with an extract which I translate from Signor Gorresio's Preface to the tenth volume of his Rámáyan, and I take this opportunity of again thankfully acknowledging my great obligations to this eminent Śanskritist from whom I have so frequently borrowed. As Mr. Muir has observed, the Bengal recension which Signor Gorresio has most ably edited is throughout an admirable commentary on the genuine Rámáyan of northern India, and I have made constant reference to the faithful and elegant translation which accompanies the text for assistance and confirmation in difficulties:

"Towards the southern extremity and in the island of Lanká (Ceylon) there existed undoubtedly a black and ferocious race, averse to the Aryans and hostile to their mode of worship: their ramifications extended through the islands of the Archipelago, and some traces of them remain in Java to this day.

The Sanskrit-Indians, applying to this race a name expressive of hatred which occurs in the Vedas as the name of hostile, savage and detested beings, called it the Rákshas race: it is against these Rákshases that the expedition of Ráma which the Rámáyan celebrates is directed. The Sanskrit-Indians certainly altered in their traditions the real character of this race: they attributed to it physical and moral qualities not found in human nature; they transformed it into a race of giants; they represented it as monstrous, hideous, truculent, changing forms at will, blood-thirsty and ravenous, just as the Semites represented the races that opposed them as impious, horrible and of monstrous size. But notwithstanding these mythical exaggerations, which are partly due to the genius of the Aryans so prone to magnify everything without measure, the Rámáyan in the course of its epic narration has still preserved and noted here and there some traits and peculiarities of the race which reveal its true character. It represents the Rákshases as black of hue, and compares them with black clouds and masses of black collyrium; it attributes to them curly woolly hair and thick lips, it depicts them as loaded with chains, collars and girdles of gold, and the other bright ornaments which their race has always loved, and in which the kindred races of the Soudan still delight. It describes them as worshippers of matter and force. They are hostile to the religion of the Aryans whose rites and sacrifices they disturb and ruin ... Such is the Rákshas race as represented in the Rámáyan; and the war of the Aryan Ráma forms the subject of the epic, a subject certainly real and historical as far as regards its substance, but greatly exaggerated by the ancient myth. In Sanskrit-Indian tradition are found traces of another struggle of the Aryans with the Rákshas races, which preceded the war of Ráma. According to some pauranic legends, Kárttavírya, a descendant of the royal tribe of the Yádavas, contemporary with Parasurama and a little anterior to Ráma, attacked Lanká and took Rávaṇ prisoner. This well shows how ancient and how deeply rooted in the Aryan race is the thought of this war which the Rámáyan celebrates.

"But," says an eminent Indianist 1181 whose learning I highly appreciate, "the Rámáyan is an allegorical epic, and no precise and historical value can be assigned to it. Sítá signifies the furrow made by the plough, and under this symbolical aspect has already appeared honoured with worship in the hymns of the Rig-veda; Ráma is the bearer of the plough (this assertion is entirely gratuitous); these two allegorical personages represented agriculture introduced to the southern regions of India by the race of the Kosalas from whom Ráma was descended; the Rákshases on whom he makes war are races of demons and giants who have little or nothing human about them; allegory therefore predominates in the poem, and the exact reality of an historical event must not be looked for in it." Such is Professor Weber's opinion. If he means to say that mythical fictions are mingled with real events,

Forsan in alcun vero suo arco percuote,

as Dante says, and I fully concede the point. The interweaving of the myth with the historical truth belongs to the essence, so to speak, of the primitive epopeia. If Sítá is born, as the Rámáyan feigns, from the furrow which King Janak opened when he ploughed the earth, not a whit more real is the origin of Helen and Æneas as related in Homer and Virgil, and if the characters in the Rámáyan exceed human nature, and in a greater degree perhaps than is the case in analogous epics, this springs in part from the nature of the subject and still more from the symbol-loving genius of the orient. Still the characters of the Rámáyan, although they exceed more or less the limits of human nature, act notwithstanding in the course of the poem, speak, feel, rejoice and grieve according to the natural impulse of human passions. But if by saying that the Rámáyan is an allegorical epic, it is meant that its fundamental subject is nothing but allegory, that the war of the Aryan Ráma against the Rákshas race is an allegory, that the conquest of the southern region and of the island of Lanká is an allegory, I do not hesitate to answer that such a presumption cannot be admitted and that the thing is in my opinion impossible. Father Paolíno da S. Bartolommeo, 1182 had already, together with other strange opinions of his own on Indian matters, brought forward a similar idea, that is to say that the exploit of Ráma which is the subject of the Rámáyan was a symbol and represented the course of the sun: thus he imagined that Brahmá was the earth, Vishṇu the water, and that his avatárs were the blessings brought by the fertilizing waters, etc. But such ideas, born at a time when Indo-sanskrit antiquities were enveloped in darkness, have been dissipated by the light of new studies. How could an epic so dear in India to the memory of the people, so deeply rooted for many centuries in the minds of all, so propagated and diffused through all the dialects and languages of those regions, which had become the source of many dramas which are still represented in India, which is itself represented every year with such magnificence and to such crowds of people in the neighbourhood of Ayodhyá, a poem welcomed at its very birth with such favour, as the legend relates, that the recitation of it by the first wandering Rhapsodists has consecrated and made famous all the places celebrated by them, and where Ráma made a shorter or longer stay, how, I ask, could such an epic have been purely allegorical? How, upon a pure invention, upon a simple allegory, could a poem have been composed of about fifty thousand verses, relating with such force and power the events, and giving details with such exactness? On a theme purely allegorical there may easily be composed a short mythical poem, as for example a poem on Proserpine or Psyche: but never an epic so full of traditions and historical memories, so intimately connected with the life of the people, as the Rámáyan. 1183 Excessive readiness to find allegory whenever some traces of symbolism occur, where the myth partly veils the historical reality, may lead and often has led to error. What poetical work of mythical times could stand this mode of trial? could there not be made, or rather has there not been made a work altogether allegorical, out of the Homeric poems? We have all heard of the ingenious idea of the anonymous writer, who in order to prove how easily we may pass beyond the truth in our wish to seek and find allegory everywhere, undertook with keen subtlety to prove that the great personality of Napoleon I. was altogether allegorical and represented the sun. Napoleon was born in an island, his course was from west to east, his twelve marshals were the twelve signs of the zodiac, etc.

I conclude then, that the fundamental theme of the Rámáyan, that is to say the war of the Aryan Ráma against the Rákshases, an Hamitic race settled in the south, ought to be regarded as real and historical as far as regards its substance, although the mythic element intermingled with the true sometimes alters its natural and genuine aspect.

How then did the Indo-Sanskrit epopeia form and complete itself? What elements did it interweave in its progress? How did it embody, how did it clothe the naked and simple primitive datum? We must first of all remember that the Indo-European races possessed the epic genius in the highest degree, and that they alone in the different regions they occupied produced epic poetry ... But other causes and particular influences combined to nourish and develop the epic germ of the Sanskrit-Indians. Already in the Rig-veda are found hymns in which the Aryan genius preluded, so to speak, to the future epopeia, in songs that celebrated the heroic deeds of Indra, the combats and the victories of the tutelary Gods of the Aryan races over enemies secret or open, human or superhuman, the exploits and the memories of ancient heroes. More recently, at certain solemn occasions, as the very learned A. Weber remarks, at the solemnity, for example of the Aśvamedha or sacrifice of the horse, the praises of the king who ordained the great rite were sung by bards and minstrels in songs composed for the purpose, the memories of past times were recalled and honourable mention was made of the just and pious kings of old. In the *Bráhmaṇas*, a sort of prose commentaries annexed to the Vedas, are found recorded stories and legends which allude to historical events of the past ages, to ancient memories, and to mythical events. Such popular legends which the *Bráhmaṇas* undoubtedly gathered from tradition admirably suited the epic tissue with which they were interwoven by successive hands.... Many and various mythico-historical traditions, suitable for epic development, were diffused among the Aryan races, those for example which are related in the four chapters containing the description of the earth, the Descent of the Ganges, etc. The epic genius however sometimes created beings of its own and gave body and life to ideal conceptions. Some of the persons in the Rámáyan must be, in my opinion, either personifications of the forces of nature like those which are described with such vigour in the *Sháhnámah*, or if not exactly created, exaggerated beyond human proportions; others, vedic personages much more ancient than Ráma, were introduced into the epic and woven into its narrations, to bring together men who lived in different and distant ages, as has been the case in times nearer to our own, in the epics, I mean, of the middle ages.

In the introduction I have discussed the antiquity of the Rámáyan; and by means of those critical and inductive proofs which are all that an antiquity without precise historical dates can furnish I have endeavoured to establish with all the certainty that the subject admitted, that the original composition of the Rámáyan is to be assigned to about the twelfth century before the Christian era. Not that I believe that the epic then sprang to life in the form in which we now possess it; I think, and I have elsewhere expressed the opinion, that the poem during the course of its rhapsodical and oral propagation appropriated by way of episodes, traditions, legends and ancient myths.... But as far as regards the epic poem properly so called which celebrates the expedition of Ráma against the Rákshases I think that I have sufficiently shown that its origin and first appearance should be placed about the twelfth century B.C.; nor have I hitherto met with anything to oppose this chronological result, or to oblige me to rectify or reject it.... But an eminent philologist already quoted, deeply versed in these studies, A. Weber, has expressed in some of his writings a totally different opinion; and the authority of his name, if not the number and cogency of his arguments, compels me to say something on the subject. From the fact or rather the assumption that Megasthenes 1184 who lived some time in India has made no mention either of the Mahábhárat or the Rámáyan Professor Weber argues that neither of these poems could have existed at that time; as regards the Rámáyan, the unity of its composition, the chain that binds together its different parts, and its allegorical character, show it, says Professor Weber, to be much more recent than the age to which I have assigned it, near to our own era, and according to him, later than the Mahábhárat. As for Megasthenes it should be observed, that he did not write a history of India, much less a literary history or anything at all resembling one, but a simple description, in great part physical, of India: whence, from his silence on literary matters to draw inferences regarding the history of Sanskrit literature would be the same thing as from the silence of a geologist with respect to the literature of a country whose valleys, mountains, and internal structure he is exploring, to conjecture that such and such a poem or history not mentioned by him did not exist at his time. We have only to look at the fragments of Megasthenes collected and published by Schwanbeck to see what was the nature and scope of his *Indica*.... But only a few fragments of Megasthenes are extant; and to pretend that they should be argument and proof enough to judge the antiquity of a poem is to press the laws of criticism too far. To Professor Weber's argument as to the more or less recent age of the Rámáyan from the unity of its composition, I will make one sole reply, which is that if unity of composition were really a proof of a more recent age, it would be necessary to reduce by a thousand years at least the age of Homer and bring him down to the age of Augustus and Virgil; for certainly there is much more unity of composition, a greater accord and harmony of parts in the Iliad and the Odyssey than in the Rámáyan. But in the fine arts perfection is no proof of a recent age: while the experience and the continuous labour of successive ages are necessary to extend and perfect the physical or natural sciences, art which is spontaneous in its nature can produce and has produced in remote times works of such perfection as later ages have not been able to equal."

INDEX OF PRINCIPAL NAMES

Ananta

Anaraṇya

Anasúyá

Andhak

Andhras

Anga

Angad

Angas

Angiras

Anjan

Anjaná

Anśudhána

Anśumán

Anuhláda

Aparparyat

Apartála

Apsarases

Aptoryám

Arishta

Aríshṭanemi

Arjun

Arjuna

Arthasádhak

Aruṇ,

Arundhatí

Aryaman

Áryan

Asamanj

Asit

Aśok

Aśoka

Asta note

Asurs

Aśvagríva

Aśvamedh note
Aśvapati
Aśvatarí
Aśvin
Aśvíní
Aśvins
Atikáya
Atirátra
Atri
Aurva note
Avantí
Avindhya
Ayodhyá *passim*
Ayomukh
Ayomukhi

Báhíka

Bahuputra
Bala
Bálakhilyas
Bali
Báli
Barbars
Beauty
Bhadamadrá
Bhadra
Bhaga
Bhagírath
Bhágírathí
Bharadvája
Bharat *passim*
Bharatas
Bháruṇḍa
Bhásí
Bhásakarṇa

Bhava

Bhímá

Bhogavatí note

Bhrigu

Brahmá *passim*

Brahmadatta

Brahmádikas note

Bhrahmamálas

Budha

Buddhist

Cancer

Ceylon note

Chaitra

Chaitraratha

Chakraván

Champá

Chaṇḍa

Chaṇḍála

Chandra

Chatushṭom

Chitrá

Chitrakúṭa

Chitraratha

Cholas

Chúli

Chyavan

Dadhimukh

Dadhivakra note

Daitya

Daksha

Dánav

Daṇḍak

Daṇḍaká

Danú
Dapple skin
Dardar
Dardur
Darímukha
Daśárṇa
Dasáratha *passim*
Dasyus
Devamíḍha
Devántak
Devarát
Devasakhá
Devavatí
Dhanvantari note
Dhanyamáliní
Dharmabhrit
Dharmapál
Dharmáraṇya
Dharmavardhan
Dhritaráshṭrí
Dhrishṭaketu
Dhrishṭi
Dhruvasandhi
Dhúmra
Dhúmráksha note
Dhúmráśva
Dhundhumár
Dikshá
Dilípa note
Diti
Dragon
Driḍhanetra
Drishṭi
Droṇa

Drumakulya

Dundubhi

Durdhar

Durdharsha note

Durjaya note

Durmukha note

Durvásas

Dúshaṇ

Dwida note

Dwijihva

Dwivid

Dwivida

Dyumatsena

Ekapádakas

Ekaśála

Fame

Fate

Fire

Fortune

Fire-god

Gádhi

Gaja note

Gálava

Gandhamádan

Gandharva

Gandharvas

Gandharví

Gangá *passim*

Garga

Garuḍ

Gautam

Gautama

Gaváksha note

Gavaya note
Gaya
Gayá
Gáyatrí
Ghoralohamukhas
Ghritáchí
Girivraja
Glory
Godávarí
Gokarna
Golabh
Gomatí
Gopa
Guha
Guhyakas

Háhá

Haihayas
Hanúmán note
Hara
Harí
Háritas
Haryaśva
Hástinapura
Hastiprishṭhak
Havishyand
Hayagriva
Hemá
Hemachandra
Heti
Himálaya
Himaváu
Hiraṇyakaśipu note
Hiraṇyanábha
Hládini

Honour

Hotri

Hraśvaromá

Huhú

Ikshumatí,

Ikshváku

Ilval

Indra *passim*

Indrajánu note

Indrajít

Indraśatru note

Indraśira

Irávatí

Jábáli

Jahnu

Jáhnaví

Jamadagni

Jámbaván

Jambudvip

Jambumálí

Jambuprastha

Jámbuvatu note

Janak *passim*

Janamejaya

Janasthán

Játarúpa

Jaṭáyu

Jaṭáyus

Java

Jáváli

Jayá

Jayanta

Jumna

Jupiter

Justice

Jyotishṭom

Kabandha,

Kadrú

Kadrumá

Kaikasí

Kaikeyí, *passim*

Kailása

Kakustha

Kalá

Kálak

Kálaká

Kálakámuka note

Kálamahí

Kalinda

Kálindí

Kalinga

Kalingas,

Kalmáshapáda

Káma

Kámboja

Kámbojas

Kámpili

Kaṇdu

Kandarpa

Kaṇva

Kanyákubja

Kapil

Kapivati

Kardam

Karṇaprávaraṇas

Kártikeya

Kárttavírya

Káśi
Kásíkosalas
Kaśyap, passim
Kátyáyan
Kátyáyana
Kauśalyá passim
Kauśámbí
Kauśikas
Kauśikí
Káverí
Kaustubha
Kávya
Kekaya
Kerala
Keralas
Kesarí
Keśini
Khara
Kinnars
Kimpurushas note
Kirátas
Kírtirát
Kirtirátha
Kishkindhá
Kośal
Kośala
Krathan
Kratu
Krauncha
Kraunchi
Kriśáśva
Krishṇa
Krishṇagiri
Krishṇveni

Krita
Krodhavaśá
Kshatriyas
Kukshi
Kulingá
Kumbha
Kumbhakarṇa
Kúmuda note
Kunjar
Kuru(s), North
Kurujángal
Kuśa
Kuśadhwaj
Kuśámba
Kuśanábha
Kuśáśva
Kuśik
Kuṭíká
Kuṭikoshṭiká
Kuvera

Lakshmaṇ, *passim*

Lakshmí
Lamba
Lanká.
Lankaṭankaṭá
Lava
Lohitya
Lokapálas
Lomapád

Mádhaví

Madhu
Madhúka
Madhushyand

Madrakas

Magadh

Mágadnas

Maghá

Mahábír

Mahábala note

Mahábhárat

Mahádeva

Mahákapála note

Mahámáli note

Mahándhrak

Mahápadma

Mahápárásva

Mahárath

Maháromá

Maháruṇ

Mahásaila

Mahendra

Maheswar

Mahí

Máhishmatí

Mahishikas

Mahodar note

Mahodaya

Maináka note

Mainda note

Makaráksha note

Malaja

Málavas

Malaya

Málí

Máliní

Malyaván

Mályavat

Mánas

Mandakarni

Mandákiní note

Mandalí

Mandar

Mandarí

Mándhátá

Mándavi

Mándavya note

Mandehas

Mandodarí

Mandra

Manibhadra

Manthará

Manu

Marícha

Máricha,

Maríchi

Maríchipas

Márkandeya

Mars

Maru

Maruts

Máshas

Mátali

Matanga

Mátangí

Mátariśva

Matsya

Maya

Máyá

Máyáví

Meghamáli note

Meghanáda

Mekhal

Mená note

Menaká

Mercury

Meru

Meruśavarṇi

Mina

Miśrakeśí

Mithi

Míthilá note

Mitraghna

Mlechchhas

Modesty

Moon

Mriga

Mrigamandá

Mrigí

Mudgalya

Nábhág

Nágadantá

Nágas

Nahush

Nairrit

Nala note

Nalá

Naliní

Namuchi

Nandá

Nandan

Nandi

Nandigráma

Nandíśvara

Nandivardhan

Nárad

Narak

Narántak

Náráyaṇ

Narmadá

Nikumbha note

Níla note

Nimi

Niśakar

Nishádas

Ocean

Oshṭhakarṇakas

Pahlavas

Páka

Pampá

Panas

Panasa note

Panchajan

Panchála

Panchápsaras

Panchavaṭa

Panchavaṭí

Páṇḍyas

Paráśara

Paraśuráma note

Paravíráksha note

Páriyátra

Parjanya

Párvati note

Paulastya

Paulomí

Pávaní

Phálguní

Pináka

Pitris

Prabháva

Prachetas

Praghas

Prágvaṭ

Prahasta

Praheti

Prahláda

Prajangha

Prajápati note

Pralamba

Pramátha note

Pramathí

Pramati note

Prasenajit

Praśravaṇ

Prasthalas

Praśuśśruka

Pratindhak

Pravargya

Prayág

Prithu

Prithuśyáma note

Proshṭhapadá

Pulah

Pulastya

Pulindas

Puloma

Punarvasu

Puṇḍaríká

Puṇḍras

Punjikasthalá

Puranda

Purandara

Purúravas
Purusha note
Purushádak
Purushottam
Púshá
Pushpak
Pushya

Rabhasa note

Rághava note
Raghu *passim*
Raghunandana
Ráhu
Rain, Lord of
Rájagriha
Ráma *passim*
Rámáyana note
Rambhá
Ramaṇá
Raśmiketu note
Rávaṇ *passim*
Reṇuká
Richíka
Right
Riksharajas
Rikshaván
Rishabh
Rishṭikas
Rishyamúka
Rishyaśring
Rohiṇí
Rohitas
Rudhiráśana note
Rudra
Rudras

Rukmiṇí

Rumá

Ruman

Sachí

Sádhyas

Sagar

Sahadeva

Sahya

Śaivya

Śakas

Śakra

Śálmalí

Śályakartan

Śáman

Śambar

Śambara

Sampáti note. note

Samprakshálas

Sanatkumár

Sandhyá

Sanháras

Sanhráda

Śaniśchar

Śankan

Śankar

Sánkáśyá

Śankha

Śankhan

Sanrochan

Śanśray

Śántá

Śarabh note

Śarabhanga

Śaradaṇḍá

Saramá

Sáraṇ

Sarandib note

Sáranga

Sarasvatí

Śárdúla

Śárdúlí

Sarjú passim

Sárvabhauma

Sarvartírtha

Śaśivindhus

Śatabali

Śatadrú

Śatahradá

Śatánanda

Śatrughna passim

Śatrunjay

Satyaván

Satyavatí

Sávitrí

Śavarí

Saumanas

Sávarṇí

Seven Rishis

Śesha

Siddhárth

Siddhas note

Śíghraga

Śilá

Śilávahá

Sindhu

Sinhiká

Śiśir(a)

Sítá. passim

Śiva

Skanda

Soma

Somadatta

Somadá

Somagiri

Śoṇa

Śringavera

Srinjay

Srutakírti

Sthánu

Sthánumatí

Sthúláksha note

Sthúlaśiras

Subáhu note

Suchakshu

Suchandra

Śuchi

Sudámá

Sudáman

Sudarśan

Sudarśandwíp

Sudhanvá

Sudhriti

Śúdras

Sugríva

Śuka

Sukeśa

Suketu

Sukí

Śukra

Sumáli

Sumágadhí

Sumantra *passim*

Sumati

Sumitrá *passim*

Sun

Sunábha

Śunahśepha

Sunda

Sunetra note

Suparṇa

Supárśva

Supátala note

Suptaghna note

Surá

Surabhí

Surapati

Suras

Surasá

Suráshṭra

Súrasenas

Śúrpaṇakhá.

Súrya

Súryáksha note

Súryaśatru note

Súryaván

Susandhi

Susheṇ note

Sutanu

Sutíkshṇa

Suváhu

Suvarat

Suvela

Suvíra

Suyajṇa

Svayambhu

Svayamprabhá

Śvetáraṇya
Swarga
Swarṇaromá
Śweta
Śyáma
Syandiká
Śyenagámí note
Śyení

Táḍaká

Táḍakeya
Taittiríya
Takshak
Takshaka
Tálajanghas
Tamasá
Támrá
Támraparṇí
Tapan
Tára note
Tárá
Tárak
Tárkshya
Ten-necked
Thirty-three Gods
Thousand-eyed
Three-eyed God
Thunderer
Titan
Toraṇ
Town-Destroyer
Trident
Trident-wielding
Trijaṭ
Trijaṭá

Trikúṭa

Triṇavindu

Trípathagá

Tripur

Tripura

Triśanku

Triśirá

Triśirás note

Tumburu

Uchchaihśravas

Udayagiri note

Udávasu

Ujjiháná

Ukthya

Umá note

Upasad

Upasunda

Upendra

Urmilá

Urvaśí

Uśanas

Utkal

Uttániká

Váhli

Váhlíka

Vahni

Vaidyut

Vaijayanta

Vaikhánasas

Vainateya

Vaiśravaṇ

Vaiśyas

Vaitaraṇí

Vajra

Vajradanshṭra note

Válmíki,

Vámadeva

Vámana

Váṇa

Vanáyu

Vangas

Varadas

Varuṇ note

Varáśya note

Varútha

Vásav

Vásava

Vaśishṭha *passim*

Vásudeva

Vásuki

Vasus

Vasvaukasárá

Vátápi

Váyu

Vedas note

Vedaśrutí

Vedavatí

Vegadarśí

Veṇá

Vibháṇḍak

Vibhíshaṇ.

Vibudh

Vidarbha

Vidarbhas

Videha

Videhan *passim*

Videhas

Vidyádharí note
Vidyujjihva
Vidyunmáli note
Vidyutkeśa
Vihangama note
Vijay
Vikaṭá
Vikrit
Vikukshi
Vinata
Vinatá
Vindhya
Vindu
Vipáśá
Vírabáhu note
Virádha
Viráj
Viramatsya
Virochan
Virtue
Virúpáksha
Viśákhás
Viśálá
Vishṇu note *passim*
Viśravas
Viśváchi
Viśvajit
Viśvakarmá
Viśvámitra. *passim*
Viśvarúpa
Viśvas
Viśvávasu
Viśvedevas
Vitardan

Vivasvat

Vraṇa

Vrihadratha

Vrihaspati

Vritra

Vulture-king

War-god

Wind

Wind-god

Yavadwípa

Yajnakopa note

Yajush

Yajnaśatru note

Yaksha note

Yáma

Yamuná

Yámun

Yavanas

Yayáti

Yudhájit

Yúpáksha

Yuvanáśva

Footnotes

895. The Sixth Book is called in Sanskrit *Yuddha-Kánda* or *The War*, and *Lanká-Kánda*. It is generally known at the present day by the latter title.

896. Váyu is the God of Wind.

897. Garuda the King of Birds.

898. Serpent-Gods.

899. The God of the sea.

900. Indra's elephant.

901. Kuvera, God of wealth.

902. Kuvera's elephant.

903. The planet Venus, or its regent who is regarded as the son of Bhrigu and preceptor of the Daityas.

904. The seven *rishis* or saints who form the constellation of the Great Bear.

905. Trisanku was raised to the skies to form a constellation in the southern hemisphere. The story in told in Book I, Canto LX.

906. The sage Visvámitra, who performed for Trisanku the great sacrifice which raised him to the heavens.

907. One of the lunar asterisms containing four or originally two stars under the regency of a dual divinity Indrágni, Indra and Agni.

908. The lunar asterism Múla, belonging to the Rákshases.

909. The Asurs or demons dwell imprisoned in the depths beneath the sea.

910. The God of Riches, brother and enemy of Rávan and first possessor of Pushpak the flying car.

911. King of the Serpents. Sankha and Takshak are two of the eight Serpent Chiefs.

912. The God of Death, the Pluto of the Hindus.

913. Literally Indra's conqueror, so called from his victory over that God.

914. Their names are Nikumbha, Rabhasa, Súryasatru, Suptaghna, Yajnakopa, Mahápársva, Mahodara, Agniketu, Rasmiketu, Durdharsha,

Indraśatru, Prahasta, Virúpáksha, Vajradanshtra, Dhúmráksha, Durmukha, Mahábala.

915. Similarly Antenor urges the restoration of Helen:

"Let Sparta's treasures be this hour restored,

And Argive Helen own her ancient lord.

As this advice ye practise or reject,

So hope success, or dread the dire effect,"

Pope's *Homer's Iliad*, Book VII.

916. The *Agnisálá* or room where the sacrificial fire was kept.

917. The exudation of a fragrant fluid from the male elephant's temples, especially at certain seasons, is frequently spoken of in Sanskrit poetry. It is said to deceive and attract the bees, and is regarded as a sign of health and masculine vigour.

918. Consisting of warriors on elephants, warriors in chariots, charioteers, and infantry.

919. Indra, generally represented as surrounded by the Maruts or Storm-Gods.

920. Janasthán, where Ráma lived as an ascetic.

921. Máyá, regarded as the paragon of female beauty, was the creation of Maya the chief artificer of the Daityas or Dánavs.

922. One of the Nymphs of Indra's heaven.

923. The Lotus River, a branch of the heavenly Gangá.

924. *Trilokanátha*, Lord of the Three Worlds, is a title of Indra.

925. The celestial elephant that carries Indra.

926. As producers of the *ghi*, clarified butter or sacrificial oil, used in fire-offerings.

927. This desertion to the enemy is somewhat abrupt, and is narrated with brevity not usual with Válmíki. In the Bengal recension the preceding speakers and speeches differ considerably from those given in the text which I follow. Vibhishan is kicked from his seat by Rávan, and then, after telling his mother what has happened, he flies to Mount Kailása where he has an interview with Śiva, and by his advice seeks Ráma and the Vánar army.

928. Vrihaspati the preceptor of the Gods.

929. In Book II, Canto XXI, Kandu is mentioned by Ráma as an example of filial obedience. At the command of his father he is said to have killed a cow.

930. A King of the Yakshas, or Kuvera himself, the God of Gold.

931. The brace protects the left arm from injury from the bow-string, and the guard protects the fingers of the right hand.

932. The story is told in Book I, Cantos XL, XLI, XLII.

933. Fiends and enemies of the Gods.

934. The Indus.

935. Cowherds, sprung from a Bráhman and a woman of the medical tribe, the modern Ahírs.

936. Barbarians or outcasts.

937. *Vraṇa* means wound or rent.

938. Here in the Bengal recension (Gorresio's edition), begins Book VI.

939. The Goomtee.

940. The Anglicized Nerbudda.

941. According to a Pauranik legend Keśarí Hanumán's putative father had killed an Asur or demon who appeared in the form of an elephant, and hence arose the hostility between Vánars and elephants.

942. Here follows the enumeration of Sugríva's forces which I do not attempt to follow. It soon reaches a hundred thousand billions.

943. I omit the rest of this canto, which is mere repetition. Rávaṇ gives in the same words his former answer that the Gods, Gandharvas and fiends combined shall not force him to give up Sítá. He then orders Śárdúla to tell him the names of the Vánar chieftains whom he has seen in Ráma's army. These have already been mentioned by Śuka and Sáraṇ.

944. Lakshmí is the Goddess both of beauty and fortune, and is represented with a lotus in her hand.

945. The poet appears to have forgotten that Śuka and Sáraṇ were dismissed with ignominy in Canto XXIX, and have not been reinstated.

946. The four who fled with him. Their names are Anala, Panasa, Sampáti, and Pramati.

947. The numbers here are comparatively moderate: ten thousand elephants, ten thousand chariots, twenty thousand horses and ten million giants.

948. The Kinśuk, also called Paláśa, is Butea Frondosa, a tree that bears beautiful red crescent shaped blossoms and is deservedly a favorite with poets. The Seemal or Śálmalí is the silk cotton tree which also bears red blossoms.

949. Varuṇa.

950. The duty of a king to save the lives of his people and avoid bloodshed until milder methods have been tried in vain.

951. I have omitted several of these single combats, as there is little variety in the details and each duel results in the victory of the Vánar or his ally.

952. Yajnaśatru, Mahápárśva, Mahodar, Vajradanshtra, Śuka, and Sáraṇ.

953. Angad.

954. A mysterious weapon consisting of serpents transformed to arrows which deprived the wounded object of all sense and power of motion.

955. On each foot, and at the root of each finger.

956. Varuṇ.

957. The name of one of the mystical weapons the command over which was given by Viśvámitra to Ráma, as related in Book I.

958. One of Sítá's guard, and her comforter on a former occasion also.

959. The preceptor of the Gods.

960. Ráma's grandfather.

961. The Gandharvas are warriors and Minstrels of Indra's heaven.

962. "It is to be understood," says the commentator, "that this is not the Akampan who has already been slain."

963. Rávaṇ's son, whom Hanumán killed when he first visited Lanká.

964. Níla was the son of Agni the God of Fire, and possessed, like Milton's demons, the power of dilating and condensing his form at pleasure.

965. An ancient king of Ayodhyá said by some to have been Prithu's father.

966. The daughter of King Kuśadhwaja. She became an ascetic, and being insulted by Rávaṇ in the woods where she was performing penance, destroyed herself by entering fire, but was born again as Sítá to be in turn the destruction of him who had insulted her.

967. Nandíśvara was Śiva's chief attendant. Rávaṇ had despised and laughed at him for appearing in the form of a monkey and the irritated Nandíśvara cursed him and foretold his destruction by monkeys.

968. Rávaṇ once upheaved and shook Mount Kailása the favourite dwelling place of Śiva the consort of Umá, and was cursed in consequence by the offended Goddess.

969. Rambhá, who has several times been mentioned in the course of the poem, was one of the nymphs of heaven, and had been insulted by Rávaṇ.

970. Punjikasthalá was the daughter of Varuṇ. Rávaṇ himself has mentioned in this book his insult to her, and the curse pronounced in consequence by Brahmá.

971. Pulastya was the son of Brahmá and father of Viśravas or Paulastya the father of Rávaṇ and Kumbhakarṇa.

972. I omit a tedious sermon on the danger of rashness and the advantages of prudence, sufficient to irritate a less passionate hearer than Rávaṇ.

973. The Bengal recension assigns a very different speech to Kumbhakarṇa and makes him say that Nárad the messenger of the Gods had formerly told him that Vishṇu himself incarnate as Daśaratha's son should come to destroy Rávaṇ.

974. Mahodar, Dwijihva, Sanhráda, and Vitardan.

975. A name of Vishṇu.

976. There is so much commonplace repetition in these Sallies of the Rákshas chieftains that omissions are frequently necessary. The usual ill omens attend the sally of Kumbhakarṇa, and the Canto ends with a description of the terrified Vánars' flight which is briefly repeated in different words at the beginning of the next Canto.

977. Kártikeya the God of War, and the hero and incarnation Paraśuráma are said to have cut a passage through the mountain Krauncha, a part of the Himálayan range, in the same way as the immense gorge that splits the Pyrenees under the towers of Marboré was cloven at one blow of Roland's sword Durandal.

978. Rishabh, Śarabh, Níla, Gaváksha, and Gandhamádan.

979. Angad. The text calls him the son of the son of him who holds the thunderbolt, *i.e.* the grandson of Indra.

980. Literally, weighing a thousand *bháras*. The *bhára* is a weight equal to 2000 *palas*, the *pala* is equal to four *karśas*, and the *karśa* to 11375 French grammes or about 176 grains troy. The spear seems very light for a warrior of Kumbhakarṇa's strength and stature and the work performed with it.

981. The custom of throwing parched or roasted grain, with wreaths and flowers, on the heads of kings and conquerors when they go forth to battle and return is frequently mentioned by Indian poets.

982. Lakshmaṇ.

983. I have abridged this long Canto by omitting some vain repetitions, commonplace epithets and similes and other unimportant matter. There are many verses in this Canto which European scholars would rigidly exclude as unmistakeably the work of later rhapsodists. Even the reverent

Commentator whom I follow ventures to remark once or twice: *Ayam śloka prak shipta iti bahavah*, "This *śloka* or verse is in the opinion of many interpolated."

984. Narak was a demon, son of Bhúmi or Earth, who haunted the city Prágjyotisha.

985. Śambar was a demon of drought.

986. Indra.

987. Devántak (Slayer of Gods) Narántak (Slayer of Men) Atikáya (Huge of Frame) and Triśirás (Three Headed) were all sons of Rávaṇ.

988. The demon of eclipse who seizes the Sun and Moon.

989. Lakshmaṇ.

990. In such cases as this I am not careful to reproduce the numbers of the poet, which in the text which I follow are 670000000; the Bengal recension being content with thirty million less.

991. The discus or quoit, a sharp-edged circular missile is the favourite weapon of Vishṇu.

992. To destroy Tripura the triple city in the sky, air and earth, built by Maya for a celebrated Asur or demon, or as another commentator explains, to destroy Kandarpa or Love.

993. The Lokapálas are sometimes regarded as deities appointed by Brahmá at the creation of the word to act as guardians of different orders of beings, but more commonly they are identified with the deities presiding over the four cardinal and four intermediate points of the compass, which, according to Manu V. 96, are 1, Indra, guardian of the East; 2, Agni, of the South-east; 3, Yáma, of the South; 4, Súrya, of the South-west; 5, Varuṇa, of the West; 6, Pavana or Váyu, of the North-west; 7, Kuvera, of the North; 8, Soma or Chandra, of the North-east.

994. The chariots of Rávaṇ's present army are said to have been one hundred and fifty million in number with three hundred million elephants, and twelve hundred million horses and asses. The footmen are merely said to have been "unnumbered."

995. It is not very easy to see the advantage of having arrows headed in the way mentioned. Fanciful names for war-engines and weapons derived from their resemblance to various animals are not confined to India. The "War-wolf" was used by Edward I. at the siege of Brechin, the "Cat-house" and the "Sow" were used by Edward III. at the siege of Dunbar.

996. Apparently a peak of the Himalaya chain.

997. This exploit of Hanumán is related with inordinate prolixity in the Bengal recension (Gortesio's text). Among other adventures he narrowly

escapes being shot by Bharat as he passes over Nandigrama near Ayodhyá. Hanumán stays Bharat in time, and gives him an account of what has befallen Ráma and Sítá in the forest and in Lanká.

998. As Garuḍ the king of birds is the mortal enemy of serpents the weapon sacred to him is of course best calculated to destroy the serpent arrows of Rávaṇ.

999. The celebrated saint who has on former occasions assisted Ráma with his gifts and counsel.

1000. Indra.

1001. Yáma.

1002. Kártikeya.

1003. Kubera.

1004. Varuṇ.

1005. The Pitris, forefathers or spirits of the dead, are of two kinds, either the spirits of the father, grandfathers and great-grandfathers of an individual or the progenitors of mankind generally, to both of whom obsequial worship is paid and oblations of food are presented.

1006. The Maruts or Storm-Gods.

1007. The Heavenly Twins, the Castor and Pollux of the Hindus.

1008. The Man *par excellence*, the representative man and father of the human race regarded also as God.

1009. The Vasus, a class of deities originally personifications of natural phenomena.

1010. A class of celestial beings who dwell between the earth and the sun.

1011. The seven horses are supposed to symbolize the seven days of the week.

1012. One for each month in the year.

1013. The garden of Kuvera, the God of Riches.

1014. The consort of Indra.

1015. The Swayamvara, Self-choice or election of a husband by a princess or daughter of a Kshatriya at a public assembly of suitors held for the purpose. For a description of the ceremony see *Nala and Damayantí* an episode of the Mahábhárat translated by the late Dean Milman, and *Idylls from the Sanskrit.*

1016. The Pitris or Manes, the spirits of the dead.

1017. Kuvera, the God of Wealth.

1018. Varuṇ, God of the sea.

1019. Mahádeva or Śiva whose ensign is a bull.

1020. The Address to Ráma, both text and commentary, will be found literally translated in the Additional Notes. A paraphrase of a portion is all that I have attempted here.

1021. Rávaṇ's queen.

1022. Or Maináka.

1023. Here, in the North-west recension, Sítá expresses a wish that Tárá and the wives of the Vánar chiefs should be invited to accompany her to Ayodhyá. The car decends, and the Vánar matrons are added to the party. The Bengal recension ignores this palpable interruption.

1024. The *arghya*, a respectful offering to Gods and venerable men consisting of rice, dúivá grass, flowers etc., with water.

1025. I have abridged Hanumán's outline of Ráma's adventures, with the details of which we are already sufficiently acquainted.

1026. In these respectful salutations the person who salutes his superior mentions his own name even when it is well known to the person whom he salutes.

1027. I have omitted the chieftains' names as they could not be introduced without padding. They are Mainda, Dwivid, Níla, Rishabh, Susheṇ, Nala, Gaváksha, Gandhamádan, Śarabh, and Panas.

1028. The following addition is found in the Bengal recension: But Vaiśravaṇ (Kuvera) when he beheld his chariot said unto it: "Go, and carry Ráma, and come unto me when my thought shall call thee, And the chariot returned unto Ráma;" and he honoured it when he had heard what had passed.

1029. Here follows in the original an enumeration of the chief blessings which will attend the man or woman who reads or hears read this tale of Ráma. These blessings are briefly mentioned at the end of the first Canto of the first book, and it appears unnecessary to repeat them here in their amplified form. The Bengal recension (Gorresio's edition) gives them more concisely as follows: "This is the great first poem blessed and glorious, which gives long life to men and victory to kings, the poem which Válmíki made. He who listens to this wondrous tale of Ráma unwearied in action shall be absolved from all his sins. By listening to the deeds of Ráma he who wishes for sons shall obtain his heart's desire, and to him who longs for riches shall riches be given. The virgin who asks for a husband shall obtain a husband suited to her mind, and shall meet again her dear kinsfolk who are far away. They who hear this poem which Válmíki made shall obtain all their desires and all their prayers shall be fulfilled."

1030.   *The Academy*, Vol. III., No 43, contains an able and interesting notice of this work from the pen of the Professor of Sanskrit in the University of Cambridge: "The *Uttarakáṇḍa*," Mr. Cowell remarks, "bears the same relation to the *Rámáyaṇa* as the Cyclic poems to the *Iliad*. Just as the *Cypria* of Stasinus, the *Æthiopis* of Arctinus, and the little *Iliad* of Lesches completed the story of the *Iliad*, and not only added the series of events which preceded and followed it, but also founded episodes of their own on isolated allusions in Homer, so the *Uttarakáṇḍa* is intended to complete the *Rámáyaṇa*, and at the same time to supplement it by intervening episodes to explain casual allusions or isolated incidents which occur in it. Thus the early history of the giant Rávaṇa and his family fills nearly forty Chapters, and we have a full account of his wars with the gods and his conquest of Lanká, which all happened long before the action of the poem commences, just as the *Cypria* narrated the birth and early history of Helen, and the two expeditions of the Greeks against Troy; and the latter chapters continue the history of the hero Ráma after his triumphant return to his paternal kingdom, and the poem closes with his death and that of his brothers, and the founding by their descendants of various kingdoms in different parts of India."

1031.   Muir, *Sanskrit Texts*, Part IV., pp. 414 ff.

1032.   Muir, *Sanskrit Texts*, Part IV., 391, 392.

1033.   See *Academy*, III., 43.

1034.   *Academy*, Vol. III., No. 43.

1035.   E. B. Cowell. *Academy*, No. 43. The story of Sítá's banishment will be found roughly translated from the *Raghuvaṇśa*, in the Additional Notes.

1036.   E. B. Cowell. *Academy*, Vol, III, No. 43.

1037.   Muir, *Sanskrit Texts*, Part IV., Appendix.

1038.   Ghí: clarified butter. Gur: molasses.

1039.   Haridwar (Anglicè Hurdwar) where the Ganges enters the plain country.

1040.   Campbell in "Journ. As. Soc. Bengal," 1866, Part ii. p. 132; Latham, "Descr. Eth." Vol. ii. p. 456; Tod, "Annals of Rajasthan," Vol. i. p. 114.

1041.   Said by the commentator to be an eastern people between the Himálayan and Vindhyan chains.

1042. Videha was a district in the province of Behar, the ancient Mithilá or the modern Tirhoot.

1043. The people of Malwa.

1044. "The Kásikosalas are a central nation in the Váyu Puráṇa. The Rámáyaṇa places them in the east. The combination indicates the country between Benares and Oude.... Kośala is a name variously applied. Its earliest and most celebrated application is to the country on the banks of the Sarayú, the kingdom of Ráma, of which Ayodhyá was the capital.... In the Mahábhárata we have one Kośala in the east and another in the south, besides the Prák-Kośalas and Uttara Kośalas in the east and north. The Puráṇas place the Kośalas amongst the people on the back of Vindhya; and it would appear from the Váyu that Kuśa the son of Ráma transferred his kingdom to a more central position; he ruled over Kośala at his capital of Kúśasthali of Kuśavatí, built upon the Vindhyan precipices." Wilson's *Vishnṇu Púraṇa*, Vol. II. pp. 157, 172.

1045. The people of south Behar.

1046. The Puṇḍras are said to be the inhabitants of the western provinces of Bengal. "In the *Aitareyabráhmaṇa*, VII. 18, it is said that the elder sons of Viśvamitra were cursed to become progenitors of most abject races, such as Andhras, Puṇḍras, Śabaras, Pulindas, and Mútibas." Wilson's *Vishṇu Puráṇa* Vol. II. 170.

1047. Anga is the country about Bhagulpore, of which Champá was the capital.

1048. A fabulous people, "men who use their ears as a covering." So Sir John Maundevile says: "And in another Yle ben folk that han gret Eres and long, that hangen down to here knees," and Pliny, lib. iv. c. 13: "In quibus nuda alioquin corpora prægrandes ipsorum aures tota contegunt." Isidore calls them Panotii.

1049. "Those whose ears hang down to their lips."

1050. "The Iron-faces."

1051. "The One-footed."

"In that Contree," says Sir John Maundevile, "ben folk, that han but o foot and thei gon so fast that it is marvaylle: and the foot is so large that it schadeweth alle the Body azen the Sonne, when thei wole lye and rest hem." So Pliny, Natural History, lib. vii. c. 2: speaks of "Hominumn gens ... singulis cruribus, miræ pernicitatis ad saltum; eosdemque Sciopodas vocari, quod in majori æstu, humi jacentes resupini, umbrâ se pedum protegant."

These epithets are, as Professor Wilson remarks, "exaggerations of national ugliness, or allusions to peculiar customs, which were not literally intended, although they may have furnished the Mandevilles of ancient and modern times."

Vishnu Purána, Vol. II. p. 162.

1052. The Kirrhadæ of Arrian: a general name for savage tribes living in woods and mountains.

1053. Said by the commentator to be half tigers half men.

1054. The kingdom seems to have corresponded with the greater part of Berar and Khandesh.

1055. The Bengal recension has Kishikas, and places them both in the south and the north.

1056. The people of Mysore.

1057. "There are two Matsyas, one of which, according to the Yantra Samráj, is identifiable with Jeypoor. In the Digvijaya of Nakula he subdues the Matsyas further to the west, or Gujerat." Wilson's *Vishnu Purána*, Vol. II. 158. Dr. Hall observes: "In the *Mahábhárata Sabhá-parwan*, 1105 and 1108, notice is taken of the king of Matsya and of the Aparamatsyas; and, at 1082, the Matsyas figure as an eastern people. They are placed among the nations of the south in the *Rámáyana Kishkindhá-kánda*, XLI., II, while the Bengal recension, *Kishkindhá-kánda*, XLIV., 12, locates them in the north."

1058. The Kalingas were the people of the upper part of the Coromandel Coast, well known, in the traditions of the Eastern Archipelago, as Kling. Ptolemy has a city in that part, called Caliga; and Pliny Calingæ proximi mari. Wilson's *Vishnu Purána*, Vol. II. 156, Note.

1059. The Kauśikas do not appear to be identifiable.

1060. The Andhras probably occupied the modern Telingana.

1061. The Pundras have already been mentioned in Canto XL.

1062. The inhabitants of the lower part of the Coromandel Coast; so called, after them, Cholamandala.

1063. A people in the Deccan.

1064. The Keralas were the people of Malabar proper.

1065. A generic term for persons speaking any language but Sanskrit and not conforming to the usual Hindu institutions.

1066. "Pulinda is applied to any wild or barbarous tribe. Those here named are some of the people of the deserts along the Indus; but Pulindas are met with in many other positions, especially in the mountains and forests across Central India, the haunts of the Bheels and Gonds. So Ptolemy places the Pulindas along the banks of the Narmadá, to the frontiers of Larice, the Látá or Lár of the Hindus,—Khandesh and part of Gujerat." Wilson's *Vishnu Purána*, Vol. II. 159, Note.

Dr. Hall observes that "in the Bengal recension of the *Rámáyana* the Pulindas appear both in the south and in the north. The real *Rámáyana* K.-k., XLIII., speaks of the northern Pulindas."

1067. The Súrasenas were the inhabitants of Mathurá, the Suraseni of Arrian.

1068. These the Mardi of the Greeks and the two preceding tribes appear to have dwelt in the north-west of Hindustan.

1069. The Kámbojas are said to be the people of Arachosia. They are always mentioned with the north-western tribes.

1070. "The term Yavanas, although, in later times, applied to the Mohammedans, designated formerly the Greeks.... The Greeks were known throughout Western Asia by the term Yavan, or Ion. That the Macedonian or Bactrian Greeks were most usually intended is not only probable from their position and relations with India, but from their being usually named in concurrence with the north-western tribes, Kámbojas, Daradas, Páradas, Báhlíkas, Śakas &c., in the Rámáyana. Mahábhárata, Puránas, Manu, and in various poems and plays." Wilson's *Vishnu Purána* Vol. II. p. 181, Note.

1071. These people, the Sakai and Sacæ of classical writers, the Indo-Scythians of Ptolemy, extended, about the commencement of our era, along the west of India, from the Hindu Kosh to the mouths of the Indus.

1072. The corresponding passage in the Bengal recension has instead of Varadas Daradas the Dards or inhabitants of the modern Dardistan along the course of the Indus, above the Himálayas, just before it descends to India.

1073. From the word yonder it would appear that the prayer is to be repeated at the rising of the Sun.

1074. The creator of the world and the first of the Hindu triad.

1075. He who pervades all beings; or the second of the Hindu triad who preserves the world.

1076. The bestower of blessings; the third of the Hindu triad and the destroyer of the world.

1077. A name of the War-God; also one who urges the senses to action.

1078. The lord of creatures; or the God of sacrifices.

1079. A name of the King of Gods; also all-powerful.

1080. The giver of wealth. A name of the God of riches.

1081. One who directly urges the mental faculties to action.

1082. One who moderates the senses, also the God of the regions of the dead.

1083. One who produces nectar (amrita) or one who is always possessed of light; or one together with Umá (Ardhanáríśvara).

1084. The names or spirits of departed ancestors.

1085. Name of a class of eight Gods, also wealthy.

1086. They who are to be served by Yogís; or a class of Gods named Sádhyas.

1087. The two physicians of the Gods: or they who pervade all beings.

1088. They who are immortal; or a class of Gods forty-nine in number.

1089. Omniscient; or the first king of the world.

1090. He that moves; life; or the God of wind.

1091. The God of fire.

1092. Lord of creatures.

1093. One who prolongs our lives.

1094. The material cause of knowledge and of the seasons.

1095. One who shines. The giver of light.

1096. The hymn entitled the Ádityahridaya begins from this verse and the words, thou art, are understood in the beginning of this verse.

1097. One who enjoys all (pleasurable) objects; The son of Aditi, the lord of the solar disk.

1098. One who creates the world, i.e., endows beings with life or soul, and by his rays causes rain and thereby produces corn.

1099. One who urges the world to action or puts the world in motion, who is omnipresent.

1100. One who walks through the sky; or pervades the soul.

1101. One who nourishes the world, i.e., is the supporter.

1102. One having rays (Gabhasti) or he who is possessed of the all-pervading goddess Lakshmí.

1103. One resembling gold.

1104. One who is resplendent or who gives light to other objects.

1105. One whose seed (Retas) is gold; or quicksilver, the material cause of gold.

1106. One who is the cause of day.

1107. One whose horses are of tawny colour; or one who pervades the whole space or quarters.

1108. One whose knowledge is boundless or who has a thousand rays.

1109. One who urges the seven (Prápas) that is the two eyes, the two ears, the nostrils and the organ of speech, or whose chariot, is drawn by seven horses.

1110. Vide Gabhastimán.

1111. One who destroys darkness, or ignorance.

1112. One from whom our blessings or the enjoyments of Paradise come.

1113. The architect of the gods; or one who lessens the miseries of our birth and death.

1114. One who gives life to the lifeless world.

1115. One who pervades the internal and external worlds; or one who is resplendent.

1116. He who is identified with the Hindu triad, i.e. the creator (Brahmá) the supporter (Vishnu) and the destroyer (Śiva).

1117. Cold or good natured. He is so called because he allays the three sorts of pain.

1118. One who is the lord of all.

1119. Vide Divákara.

1120. One who teaches Brahmá and others the Vedas.

1121. One from whom Rudra the destroyer or the third of the Hindu triad springs.

1122. One who is knowable through Aditi, i.e., the eternal Brahmavidyá.

1123. Great happiness or the sky.

1124. The destroyer of cold or stupidity.

1125. The Lord of the sky.

1126. Vide Timironmathana.

1127. One who is known through the Upanishads.

1128. He who is the cause of heavy rain.

1129. He who is a friend to the good, or who is the cause of water.

1130. One who moves in the solar orbit.

1131. One who determines the creation of the world; or who is possessed of heat.

1132. One who has a mass of rays; or who has Kaustubha and other precious stones as his ornaments.

1133. He who urges all to action; or who is yellow in colour.

1134. One who is the destroyer of all.

1135. One who is omniscient; or a poet.

1136. One who is identified with the whole world.

1137. One who is of huge form.

1138. One who pleases all by giving nourishment; or who is red in colour.

1139. One who is the cause of the whole world.

1140. One who protects the whole world.

1141. The most glorious of all that are glorious.

1142. One who is identical with the twelve months.

1143. One who gives victory over all the worlds to those who are faithfully devoted to him; or the porter of Brahmá, named Jaya.

1144. One who is identical with the blessing which can be obtained by conquering all the worlds; or with the porter of Brahmá named Jayabhadra.

1145. One who has Hanúmán as his conveyance.

1146. One who controls the senses; or is furious with those who are not his devotees.

1147. He who is free in moving the senses; or urges all beings to action.

1148. He who can be known through the Pranava (the mystical Om-kára.)

1149. One who is the knowledge of Brahmá.

1150. One who devours all things.

1151. He who is the destroyer of all pains; and of love, and hate, the causes of pain; and ignorance which is the cause of love and hate.

1152. One who is bliss; or the mover.

1153. One who destroys ignorance and its effects.

1154. The doer of all actions.

1155. One who beholds the universe; who is a witness of good and bad actions.

1156. Sacrifice of the five sensual fires.

1157. According to Ápastamba (says the commentator) "it should have been placed on the nose: this must therefore have been done in conformity with some other Sútras."

1158. A class of eight gods.

1159. A class of eleven gods called Rudras.

1160. Named Víryaván.

1161. A class of divine devotees named Sádhyas.

1162. One who resides in the water.

1163. The third incarnation of Vishṇu, that bore the earth on his tusk.

1164. One whose armies are everywhere.

1165. One who controls the senses.

1166. He who resides in the heart, or who is full, or all-pervading.

1167. Vámana, or the Dwarf incarnation of Vishṇu.

1168. The killer of Madhu, a demon.

1169. He from whose navel, the lotus, from which Brahmá was born, springs.

1170. He who has a thousand horns. The horns are here the Sákhás of the Sáma-veda.

1171. One who has a hundred heads. The heads are here meant to devote a hundred commandments of the Vedas.

1172. Siddhas are those who have already gained the summit of their desires.

1173. Sádhyas are those that are still trying to gain the summit.

1174. A mystic syllable uttered in Mantras.

1175. A mystic syllable made of the letters which respectively denote Brahmá, Vishnu, and Śiva.

1176. A class of divine gods.

1177. Sanskáras are those sacred writings through which the divine commands and prohibitions are known.

1178. Bali, a demon whom Vámana confined in Pátála.

1179. Vishnu, the second of the Hindu triad.

1180. Krishna, (black coloured) one of the ten incarnations of Vishnu.

1181. A. Weber, *Akademische Vorlesungen*, p. 181.

1182. Systema brahmanicum, liturgicum, mythologicum, civile, exmonumentis Indicis, etc.

1183. Not only have the races of India translated or epitomized it, but foreign nations have appropriated it wholly or in part, Persia, Java, and Japan itself.

1184. In the third century B.C.